D1600377

WAR, LITERATURE,
AND POLITICS IN THE
LATE MIDDLE AGES

War, Literature, and Politics in the Late Middle Ages

EDITED BY
C. T. ALLMAND

BARNES & NOBLE BOOKS·NEW YORK
A division of Harper and Row Publishers, Inc.

1976

Published in the U.S.A. 1976 by
HARPER & ROW PUBLISHERS, INC.
BARNES & NOBLE IMPORT DIVISION

Copyright © 1976 by
Liverpool University Press

ISBN 0-06-490159-9

First published 1976

PRINTED IN GREAT BRITAIN BY
HAZELL WATSON AND VINEY LTD, AYLESBURY, BUCKS

PREFACE

The essays forming this volume, all concerned with aspects of war, literature, and politics in the late Middle Ages, have been written with the intention of doing honour to one man, G. W. Coopland. The list of his published works, if not long by the standards of some, is an impressive one. The influence of an academic teacher, in this case that of one whose main preoccupation has been the analysis and editing of texts, can largely be measured by the work which he inspires, and this, in turn, depends to a considerable extent upon the significance of the texts which he selects for study and publication.

Coopland's great service to scholarship, through which he will surely continue to exercise considerable influence, was to make available, primarily but not exclusively for the benefit of the English-speaking world, some major texts of law and social commentary which owed their inspiration to the long conflict between England and France which dominated the end of the Middle Ages. War brought about change, and change provoked discussion and comment. Were the means being employed to wage war legal and proper, and how could the moral dilemmas of the fighting man and others best be resolved? How should both the governors and the governed face the developments which French society was experiencing not without bitterness and dissension? These were matters of great moment which raised big questions, and it needed men of wide experience, wisdom, and vision to attempt to answer them.

Clearly, we are not concerned here with history confined to political events, but rather with materials which tell us how men of a particular period of the past faced up to and discussed the ills which beset their society in general and that of France in particular. The historian's task of analysis, apportionment of responsibility, and judgement is made easier by his ability to draw upon the opinions of men of the past regarding what they saw around them, especially if these ideas were expressed by persons of insight and sympathy holding, perhaps, positions of influence within their society. To achieve their fullest impact upon students of our own day, however, these opinions and generalizations must be tested, for only then can their true worth be properly estimated and understood. It is here that the student who uses other methods and other sources for appraising the past has a positive role to play: the use of materials found in archives, for instance, can in many cases complement or bring light to bear upon observations on the social, military, and political scenes whose significance has, so far, not been properly and fully appreciated. Used in this way, very different kinds of sources can assist us to arrive at something like the truth.

In some of the contributions which follow, the influence of Coopland's work can be directly seen. The authors of those essays in which the names of Honoré Bouvet, Philippe de Mézières, and Jean de Bueil do not appear will, however, be the first to acknowledge that Coopland's writings, in addition to the texts which he published, have played a significant part in making the Hundred Years War an important area of study among historians of our day. It is in recognition of this fact that these essays, united around the theme of war in the late Middle Ages so much illumined by Coopland, were prepared for presentation to him on his hundredth birthday.

It is a source of deep regret to all the contributors that G. W. Coopland died suddenly just three months short of his hundredth birthday. This book was by then at press, and under the circumstances the biographical appreciation of Professor Coopland by A. R. Myers appears unaltered in its original form.

CONTENTS

CONTENTS

ACKNOWLEDGEMENTS

I should like to thank Professor A. R. Myers and all the contributors for their help and generous co-operation in the preparation of this volume.

A book containing essays by a number of contributors needs careful sub-editing, and I am glad to acknowledge the most able work of Mrs. Janet Godden in this aspect of the book's production. By happy coincidence she had previously worked on one of Professor Coopland's major publications and was therefore closely acquainted with the nature of the material. Between many other commitments Mrs. Alison Quinn has found time to compile the index.

Every author or editor realizes as he goes along how his task can be lightened by the practical advice and enthusiasm he receives from his publisher, and I should like to thank the staff of Liverpool University Press for their thoughtful assistance at every stage of this book's production.

C.T.A.

ABBREVIATIONS

A.A.S.R.P.	*Associated Architectural Societies Reports and Papers*
A.B.	*Annales de Bourgogne*
A. Bret.	*Annales de Bretagne*
Add. Ch.	Additional Charter
Add. MS.	Additional Manuscript
A.H.G.	*Archives Historiques de la Gironde*
A.M.B.	*Archives Municipales de Bordeaux*
Annales E.S.C.	*Annales, Économies, Sociétés, Civilisations*
Arch. Dép.	Archives Départementales
Arch. Nat.	Archives Nationales
B.E.C.	*Bibliothèque de l'École des Chartes*
B.E.F.A.R.	*Bibliothèque des Écoles Françaises d'Athènes et de Rome*
B.I.H.R.	*Bulletin of the Institute of Historical Research*
B.L.	British Library (formerly British Museum)
B.N.	Bibliothèque Nationale
C.C.R.	*Calendar of Close Rolls*
C.P.R.	*Calendar of Patent Rolls*
C.S.	Camden Series
C. & Y.S.	Canterbury and York Society
E.E.T.S.	Early English Text Society
E.H.R.	*English Historical Review*
Foedera	*Foedera, Conventiones, Litterae, etc.* of Thomas Rymer, various editions
M.A.	*Le Moyen Âge*
Morice, *Preuves*	Dom P. H. Morice, *Mémoires pour servir de preuves à l'histoire ecclésiastique et civile de Bretagne* (3 vols., Paris, 1742–6)
MS. fr.	Manuscrit français
MS. lat.	Manuscrit latin

nouv. acqs. frs.	nouvelles acquisitions françaises
P.P.C.	*Proceedings and Ordinances of the Privy Council of England*, ed. N. H. Nicolas (7 vols., Record Commission, 1834–7).
P.R.O.	Public Record Office
Reg. Vat.	[Archivio Segreto Vaticano], Registra Vaticana.
Rev. Hist.	*Revue Historique*
Rot. Parl.	*Rotuli Parliamentorum . . . 1278–1503*
R.S.	Rolls Series
S.A.T.F.	Société des Anciens Textes Français
S.H.F.	Société de l'Histoire de France
S.T.S.	Scottish Text Society
T. R. Hist. S.	*Transactions of the Royal Historical Society*

G. W. COOPLAND

Photograph taken in 1975

I

George William Coopland:
A Biographical Appreciation

A. R. MYERS

George William Coopland was born on 8 July 1875, in Caernarvon, the eldest child of Thomas Paul Coopland, whose father came from Lincolnshire and whose mother was born in Anglesey. George's mother, Mary Jane McIver, came from Liverpool, to which the family soon returned after his birth. His childhood memories are very hazy; though he remembers vividly being told of his mother's death, when he was quite small, as he was sitting up in bed, reading. Thereafter there was a vague period when a housekeeper was looking after the house for his father. His earliest public memory is of the Phoenix Park murders in 1882 and the subsequent Fenian atrocities in Ireland.

It was at about this time that he went to live in London with his father's sister, Mrs. Julian, whose husband was a mining engineer and spent most of his time abroad in Brazil and then in the United States of America. Coopland was reading prodigiously by this time. He was already devouring such adult works as those of Dickens; but he was still young enough to compel the unfortunate maidservant to play the part of a Red Indian tied to the stake, after his reading of Red Indian stories, while he advanced upon her as a brave white frontiersman. After some years in London the whole family, now increased by the birth of his cousin Tom, ten years younger than himself, moved north, first to Liverpool then to Preston.

Most of Coopland's schooldays were spent at a Church of England school in Preston attached to St. Matthew's Church. He stood out from the rank and file, for at the age of thirteen he was selected, along with two or three others, to become a 'pupil teacher'. In the first year he was a monitor, an office which included the duty of stoking up the furnace in the cellar. As it was warm and fuggy down there, the monitors made the job spin out on cold winter days. At the age of fourteen he became a fully fledged pupil teacher; half the working day was spent in study, and half in charge of a class, where the ages of the children ranged from the quite small to those of nearly leaving age. About ninety per cent of the children went into the mills: half-time to begin with and then full-time when they were old enough; though as far as Coopland can remember, no child left school unable to read, write, and do simple arithmetic. The pupil teachers received a small salary which rose progressively over the three to four years in which they served. School hours started for them at 8.15 a.m. and ended when they had finished their work for the day after 6 p.m. After school Coopland often took part in various courses at the Harris Institute. There he met a boy slightly older than himself, Jack Tomlinson, who became his lifelong friend. Tomlinson was working in a mill, in charge of four looms and, like David Livingstone in an earlier generation, worked at his lessons as he minded the looms. Later on he matriculated to Owens College, Manchester, and graduated in the Victoria University. Later still at Coopland's prompting, he became a master at Dover County School, where Coopland was already working. Such was the determination which resulted in the achievements of the Victorian age.

Apart from this, Coopland seems to have been a somewhat solitary and contemplative boy, whose main recreations were fishing, walking, and, above all, reading. At the age of seventeen he sat for the 'Queen's Scholarship' examination, and came 143rd out of some thousands of candidates. This gave him the chance of entering a recognized teachers' training college, in his case the University College at Liverpool, which he did in 1893. During term-time he lived in the teachers' training hostel in Croxteth Road; in the vacations he went back to his aunt's home in Preston.

The degree course lasted for three years, divided into Preliminary, Intermediate, and Final. It has to be remembered that in addition to studying four academic subjects—in Coopland's case English, History, Latin, and French—the prospective teacher had to study simultaneously for his teaching certificate. Coopland obtained his degree, of the federal Victoria University, before his twenty-first birthday, and took his teaching certificate (with a 'First') during the following vacation. Some of his university teachers were not only pioneers of the still young University College but also men of intellectual distinction, like Sir Walter Raleigh, Professor of English Literature, and Kuno Meyer, Professor of Teutonic Languages. The Professor of History, John Macdonald Mackay, was one of the chief promoters of the movement for the creation of an independent University of Liverpool in 1903, and the more adequate endowment of the new foundation by a fresh appeal fund, raised from the citizens of Liverpool. Coopland was friendly with a son of Sir Oliver Lodge, then Professor of Physics. But stimulating and heroic as those pioneer days may have been, there was no money to spare for those who were teachers in training, and Coopland's re-creations had to be reading, observing the shipping on the river (during years when Liverpool was at the height of its world importance), and walking. During his undergraduate days he went on several walking tours with fellow-students and with Jack Tomlinson.

From the autumn of 1896 until that of 1913 Coopland was teaching in various schools, first of all for some years in Leeds. In his first school he was faced by a tough class of 121. The head was pompous and told him that 'History was all right as a hobby', so he had to attend evening classes in chemistry and drawing, in neither of which was he able to muster any interest or aptitude. Fortunately he escaped soon afterwards to a more congenial school in a pleasanter area. Then he taught for a short while in Preston, before going on to Grimsby. There Coopland met Emily Barlow, headmistress of an infants' school, whom he married in 1902; she died in 1961. While at Grimsby he was still working very hard and won his M.A. by examination (at Manchester). He gained promotion by moving to Norwich in 1902, but in the next year he transferred to Dover, to a school which had been started as an art school and had been then extended into a secondary school. Here there were higher teaching standards, and Coopland was able to teach some senior pupils, preparing them for College entry, through the Oxford and Cambridge examinations, with considerable success. All this was a very good training in the arts of verbal exposition, for which he was to become so renowned at Liverpool. His only child, Gwen, was born while he was at Dover. She now lives in Somerset. While he was at Dover, Coopland worked for and gained the degree of B.Sc. (Econ.) of the University of London in 1909.

One of the members of the staff of Dover School was a Miss Chapman, who had been a school friend of the niece of Frederick Seebohm. It was through her that Coopland gained an introduction to Seebohm at Hitchin in 1907, and subsequently paid him several visits. The famous scholar was then in his early seventies, and something of an invalid; but he welcomed Coopland, and suggested to him two possible lines of research. One was an investigation into the society of the olive country in the south of France; the other was into the social and administrative history of the villages surrounding the Abbey of Saint-Bertin, in the Pas-de-Calais. The choice fell on the latter theme, and it was decided that Coopland should spend as much as possible of the Easter and summer holidays at Saint-Omer. There, through the good offices of the Abbé Bled, he was given permission to study the relevant documents, which were housed in the local *lycée*. These documents were guarded by a man of benign disposition. He saw that Coopland was pressed for time, and if the researcher had not finished with a particular document at the closing hour, the custodian would urge him to take it home and return it the next day.

The Abbé Bled also obtained for him, for the sum of three francs a day, accommodation and meals at the restaurant Jean Bauer, kept by M. and Mme Hercent, the son-in-law and daughter of the founder. Cigars cost 1*d.* and a glass of white wine 1½*d.* This modest restaurant had a permanent clientèle of commercial travellers, the *sous-officiers* from the local barracks, and a group of young clerks from the Banque de France. They soon brought Coopland into their circle of middle-class male society in a small French town. His recollection of the men he came to know at the restaurant illustrates his sharp memory and also his gift for the telling anecdote. Among these men were several who had fought at Sedan. One had been through the siege of Paris in 1870, and had been a member of a group who had made a sortie. The cold had been so bitter that they had been unable to dig up the turnips in the fields. They were so hungry and miserable that had not some Germans come along, the Frenchmen would assuredly have fallen to fighting among themselves. This man had been wounded and had been put in hospital in Paris; but conditions were so bad that he would certainly have died if he had stayed there. He had had to crawl away to the house of friends in the city, to be nursed back to health there.

During his visits to Saint-Omer Coopland made periodic trips to Arras to examine documents of the Revolution connected with the sale of church lands. He often took his bicycle to France and cycled round to all the villages connected with the Abbey, talking to the *greffiers*, local farmers, and other inhabitants, thus obtaining a close knowledge of French customs and habits of thought. Some of the farmers were astonished that he should know about and be able to discuss the differing sizes of land measures. Some people thought he was a government official from Paris, examining the possibilities of introducing a railway line. Between these visits to France Coopland devoted all his spare time to reading large numbers of cartularies and other relevant documents, which he obtained in great quantity from the London Library. Finally the work was finished in 1912.

During his meetings with Seebohm the famous scholar had promised to see to the publication of Coopland's work and finance the printing. Unfortunately Seebohm died in February 1912, and as he had left no written directions for such aid, the family did not feel under any obligation to undertake the task. Seebohm's literary legatee was Sir Paul Vinogradoff, with whom Coopland had two meetings. The first was somewhat patronizing; but at the second, when Vinogradoff had read the work, the air of patronage had disappeared. The work was published in the series of Oxford Studies in Social and Legal History, edited by Vinogradoff. But alas, the year was 1914, and the world had other things to think about. Hence the work did not make the immediate impact on historical circles which its merits demanded.

Its quality had, however, won recognition in Liverpool. It was on this piece of research that Coopland was awarded his Litt.D. at Liverpool; the conferment of the degree was approved by the Senate on 19 June 1914. The work was assessed by Professor Charles Bonnier, in charge of the French Department until the end of the session 1912–13. Bonnier was very impressed by the scope of the work and by its execution. In the summer of 1913, after Coopland had applied for and been appointed to the post of Lecturer in Medieval History in the University of Liverpool, he cycled from Saint-Omer to Templeuve, to which Bonnier had just returned. At Templeuve he spent a pleasant afternoon with this outstanding scholar. Next year Bonnier was to be caught up in the sudden and overwhelming onrush of the German army and exiled to Belgium, where he died during the war.

When Coopland came to Liverpool, the Faculty of Arts had polarized into two parties: a dominant conservative group, and a protesting radical group, known as the New Testament. Coopland was attracted to the New Testament, whose leader was Oliver Elton, the King Alfred Professor of English Literature. Elton became and remained one of his closest friends. Unlike the members of the old school, Elton valued a scholar for what he was, and did not despise him because he had not reached his position by the conventional route of public school and 'Oxbridge'. And like other members of the New Testament, Elton wanted to foster the study of modern languages and medieval and

modern history. The then unconventional route by which Coopland
had attained his university lectureship proved invaluable in at least one
important respect: he had been compelled to study, as some lecturers
had not, how to present a subject so as to make it both interesting and
stimulating to his hearers. He rapidly acquired, and retained until his
retirement, a well-deserved reputation as a brilliant lecturer.

Mr. J. J. Bagley, Reader in Extension Studies in the University of
Liverpool, who has himself earned a wide and well-founded reputation
as an outstanding lecturer and is therefore well-qualified to judge what
good lecturing can be, was one of the distinguished pupils whom Coopland inspired. Mr. Bagley wrote to me in a letter of 19 March 1974:

When it comes to recalling Coopland in the lecture room, it is surprising how clear
my mental picture of him is, considering that I sat at his feet in the 1927–8 session for
the outline course in medieval history and again in the following session for his
special period, 'France in the Fifteenth Century'. When I went up to Liverpool in
1927, I fully intended to specialize in Stuart History. I ended up, as you know, with a
thesis on Charles the Bold. It was Coopland's contagious enthusiasm that made me
change my mind. . . . I never heard Coopland read a lecture. He brought in notes, put
them on the lectern, and then walked away. He did quite a bit of walking during a
lecture—but never in an irritating way—and as he passed the lectern he frequently
paused and glanced at his notes. He was a fluent lecturer but his main asset was
enthusiasm for the subject, and, I suspect, for the art of lecturing. He obviously
enjoyed conveying his own enthusiasm to his students; his eyes shone with pleasure
as he unfolded his tale with skill and zeal. We took fewer notes than in most other
lectures, but we saw the pattern of events, particularly in fifteenth-century France.
As Coopland said more than once, 'Lavisse will give you the details'. He did not
encourage students to ignore facts—facts were as sacred to him as they were to C. P.
Scott—but narrative was not his chief concern when lecturing. I still remember him
beginning his opening lecture on 'France in the Fifteenth Century' with: 'This
course begins in 1380, and goes on until 14–, er, 14–, oh, whenever it was that Louis
XI died.' I am sure he did that deliberately to show there were more important matters than dates in historical studies. He made his main characters really live, and at
the end of that session I felt I knew the feelings of the Armagnacs, Burgundians and
Bretons, and had actually met men like Philip the Good, Louis XI, and Charles the
Bold. . . . Just as theology was the queen of subjects in the Middle Ages, so Coopland regards the later Middle Ages, especially in Western Europe, as the most satis-
fying historical study available; and from him the student appreciated the significance
of the period in the evolution of Europe. . . . I dedicated my *Margaret of Anjou* to
him, and I still regard him as the most influential of my many teachers.

Though Coopland so quickly made a name for himself as a lecturer
inside the University, and though from 1914 he was in charge of the
Department of Medieval History, for several years without an assistant,

he did not forget the University's responsibilities to the wider world, of which he had seen so much. Soon after his appointment as lecturer he became secretary to the University Extension Board, and himself taught with great effect extramural classes in Lancashire and Cheshire. During the First World War he took one W.E.A. class at Crewe (mainly of school teachers) on two evenings a week, and the other at Haslingden (mainly of railway workers) on another evening. After a snack at the railway station he would travel in an unheated railway carriage to his destination; the wartime trains often failed to run to time, and after the classes he sometimes had to walk home from the station in Liverpool after midnight to his home in the suburb of Aigburth four miles away. There he had to look after himself, for he had sent his wife and daughter to North Wales for the period of the war, and frequently cycled at the weekends to see them.

After the First World War he gradually developed a special relationship with Egypt. A number of Egyptian students came to study in his classes in Liverpool, and some of them later achieved great distinction in the academic world. One of them was M. M. Ziada, who became Professor of Medieval History at Fuad I University in Cairo and an authority on the Mamelukes. Another was A. S. Atiya, who, after being Professor of Medieval History in the University of Alexandria, was invited to build up a great centre of African and Near Eastern studies in the University of Utah, United States of America, and is a scholar of international reputation on the history of the Crusades. A third was Shafik Gharbal, who, after teaching in the University of Cairo, was for a while Minister of Education in Egypt. In 1929 Coopland went out to Cairo and spent a full academic session there as visiting Professor of Medieval History. He was to return to Egypt on more than one occasion after his retirement from Liverpool, each visit lasting four to five months: in 1946–7, 1948, and 1954–5 to Alexandria, and in 1949–50 and 1950–1 to Cairo. His scholarship and services to Egyptian universities were recognized by the award in 1950 of an Honorary Litt.D. by the University of Cairo.

Corresponding recognition by the University of Liverpool of Coopland's services to scholarship was, however, slower to come. In 1924 he was made an Associate Professor, a term more familiar in the United States of America than in Britain. When someone asked him what an Associate Professor was, it provoked from him the quip that it was one who was allowed to associate with professors, but not in public. While he was in Egypt in 1929–30 there was a move to make him a professor in Liverpool on his return. But the country was then in the throes of a great economic depression and the University was in serious financial difficulties. Moreover, some of the 'old school', still influential in the University, continued to disapprove of a scholar who had attained distinction by a route less traditional than that of public school and 'Oxbridge'. And Coopland had never set out to win supporters in University governing circles. Sir James Mountford, Vice-Chancellor of the University from 1945 to 1963, and Professor of Latin from 1932 to 1945, writes of him:

My general recollection of Coopland here is that he was a man of vigorous intellect, interested much more in teaching and scholarship than in academic politics, shrewd and firm in his opinions on basic issues of Faculty and University policy. He was not likely to be the first to rise to his feet in debate; but if he felt that something needed to be said, he had no hesitation in saying it concisely and effectively.

So the proposal to make Coopland a professor in 1930 failed, but in 1937 a second attempt succeeded, and a personal Chair of Medieval History was created for him. He was to occupy it longer than he can have foreseen. He was due to retire in the summer of 1940, but it seemed at that moment very inopportune to make arrangements for appointing a successor, when France had capitulated to the Nazi onslaught and the invasion of Britain was expected at any moment. So he was asked to remain in charge of the Department of Medieval History until the end of the war. The University then decided to make his Chair a permanent one, and appointed to it in 1945 Geoffrey Barraclough, who in 1946 took over the Department from Professor Coopland. The University had already conferred on Professor Coopland the title of Emeritus Professor.

Throughout his university career Professor Coopland gave many lectures to outside bodies—historical societies, literary societies, Rotary clubs, and so on—and was successful in getting across to the most diverse audiences. One of his most memorable lectures was that given to a densely packed Arts Theatre in 1924 on 'St. Thomas and his View of History' during the celebrations in Liverpool to mark the seven-hundredth anniversary of the birth of Aquinas.

Coopland lived in Blackpool for several years after the war and then moved to Harrold, Bedfordshire, in 1950. Thence he migrated to Robertsbridge in Sussex in 1955, and transferred to his present home at Broad Oak, near Rye, in 1962. Much of his time since retirement has been taken up by the research for which he had too little time during his teaching years. He has pursued this aim to very impressive effect. There can be few scholars who have published the bulk of their work after passing the age of seventy and there can be fewer still who at the age of ninety-four have seen the publication of a powerful edition, in 1,150 pages, of a very important work. And it must surely be unique to have presented to the Press at the age of ninety-seven the manuscript of another interesting work, this time of about 80,000 words. In all his literary activities since 1933 Professor Coopland has had the invaluable help of his secretary, Miss Gertrude Winter. He would be the first to acknowledge that her assistance has become more indispensable as the years have gone by. I certainly could not have attempted this personal appreciation without her aid, which I hereby gratefully and warmly acknowledge.

Perhaps the most characteristic feature of Professor Coopland's scholarly work has been his ability to combine a meticulous analysis of detail with his power to discern the large-scale aspects and the significant features of his sources. Thus in his first book, *The Abbey of Saint-Bertin and its Neighbourhood, 900–1350*, much of the long introduction is concerned with a precise analysis of forms of land-measurement and of land-tenure, and categories of rent, taxes, and other exactions; yet we are not allowed to forget the political setting, the big economic forces, the chief features, and the picture of a society which results. All his later books have been editions or discussions of more speculative and intellectual works; but these traits remain. Thus in his edition of the *Tree of Battles* by Honoré Bonet (or Bouvet) Professor Coopland naturally tries to tell us something of the author, of his sources, and his influence; but he is also concerned to show us the light which the treatise throws on themes such as the medieval view of history, of international law, and of the conduct of war. Then in his edition of the much bigger work, *Le Songe du Vieil Pèlerin*, he is similarly concerned with the life of the author, the sources he used for his work, the manuscripts that exist and the very complicated plan of the treatise; but he also seeks to illuminate from the work the modes of thought of the late fourteenth century, such as allegory, the ideals of institutions such as kingship held at that time, and the structure of contemporary European societies, especially that of France. The result of this happy combination of precise detail and large views is to engage the reader's interest and to convince him that he is being given an insight into the history of that age.

Finally, a few words should be attempted about the man himself. He has always been so intent on scholarship that administrative details, and the minutiae of living have meant little to him. He once told me that he was not nearly so attached to particular places as most people appear to be. Yet this does not mean that he is a remote and desiccated scholar. On the contrary the impression that his friends have always had of this tall, lean, and wiry figure, with the striking large brown eyes, is one of great liveliness and wit. He has always retained a strong and shrewd interest in people, both past and present. Indeed his sympathy for other lives extends to those of animals; he has always regarded his cats and dogs not just as 'pets' but as very real individuals, with their own personalities and rights. He has often kept several cats simultaneously because he has found the differences in their characters as fascinating a study in its way as the differences in character between human beings. He is a great raconteur, whose ready conversation is constantly sparkling with sardonic humour and penetrating observations. The Secretary of the Liverpool University Press who went to see him in 1974 about his latest work came away confessing himself quite exhausted by several hours conversation with the nonagenarian. Professor Coopland seems indeed to have succeeded in that medieval quest, the search for the elixir of life. In admiration for his long and distinguished service of Clio, and in gratitude for the light he has shed on the Middle Ages, especially the fourteenth and fifteenth centuries, a group of scholars of this period has combined to write and to present to him this volume of essays, to celebrate his hundredth birthday. As he himself said of the Old Pilgrim, 'Our final impression is of a man, noble and sincere, many-sided, shrewd and practical ... one of the many who have attempted the impossible and, so doing, have helped to hearten and perhaps reassure mankind'.

The Principal Writings
of G. W. Coopland

The Abbey of Saint-Bertin and its Neighbourhood, 900–1350, Oxford Studies in Social and Legal History 4, ed. Sir Paul Vinogradoff (Oxford, 1914).

'Notes on Domainal Administration, Monastic and Collegiate', *A Miscellany presented to John Macdonald Mackay, LL.D., July, 1914*, ed. O. Elton (Liverpool and London, 1914), pp. 120–7.

'The Franco-Belgian Frontier', *The Geographical Teacher*, viii (1916), 266–70.

'The Tree of Battles and Some of its Sources', *Tijdschrift voor Rechtsgeschiedenis: Revue d'Histoire du Droit*, v (1923), 173–207.

'An Unpublished Work of John of Legnano; The "Somnium" of 1372', *Nuovi Studi Medievali*, ii (1925), 65–88.

'Eustache Deschamps and Nicholas Oresme. A Note on the *Demoustracions contre Sortileges*', *Romania*, lii (1926), 355–61.

'Nicholas Oresme's Livre de Divinacion', *The Monist*, xxxvii (1927), 578–600.

'Serfdom and Feudalism', *Universal History of the World*, ed. J. A. Hammerton, (London, 1928), v. 5, pp. 2661–73.

The Tree of Battles of Honoré Bonet. An English Version with Introduction (Liverpool, 1949).

Nicole Oresme and the Astrologers. A Study of his Livre de Divinacions (Liverpool, 1952).

'*Le Jouvencel* (Re-visited)', *Symposium*, v (1951), 137–86.

'A Glimpse of Late-Fourteenth-Century Ships and Seamen, from *Le Songe du Vieil Pelerin* of Philippe de Mézières (1327–1405)', *Mariner's Mirror*, xlviii (1962), 186–92.

Philippe de Mézières, Chancellor of Cyprus, *Le Songe du Vieil Pelerin* (2 vols., Cambridge, 1969).

'Crime and Punishment in Paris, September 6, 1389–May 18, 1390', *Medieval and Middle Eastern Studies in Honor of Aẓīẓ Suryal Atiya*, ed. S. A. Hanna (Leiden, 1972), pp. 64–85.

Philippe de Mézières, Chancellor of Cyprus, *Letter to Richard II*. An English version of *Epistre au Roi Richart, 1395* (Liverpool, 1975).

2

The *Tree of Battles* of Honoré Bouvet and the Laws of War

N. A. R. WRIGHT

The *Tree of Battles*,[1] written by an obscure Benedictine monk during the last quarter of the fourteenth century, achieved a remarkable measure of popularity during the fifteenth century and is still read with great interest by historians and international lawyers. The initial publicity work was done by Honoré Bouvet[2] himself who sent finely illuminated copies of the *Tree* to King Charles VI of France, and to his uncles, the dukes of Berry and Burgundy. Before very long the work became known to heralds and pursuivants on both sides of the Pyrenees; to officers and clerks of the military courts at the *Table de Marbre* in Paris and at the Court of Chivalry in London; and, above all, to the higher aristocracies of France, England, and Spain. In the wars which plagued western Europe during the late Middle Ages, it accompanied rival military commanders to battle with one another. Thus while John II, duke of Bourbon, and Arthur of Brittany, constable of France, possessed copies of the *Tree*, so did their respected rival John Talbot, earl of Shrewsbury;[3] while John Howard, duke of Norfolk, was boarding his ship in 1481, along with his copy of the *Tree of Battles*, with intent

---

1. Unless otherwise specified references are to the edition by G. W. Coopland, *The Tree of Battles of Honoré Bonet* (Liverpool, 1949). Book and chapter numbers have been incorporated into the text thus: (4:61), indicating book 4, chapter 61.

2. Until G. Ouy published a short article entitled 'Honoré Bouvet (appelé à tort Bonet) prieur de Selonnet' (*Romania*, lxxxv (1959), 255–9), the surname of the *Tree*'s author was generally considered to have been Bonet. His alias *Carobovis* (see N. A. R. Wright, 'Honoré Bouvet and the Abbey of Île-Barbe', *Recherches de théologie ancienne et médiévale*, xxxix (1972), 116), confirms Ouy's thesis that the prior's name was somehow connected with that of an ox or bullock (*bouvet* or *bovet*), but whether the *u* should be included in the surname must remain something of an open question.

3. Respectively B.N., MS. fr. 1274; Bibliothèque de l'Arsenal, Paris, MS. 2695; and B.L., MS. Royal 15 E VI, fos. 293 ff.

'to brenne the Lith and other vilages along the Scottisch see',[4] his intended victims might also have been browsing through Gilbert of the
Haye's Scots translation of the work executed in 1456;[5] while Alvaro de
Luna, constable of Castile, was employing Diego de Valera in the task
of translating the *Tree* into his native language, his deadly enemy Don
Inigo Lopez de Mendoza had engaged another translator to do exactly
the same task for him.[6]

By the time that the new presses of Paris and of Lyons started producing printed editions of the *Tree of Battles* (nine in the forty or so
years after 1477), there was a very large number of manuscript copies
indeed in at least four different languages: Anglo-Scots, Castilian,
Catalan, and Provençal, in addition to the original French. The *Tree*
had been quoted in legal disputes,[7] used as a manual in the instruction of
prospective heralds,[8] and plundered by Christine de Pisan in the preparation of her *Lavision-Christine* and *Livre des faits d'armes et de
chevalerie*. There can be little doubt that the *Tree* was a popular and
widely read book during the late medieval and early modern period.
This popularity has revived over the last hundred years, though perhaps among a more scholarly public, thanks to Ernest Nys, who published the original French text in 1883,[9] and to George Coopland, who
provided an excellent English translation of the work in 1949.[10]

Modern interpretations of Bouvet's *Tree of Battles* have tended to fall
within two broad categories: the one observing the *Tree* in the context
of modern international law, the other in terms of a more ancient 'law of
arms'. Nys was the main spokesman for the international lawyers, and
his main object in publishing the *Tree* was 'to set before the eyes of
those who study international law the oldest doctrinal monument of
this legal discipline'.[11] It was, as Johan Huizinga pointed out, an
essentially theoretical treatise whose 'fine rules ... were too rarely
observed' but were to have a dynamic effect on the developing 'law of

4. *The Household Books of John, Duke of Norfolk, and Thomas, Earl of Surrey.
1481–1490*, ed. J. P. Collier (Roxburghe Club, 1844), p. 277.
5. *Gilbert of the Haye's Prose Manuscript: The Buke of the Law of Armys or Buke
of Bataillis*, ed. J. H. Stevenson (S.T.S., 1901).
6. Respectively Biblioteca Nacional, Madrid, MS. 6.605 and Escorial, H II 19. Both
translations were made in the year 1441.
7. Duke of Norfolk versus duke of Somerset, 1453. See *The Tree*, p. 23, where
reference is made to the Paston Letters.
8. Jacques d'Enghien, *dit* Sicile, *Le Blason des couleurs en armes, livrées et devises*, ed.
H. Cocheris (Paris, 1860), p. 19.
9. *L'Arbre des Batailles d'Honoré Bonet*, ed. E. Nys (Brussels and Leipzig, 1883).
10. See above, p. 12, n. 1.   11. *L'Arbre*, ed. Nys, p. xxviii.

nations'.[12] G. W. Coopland, on the other hand, asserted 'from the standpoint of the medievalist' that the *Tree* marks 'not the rudimentary beginnings of International Law, but a phase near to the declared and accepted end of an older system'.[13] This 'older system' has been described in great detail by M. H. Keen who recognized the *Tree* as an authority on a very ancient system of war theory and soldierly custom which was variously called the 'laws of war' or the 'law of arms'.[14] The implication here is that the *Tree* might have been used as a legal handbook for the soldier of Bouvet's own day and R. Kilgour even went so far as to describe it as a 'working manual for the knight'.[15] It is this latter theory, which relates the *Tree of Battles* to the codes and practices of warfare in the late medieval period, which will be the subject of this article.

The *Tree of Battles* is about the 'just war'—a theme popular to jurists and theologians throughout the Middle Ages—and about the position of the soldier in society, a subject which had engaged the critical talents of many a clerical commentator since the eleventh century. The first two parts of the *Tree* deal with war's historical and biblical antecedents and can be virtually disregarded for the present purposes. The remaining 140 chapters of Bouvet's work were not assembled with quite that meticulous attention to structure and consistency which is so desirable to the more orderly modern mind, and it is hoped that a rearrangement of the *Tree*'s material on a thematic basis, as is attempted below, will produce no serious distortion of what the author was trying to communicate to his fourteenth-century public.

War, according to Bouvet, is in the nature of things: it 'has arisen on account of certain things displeasing to the human will, to the end that such conflict should be turned into agreement and reason' (1:1). Antipathies and conflicts are as natural to the human world as they are to the rest of creation, animate and inanimate, because 'everything is inclined by its nature to contradict its evil form' (3:2 and 4:1). War is not only natural; it actually accords with the law of Reason, as embodied in the Canon and Civil Laws, and with Divine Law as revealed in the Old Testament, where God is shown not only to have permitted

12. J. Huizinga, *The Waning of the Middle Ages* (Harmondsworth, 1968), pp. 101–2.
13. *The Tree*, p. 68.
14. M. H. Keen, *The Laws of War in the Late Middle Ages* (London, 1965), esp. p. 157.
15. R. Kilgour, 'Honoré Bonet: A Fourteenth-Century Critic of Chivalry', *Publications of the Modern Languages Association of America*, l (1935), 352–61.

war but to have ordered and encouraged it (4:1). Clearly, since war is backed by such impeccable credentials, the evils and injustices which so often attend it are not part of its nature but usually the results of misconduct and abuse. 'And if in war', Bouvet explained, 'many evil things are done, they never come from the nature of war but from false usage; as when a man-at-arms takes a woman and does her shame and injury, or sets fire to a church' (4:1). In chapter 79 of the *Tree*'s fourth part, Bouvet divides war into three categories: the wars of princes, wars in self-defence, and wars of reprisal, and shows in this and in other chapters how the conditions which regulated their conduct differed in particular instances. Such wars could be waged according to justice and reason, or they might be perverted into illegal acts of violence according to the three-fold standard of the just war: the objectives pursued in the war must be legitimate, the parties engaged in it must be competent, and the manner in which it is conducted must be proper.

Clearly the use of physical force in self-defence was legitimate: a serf could defend himself against the lord who wished to kill him, and, in like circumstances, the monk might defend himself against his abbot, the son against his father, the accused against wrongful judgement, and the exile against arrest (4:73–77). If self-defence was a legitimate call for violent resistance, so was the defence of one's lord, one's family, and one's property (4:23–24 and 64–69), but the boundaries between legitimate defence and criminal offence had to be strictly drawn and observed. The 'law allows all just defence, so long as it does not pass beyond the bounds of the offence. If a man tried to strike me with his hand and I, being as big as he, tried to strike him with a lance or an arrow, this would not be a due or proportionate defence . . .' (4:44 and 71). The same sort of conditions applied in the case of *marque* or reprisal where the injured party was compensated only to the extent of the initial loss or injury, and no further (4:79). Over and above the right of the individual to make war in his own defence, the church had the special right to initiate war against the German emperor and against the Saracens and Jews, but only when they were considered to constitute an active threat to the Christian society (4:2, 6, and 63).

The question of which parties were competent to initiate and to participate in war received, in the *Tree of Battles*, a relatively simple and straightforward answer: 'According to written law a man cannot ordain or decide on war if he is subject to any lord, so that he who decides on war should have no sovereign' (4:82 and 84). The prince's assent was implicit in wars of self-defence, but in every other case—including that of reprisal—explicit authorization was required. It is understandable that Bouvet had to tread rather carefully when attempting the precarious distinction between sovereign and subject prince, and his treatment is equivocal. It was clear, however, that the pope, the emperor, and the king of France could be ranked in the former category (4:6 and 83), even if the kings of England and of Spain were more doubtful cases (4:84). Although a sovereign prince was entitled to initiate offensive war given reasonable cause, and defensive war in all cases, and although his subjects were bound to aid him in this war (4:15–17), there were certain classes of people who could not be compelled to participate. Clerks should not take up arms, asserted Bouvet, for 'the clerical estate and office is separate from all war, for the service of God to which clerks belong makes them unfit to carry the arms and harness of temporal battles' (4:97—though contradicted by 4:35). Also 'separate from all war' were old people, children, women, and the infirm, and these, too, could not be compelled to take up arms (4:70).

Many of the remaining chapters of the *Tree* were concerned with the thorny question of how wars should properly be conducted. Bouvet outlined the procedure whereby letters of *marque* should be granted by the prince to an individual (4:80–81), and how, in all types of war, prisoners should be ransomed at a reasonable price (4:46–47); how safe conducts should be observed in the spirit as well as in the letter (4:57), and how deceit should be shunned (4:49); how fighting during feast and rest days should be discouraged (4:50), and how it should be actively prohibited and severely punished during periods of truce (4:103–4). But these questions of military conduct were given treatment which can only be described as summary in comparison to that devoted to the question of immunities.

In the case, for example, of war between the kings of France and of England in which the English subjects give their prince aid and countenance, 'the French can make war on the English people and take their possessions and lands and all that they can seize, without being required, in the sight of God, to return them' (4:48). It is inevitable that during such a war the 'humble and innocent' will occasionally suffer harm and loss. Furthermore, in the case of *marque* and reprisal, innocence of the crime offers no security against injury, 'for on this theory one person suffers loss for another, and receives damage and molestation for the deed of another ...' (4:79). Co-citizenship with the offender presumably implies 'aid and countenance' in this instance. On the whole, however, the possibilities of a loose interpretation of the phrase 'aid and countenance', and of a casual attitude towards the sufferings of the innocent in time of war, are carefully excluded from the *Tree* by the author's firm and unequivocal stand on immunities. 'Ox-herds, and all husbandmen, and ploughmen with their oxen, when they are carrying on their business, and equally when they are going to it or returning from it, are secure, according to written law' (4:100), and 'neither emperor, king, duke nor count, nor any person whatsoever can excuse himself from keeping this law' (4:102). It is also a 'very terrible act of war' to attack a visiting foreign student (4:86 and 90), his servants (4:87), his father (4:88), or his brother (4:89), who attend or visit him. It is also forbidden under any circumstance to lay violent hands on the infirm and the insane (4:91, 92, and 95); on the very old and the very young (4:93–94); on ambassadors, on clerks, and on pilgrims (4:96–99). All these categories are entitled by their very status to the highest and most binding safe conduct of all: namely, the 'safeguard of the Holy Father of Rome'. The infringement of such a security is a mortal sin and may be punished by excommunication (4:99).

However terrible Bouvet may have felt the punishment of excommunication to be, he was well aware that ecclesiastical sanctions were not as effective as the more tangible civil form. It is for this reason that he concentrated on the sovereign prince who alone had both the right to wage war and the power to prevent others from so doing. Once the principle was generally accepted that only the king had the right to make war (a situation far removed from the France of Charles VI), then it had to be admitted also that only soldiers in the king's service or under his licence were permitted to bear arms. Once the stipulations regulating the conduct of the just war had been formulated, their application in practice would depend on how well they were understood and accepted by the prince and how well he kept control over his soldiers. The *Tree* is, therefore, addressed to a soverign prince, King Charles VI of France, and the author expresses his hope, in the prologue, that 'by a member of the high lineage of France, healing will be given to an age which is in such travail and disease'. He assures the king of God's help in providing a remedy for current abuses (4:94); he reminds him that the security of peasants is his personal responsibility (4:102), and earnestly desires that soldiers be made aware that he 'is a prince who does justice severely' (4:104). It is this emphasis on princely discipline over soldiers which is one of the most interesting and important features of the work.

Bouvet was extremely unwilling to accept the ideal of knightly virtue which was propagated by some of his contemporaries: by Jean Froissart, Geoffroy de Charny, and Jean le Seneschal. He abhorred the kind of individual heroism, senseless and immoderate, which had decimated King John's Order of the Star, and described, with obvious distaste, the 'plain and notorious' fact 'that a young knight receives more praise for attacking than for waiting' (3:5). True boldness in a knight is derived from a proper understanding of the reason and justice of his cause, not from base motives of vainglory, anger, or fear of dishonour (3:4, 6–7, and 4:52). A knight's loyalty to the crown should override all obligations to any other lord (4:15–17). He must be loyal to his lord and obedient 'to him who is acting in place of his lord as governor of the host' (4:8). Instead of engaging in spontaneous acts of individual prowess soldiers should 'go nowhere at all' without the licence of the military commander (4:9), and, amongst the numerous capital offences in the military catalogue were ranged 'striking the provost of the army with intent to injure him', disobedience to the 'governor of the host', absenting oneself from the host in order to show one's 'great courage', causing riots and dissension within the army, and desertion (4:10).

The effectiveness of princely discipline and, indeed, the fine principles of the just war where they related to the protection of non-combatants, was likely to depend to a large measure on how well-paid soldiers were. Without reasonable pay soldiers could not be expected to refrain from using their power in their own private interests. The *Tree* contains a very heavy concentration on the subject of wages paid to soldiers, although the details of who was obliged to pay (4:15 and 19), of who had the right to wages (4:29–32, 34, 36, 38, and 42), and of when wages were to be paid (4:37), were technicalities more relevant to the Italian than to the French situation. The idea, however, that soldiers who went to war for the sake of pillage were not entitled to wages (4:34), and that those who were paid wages had no rights over booty and prisoners captured in the war (4:14 and 43), held implications of the utmost significance to the military class. It implied, in fact, that any man engaged in the profession of arms, be he knight or commoner, was a paid servant of the state who 'does all that he does as a deputy of the king or of the lord in whose pay he is' (4:14).

Such then is a summary of the third and fourth books of the *Tree of*

Battles. It is a summary which perhaps obscures some of the work's major inconsistencies, ambiguities, and absurdities, and also some of its finer points such as the appeal on behalf of the peasants in chapter 102 of the fourth book. It does, however, suggest a possible reason for the *Tree*'s popularity amongst fifteenth-century military leaders who were attempting to create disciplined national chivalries in a world where chivalry had traditionally accepted neither discipline nor nationalism as virtues. It also suggests that the interpretation of the 'laws of war' presented in the *Tree of Battles* was more likely to receive an enthusiastic response from representatives of the civil authority than from the knight or soldier who made his living from war. In Italy this was the *condottiere* whose interests as a soldier and as a member of a company often ran counter to the public interests of the employer; in France it was the *homme d'armes* who was unprepared or unable to take up peaceful occupations whenever the king no longer required his services. These men may have felt powerful ties of loyalty to authorities within and outside their company; they may even have considered themselves knights worthy of the romances of chivalry, forever in search of just quarrels. But fundamentally they were an irresponsible and anarchic element in society, and they were recognized so to be.[16]

The professional soldier of the fourteenth century, while extremely unresponsive to arguments concerned with 'public duty' and 'common good', did recognize himself as subject to a law which was peculiar to his profession: namely, the 'law of arms'. The use of the term *droit d'armes* in the fourteenth century by men who were directly involved in warfare, or in the recording of deeds of arms, provides us with a surprisingly limited conception of its scope. Froissart usually employed the phrase to indicate some sort of relationship between knights in which one party was temporarily at a disadvantage with regard to another. Thus, in his account of the siege of Limoges in 1370, three French knights surrendered themselves to the duke of Lancaster, saying, 'Lord, we are yours and you have vanquished us: now treat us according to the law of arms'.[17] Earlier, Froissart had described how the

16. Not only by Bouvet, but also by many of his contemporaries at the French court: Nicolas de Clamanges, in his letters to Jean Gerson; Gerson himself, in his sermon *Vivat Rex* (1405); Jean Petit, in the *Livre du champ d'or*; Philippe de Mézières, in *Le Songe du Vieil Pèlerin*; Christine de Pisan, in *Le Livre de la paix*, and Eustache Deschamps, in several of his ballads, such as the *Lay des douze estas du monde*.

17. Froissart, *Oeuvres. Chroniques*, ed. K. de Lettenhove (29 vols., Brussels, 1870–7), viii. 43.

English left the slayer of Sir John Chandos to die of his wounds, which was 'ill done, for it is an improper thing to treat any prisoner other than as the law of arms requires'.[18] The implication was that the law of arms imposed some sort of obligation on one knight to behave with magnanimity towards another who was at his mercy.

That the law of arms was something more positive and more formal than a simple code of gentlemanly behaviour is suggested by one of the works of Geoffroy de Charny. Charny was a captain of French garrisons on the Picard and Norman frontiers when, on 6 January 1352, he was admitted to King John II's Order of the Star. This famous but short-lived order had as its centre the Noble Maison de Saint-Ouen situated between Paris and Saint-Denis, where, on 15 August, its 500 member knights held their assembly. Soon after his admission to the order Charny drew up a list of questions for discussion by his fellow-members:[19] questions important and of limited application which were aimed at establishing definite rulings in cases concerning the *droit d'armes* of jousts, of tournaments, and of war. All 134 of Charny's *Demandes* are concerned with technicalities of terminology and of the rights and duties of knights in the list and in the field. Although many of the questions are bafflingly casuistical, most conclude with the question: 'How will it be judged by the law of arms?', and therefore point to conclusions about a contemporary soldier's interpretation of the law of arms.

Charny, clearly, did not consider the law of arms to be a codified body of law as were the two great collections of written law: the Canon and Civil Laws. If he concluded many of his demands with the question 'Qu'en sera il jugie par droit d'armes?', he frequently associated it with, or replaced it by, other questions: 'Qu'en dictes vous?', or 'Qu'en sera il jugie par gens d'armes?'[20] Charny's use of these phrases as if they were interchangeable, and the fact that the *Demandes* were addressed to other knights rather than to lawyers and clerks, suggest that the law of arms was a matter of military custom and usage. No group of men would have been more competent to rule on such questions than the eminent and experienced knights of the Order of the Star. Another important

18. Froissart, *Chroniques*, vii. 459.

19. Geoffroy de Charny, *Demandes*, B.N., MS. nouv. acqs. frs. 4736. This manuscript contains thirty-four folios, of which twenty-six are concerned with questions on war. I am grateful to Professor Kenneth Fowler for making available to me his transcript of the manuscript.

20. Examples of each appear in question 42 (1st on 'war'), question 88 (47th on 'war'), and question 93 (52nd on 'war').

distinction between the law of arms, as interpreted by Charny, and more conventional positive law appears in the matter of incentives and sanctions. Like any other law, the law of arms was concerned with rights and duties (albeit of a restricted social class), but the rules were to be observed not from fear of punishment but from a desire not to be excluded from a share in the profits of war. It was a law similar to that of the joint-stock company, evolved in the interests of its members and administered by those who shared the same trade. It applied in relations between soldiers of the same side, as in the question of whether soldiers of a garrison must share booty acquired outside the walls of the castle with their fellows who remain behind; it applied in relations between soldiers and their captains in cases, for example, of indiscipline; and it applied in cases concerning soldiers of opposite sides, usually where title to ransom was at stake.[21] Charny was, in fact, so overwhelmingly preoccupied with questions of booty and ransoms that we may be justified in thinking, on the basis of his *Demandes*, that the law of arms was little more than 'rapacity working through well-organized legal channels'.[22]

The law of arms as described by Froissart and Charny was a professional code which regulated the conduct of knights, especially where this related to the acquisition and distribution of booty and prisoners. It was, as Keen described it, a 'special law' for knights, and one which made 'little distinction between the rights of public bodies and those of private persons' since it was 'formulated and applied with a view to the protection of the rights of individual soldiers . . .'.[23] It was clearly in the best interests of knights to observe its stipulations, not only because a share of war profits was at stake, but also because it imposed patterns on warfare which made it a slightly less hazardous undertaking for the professional soldier. Furthermore, it would also appear that this law of arms was not to be found in any book, but rather in the everyday practices and customs of *gens d'armes* as interpreted by eminent members of their own profession: old knights, military officers, and heralds.[24]

21. Examples in questions 81 (40th on 'war'), 51 (10th on 'war'), and 97 (56th on 'war').

22. D. Hay, 'The Division of the Spoils of War in Fourteenth-Century England', *T.R.Hist.S.*, 5th ser., iv (1954), 94.

23. Keen, *Laws of War*, pp. 15 and 245.

24. The nearest that the fourteenth century came to a codification of the law of arms was perhaps *Las Siete Partidas* which it inherited from Alfonso IX of Castile (trans. S. P. Scott, Chicago and New York, 1931). The work, however, does not appear to have had a wide circulation north of the Pyrenees. It was reported in *La Geste des nobles françois* (c. 1429) that Henry of Lancaster 'tant fut droicturier en armes et autres choses, et qui

The *Tree of Battles* had very little to do with such a law. The rules of soldierly conduct described in the *Tree* were binding upon military men whether or not they were accustomed to observe them already. In fact many of the laws embodied in this work were recognized as being contrary to contemporary soldierly custom. The 'law', for example, forbad the taking of excessive ransoms from prisoners, and especially from the common people, 'but God well knows that the soldiery of today do the opposite' (4:47); a foreign student and his relatives might not be attacked 'by law' even though, 'perhaps, soldiers will not receive this opinion very willingly' (4:88); and Bouvet expressed similar doubts about the observance of the rules of feast days (4:50), safe conducts (4:57), and immunities (4:102). The *Tree* was not a collection of knightly customs, nor was it a work which failed to make a distinction between 'private' and 'public' rights. The king's war, insisted Bouvet, 'concerns the common good of the whole kingdom, which is more important than the particular good of a barony' (4:17), and only the sovereign prince, as the representative and guardian of the 'public good' was permitted to order 'general war' (4:4). Bouvet contrasted repeatedly the selfish interests of individual knights with those of the community as a whole, and accused them of being decadent (4:132), eager to find flaws and loop-holes in the law (4:58), and of filling a rôle in this world like that of the 'devils of hell' in the other (4:54).

In the introduction to his edition of the *Tree*, Nys remarked that the work is less than explicit in its dealing with questions of the 'practices of war, of booty and ransoms of prisoners':[25] these matters were not treated with 'toute la rigeur désirable'. Such a statement is nothing short of the truth. The vexed question of how booty is to be divided among soldiers, which occupied Charny for nearly one-third of his *Demandes* on war, is concentrated into one single paragraph of the *Tree* where it is blandly stated that all booty must be handed over to the 'duke of the battle; and the duke should share the spoils out among his men, to each according to his valour' (4:43). The *Tree* does, it is true, address itself in a more businesslike fashion to problems relating to prisoners and ransoms, but most of such material deals with immunities to imprisonment

---

a l'introduction des nobles establit et fist le Livre des Droiz de Guerre', but there is no other evidence of this book or of its contents. See M. Hayez, 'Un exemple de culture historique au XVᵉ siècle: *La Geste des Nobles François*', *Mélanges d'archéologie et d'histoire de l'École Française de Rome*, lxxv (1963), 162.

25. *L'Arbre*, ed. Nys, pp. xxvii–xxviii.

rather than rights within such a relationship. Thus, while only four of the *Tree*'s questions are directly related to matters such as the scale of ransoms and the proper treatment of prisoners, at least twenty others are concerned with the classes of people entitled to immunity from imprisonment and ransom.[26] Far from devoting itself to the 'protection of the rights of individual soldiers', the *Tree* seems to have been much more concerned with protecting the rights of all other classes in society.

The content and principles of the *droit d'armes* indicated by the questions of Geoffroy de Charny are so radically different to the 'laws of war' exposed in the *Tree of Battles* that it would be fair to assume that they were derived from different sources. The law of arms, as a code which regulated the mutual relationship between knights engaged in their military calling, was the product of the different standards, interpretations, and needs of successive generations of knights. The *Tree*, on the other hand, seems to have had a permanent base in the 'written law'.

The *Tree* acknowledges many different types of authority: Divine Law, the law of nations, Canon Law, Civil Law, the Lombard Law, and the law of war, but Bouvet tended to classify them all in terms of written and unwritten law. The Lombard Law was, as he noted, 'extraordinary', and did not fit in well with either classification. The distinction was essentially between the customary *droit de guerre* and all other laws. When discussing, for example, the question of whether legates or ambassadors were permitted to bring with them into enemy territory 'things' or 'persons' superfluous to their actual requirements, Bouvet remarked that if a soldier 'had captured this thing or that man neither the laws of war nor written law would take it from him' (4:96). All written law is occasionally indicated by the simple word *droit* (4:112), whereas the laws of war appear variously, depending on the author's approval or disapproval, as *de bonne guerre* (4:56), *bonnes coutumes* (4:60), *coustumes et usaiges du monde* (4:112), or 'practices' invented by 'lords and others' (4:79). It is clear that the *Tree* was drawing upon many different sources both in written and in customary law.

The *Tree* was not, however, simply an indiscriminate collection of materials which related to the subject of war, for the sources themselves did not always agree. In the case of duels and reprisals, customary law

26. A comment in the chapter (4:56) dealing with conditions of imprisonment is revealing: 'And if a man, by his own fault, find himself in such a case [of harsh imprisonment], the peril and risk are on his own head, *for he has thereby lost the privilege of law*' (my italics).

contradicted all written law (4:79, 111, and 112); with regard to the captor's rights over his prisoner, the 'ancient law' of Rome had been humanized by Christianity (4:46); in the case of an enemy leader taken prisoner, the Civil Law and the 'decretal' disagreed over his treatment (4:13); if the son should resist his father, the 'law of nature' would allow what the Civil Law condemned (4:75). The thesis, recently advanced, that the laws relating to war (which drew upon Divine, Natural, Canon, and Civil Law, and upon the customary rules observed from old times by professional soldiers) formed a naturally coherent structure in which the laws 'were not all essentially different but supplementary to one another in particular matters',[27] appears, on the evidence of the *Tree*, to be untenable. The *Tree* was a selection from such sources and in order to understand the principles and criteria of such a selection we must first examine the direct legal sources themselves.

The *Tree* is the direct product of those developments in legal theory which took place during the late thirteenth and fourteenth centuries, and which are associated with the school of the Post-glossators.[28] This school which was French in origin had come, during the fourteenth century, to be dominated by Italian jurists, notably by Bartolus of Sassoferrato, Baldus of Ubaldis, and Lucas of Penna. The aim of the Post-glossators was no less than the creation of a new medieval Civil Law, the *usus modernus*, by combining Roman and non-Roman legal materials. Their basic principles were derived from Roman Law (the Justinian texts and glosses) and from scholastic philosophy (particularly of Aquinas and Colonna), but other sources—notably Canon Law and various feudal and customary laws—were not entirely discountenanced. When they turned their attentions to the subject of war, the Italian lawyers, with their high ideals of law based on equity ('jus est justitiae executivum'), did not always accommodate themselves easily with the primitive and barbaric customs inherited from a tribal and feudal past. The doctrine of reprisals, for example, which allowed an innocent individual to suffer for the misdeeds of another, and which was derived from Germanic tribal principles of collective responsibility for a crime,[29] did not accord well with Post-glossatorial principles. In fact Lucas of

---

27. Keen, *Laws of War*, p. 18.

28. On the Post-glossators, see W. Ullmann, *The Medieval Idea of Law as represented by Lucas da Penna* (London, 1946), and the introduction by H. Hazeltine.

29. R. de Mas Latrie, 'Du droit de marque ou droit de représailles au moyen âge', *B.E.C.*, 6ᵉ sér., ii (1866), 529–77. On the origins of the reprisal doctrine, see ibid., pp. 532–6.

Penna denounced the custom altogether, as he did also the practice of judicial combat. Other jurists, particularly those of the Bartolist school, were more realistic in their approach and attempted not to eliminate these deeply rooted customs, but to restrict their operation and to bring them securely under the control of the civil authority. One of the pioneers in this field was the Bolognese professor of law, John of Legnano, whose *Tractatus de Bello, de Represaliis et de Duello* was completed in 1360 and became, some twenty-five years later, the basic source of the *Tree of Battles*.[30]

Thanks especially to their training in Roman Law, and also to their familiarity with the *Summa Theologica* of Thomas Aquinas and the *De Regimine Principum* of Colonna, John of Legnano and the other 'subtle and strenuous legists of the [Italian] trecento' were often the 'faithful intellectual auxiliaries of the civil authority'.[31] One of the most serious problems of the 'civil authority' in fourteenth-century Italy was that of controlling the mercenary soldiers in its employ: of subordinating the private interests of the *condottieri* to the public interests of the state. The commune of Florence, for example, had been attempting with less and less success since the Biliotti commission of 1337 to impose on its stipendiary soldiers a regular system of muster and review and a strict interpretation of public rights in the spoils of war. The *usus modernus* would have been of no more than academic interest if the Post-glossators had failed to relate it to the particular problems of the society for which it was devised. The *Tractatus* of Legnano did deal with just such contemporary problems—but they were the problems of the civil authority, not those of individual soldiers who were more than adequately equipped to secure their own interests. It was no coincidence that the *Tractatus* was dedicated to Cardinal Gil Albornoz, lieutenant of the Avignon popes in Italy, and 'widely acclaimed as the leading civilian virtuoso of his generation in the management and control of mercenaries'.[32]

When the *Tractatus* was transferred to a French setting, in Bouvet's *Tree of Battles*, some of its details must have sounded strange and alien.

30. John of Legnano, *Tractatus de Bello, de Represaliis et de Duello*, ed. T. E. Holland and trans. J. L. Brierly (Oxford, 1917). For a detailed exposition of Bouvet's debt to Legnano, see G. W. Coopland, 'The Tree of Battles and Some of its Sources', *Revue d'Histoire du Droit*, v (1923), 173–207.

31. C. C. Bayley, *War and Society in Renaissance Florence: The 'De Militia' of Leonardo Bruni* (Toronto, 1961), p. 45.

32. Ibid., p. 46.

The regulations for the proper conduct of trial by combat, for example, which were derived from the Lombard law, had little relevance to French customs which had been standardized in the *Ordonnance* of Philip IV in 1306. Nevertheless, the problems which faced the French crown, as the embodiment of the public good of the realm, concerning the conduct of war and the control of soldiers, were essentially similar to those of the Italian communes, and the legal theories of the Post-glossators were as relevant to France as they were to the Italian republics. The Italians were concerned with directing the aggressive energies of the *condottieri* against the enemies of the state rather than against its own subjects in the *contado*. The French crown had similar problems, especially with its garrison troops on the frontiers of the kingdom who often compensated themselves for insufficient and irregular pay at the expense of 'friendly' non-combatants. The whole question of public interest versus private rights, which was such a dominant theme in the literature of this period, had bedevilled the Hundred Years War from its start and had effectively prevented a final peace-settlement during the 1360s.[33] These problems were eliminated, at least in theory, by the assertion, repeatedly expressed in the *Tree*, that the private interests of soldiers must never run counter to the public interests of the crown.

If the traditional 'law of arms' embodied these 'private interests' of soldiers, as certainly seems to be the case, then it is hardly surprising that it receives somewhat unsympathetic handling in the *Tree of Battles*. The customary law which Bouvet occasionally calls the 'laws of war' and which has a significant contribution to make to the *Tree*, is not coterminous with the law of arms. The customs and usages which were considered by Bouvet to have legal force were those which had been sanctioned by the civil authority and over which such an authority could maintain effective control.

In the case, for example, of trial by combat, Bouvet, who was temperamentally and professionally sceptical about any such procedure, describes how 'worldy customs and usages' ('les coustumes et usaiges

<hr />

33. It was difficult for Edward III to remove the occupants of castles which had been captured in his name during the war, but which had been returned to France by the Treaty of Brétigny; the captains claimed compensation for their losses. See P. Chaplais, 'Some Documents regarding the Fulfilment and Interpretation of the Treaty of Brétigny', *Camden Miscellany*, xix (1952), 12–15. For examples of this problem on the French side after Brétigny, see P.-C. Timbal, *La Guerre de Cent Ans vue à travers les registres du Parlement, 1337–1369* (Paris, 1961), pp. 432–67.

du monde') take precedence over all written law (4:111–12). The author
of the *Tree* recalls a duel which took place before King John II of France
at Villeneuve-les-Avignon in the spring of 1363.[34] Urban V had done
his best to ban the duel between the Gascon lord, Amanieu de Pom-
miers, and the Frenchman, Foulques d'Archiac, but, 'although the Pope
wished to keep the laws laid down by the Decretals, and commanded
that no one, under pain of excommunication, should be present at the
combat, the King did not refrain from having the combat carried out
and was unwilling to act to the prejudice of royal customs' (3:1). Thus
when Bouvet talks respectfully of 'worldly' customs he refers only to
those practices which the secular authority was prepared to permit and
to support: the 'coustumes royaulx'. This point might be further illustrated from Bouvet's treatment of the doctrine of *marque* and reprisal
which, 'according to the written law . . . is by no means permitted', but
which can be justified on the grounds that it is a 'kind of war which
princes for long have been using commonly throughout the world'
(4:79). A tightly administered law of reprisal, as defined in the *Tree of
Battles*, was very much in the interests of the civil authority anxious to
curb and eradicate the *guerre privée* and to monopolize the control of
war.[35]

If the Post-glossators present a peculiarly monarchical picture of the
function of law, and the *Tree of Battles* follows their lead, they also give
a similar twist to the concept of chivalry. The interpretation of chivalry
in the *Tree* is a decidedly unromantic one and is ultimately derived,
through the selective lens of the Post-glossators, from two quite independent sources: the military manuals of republican and imperial Rome,
and the 'peace movement' of the tenth- and eleventh-century church.

The myth that the code of chivalry originated in the Roman republic
encouraged the use of Roman military manuals by fourteenth-century
commentators. The collection of anecdotes organized by Valerius
Maximus under appropriate headings, (including 'military discipline'),
in his *Facta et Dicta Memorabilia*, became popular in the late Middle

34. The duel is referred to by Froissart (*Chroniques*, vi. 370 and 372) and by the
author of the *Chronique des règnes de Jean II et de Charles V*, ed. R. Delachenal (4 vols.,
S.H.F., 1910–20), i. 339.
35. The feudal right of the noble to engage in 'private war' whenever he considered
justice to have been denied him existed in direct proportion to the lack of central authority
and was therefore most securely based in Germany and Italy. Elsewhere, the kings of
England, France, Castile, and Aragon had attempted, with more or less success, to place
restrictions on private war. See E. Nys, *Le Droit de la guerre et les précurseurs de Grotius*
(Brussels, 1882), chapter on 'La Guerre et le Christianisme'.

Ages thanks to the commentary of Dionigi da Borgo San Sepolcro. Simon de Hesdin, chaplain of the Order of St. John of Jerusalem and one of Charles V's industrious team of translators, had started a translation and commentary of this work in 1375, and there is at least one other commentary which originated in fourteenth-century France.[36] The *Strategemata* of Sextus Julius Frontinus was also popular. By far the most celebrated of these books, however, was the handbook of military tactics compiled by Flavius Vegetius Renatus towards the end of the fourth century A.D., and entitled *De Re Militari*. This work was translated into French, first by the indefatigable Jean de Meun in 1284, then by Jean de Vignai during the second quarter of the fourteenth century. In 1380 yet another translation appeared, possibly the work of Eustache Deschamps.[37] These works provide practical advice in most areas of military activity, but the feature of Roman armies which they described, and which most impressed the fourteenth-century reader, was their discipline. This is precisely the lesson which Bouvet drew from these sources into the *Tree of Battles*, and particularly from the 'doctrine of a doctor called Monseigneur Vegetius, in his Book of Chivalry' (4:9).

The ideals of discipline and organization so universally recognized among the Roman legions were not received so willingly by the medieval knight who also recognized the ideal of the knight-errant whose vocation was the pursuit of just quarrels. The individualistic knights of Chrétien de Troyes's romances would not, and could not, have existed in an orderly and disciplined society. Yet Bouvet advocated such reforms in the very name of chivalry and showed how soldiers must accept them as 'l'ordonnance de deue chevalerie' (4:102). Bouvet's *chevalier* is loyal to his lord and obedient to the lord's deputy in the host; he is fully professional and constantly occupied with the practice of arms; he is subject to the strict discipline which the lord's officers exercise in the host. It was just such a conception of knighthood and chivalry, based on the works of Vegetius and of Bouvet himself, which formed the essential element in a book composed by Christine de Pisan in 1409, *Le Livre des faits d'armes et de chevalerie*.

---

36. M. A. Berlincourt, 'The Relationship of Some Fourteenth-Century Commentaries on Valerius Maximus', *Mediaeval Studies*, xxxiv (1972), 361–87.

37. On translations of Vegetius, see J. Camus, 'Notice d'une traduction française de Végèce faite en 1380', *Romania*, xxv (1896), 393–400, and P. Meyer, 'Les Anciens traducteurs français de Végèce et en particulier Jean de Vignai', ibid. 401–23.

The Roman war-manuals described a pattern of 'chivalrous' behaviour for the individual knight within the host, but the *Tree* also outlined other requirements of 'chivalry' which regulated the relationship between the military and non-military classes. 'I hold firmly', Bouvet said, 'according to ancient law, and according to the ancient customs of good warriors, that it is an unworthy thing to imprison either old men taking no part in the war, or women, or innocent children' (4:94). Again, in the context of soldiers who attack and rob 'poor labouring people', Bouvet remarked that 'that way of warfare does not follow the ordinances of worthy chivalry or of the ancient custom of noble warriors who upheld justice, the widow, the orphan and the poor' (4:102). It has often been pointed out that such 'ordinances' and 'ancient customs' had origins no more ancient than the councils summoned at the instigation of the church in southern France during the late tenth and eleventh centuries.[38] One of the primary objectives of the peace associations which emerged from these councils was that knights who had the right to bear arms should no longer turn them against those who did not possess such a right: clerks, peasants, and merchants. Even the sanctions which the peace associations could bring to bear were often insufficient to enforce either this, or the related principle of the 'truce of God'. Nevertheless, the principles themselves passed into Canon Law with the decree of Pope Nicholas II in 1059, whence, through a remarkable chain of revisions and repetitions, they reappeared in the pages of the *Tree of Battles*.

The *Tree of Battles*, therefore, presents a clear and uncompromising picture of the soldier's rôle in society: a picture which must have appeared a long way from reality in fourteenth-century France. The book represents a stage in the development of legal theory relating to war: a product of legal synthesis which drew upon a multitude of sources, biblical, scholastic, canonical, Roman, and customary. The selection of material from such disparate sources which appeared in the *Tree* achieved its coherence not because the sources themselves agreed, but because they had been employed selectively according to the criterion of the 'public good'. The representative of the 'public good', and its

---

38. G. Molinié, *L'Organisation judiciaire, militaire et financière des associations de la paix* (Toulouse, 1912); R. Bonnaud-Delamare, 'Fondement des institutions de paix au XIᵉ siècle', *Mélanges d'histoire du Moyen Âge dédiés à la mémoire de Louis Halphen* (Paris, 1951), pp. 19–26, and F. Duval, *De la Paix de Dieu à la Paix de Fer* (Paris, 1922), esp. p. 35: 'La Chevalerie'.

guardian, was the prince, the soldier merely his agent. Such a law, which embraced the entire community, had little time for the special laws of particular classes in the community. The long-established customs which protected the rights of individual soldiers and which had been evolved with few points of reference outside the military profession was just such a special law: it was called the law of arms. The law, which Bouvet exposed for the first time in the French language, and which might be distinguished by the title 'laws of war', did incorporate certain emasculated elements of the old law of arms which related to the conduct of duels and the treatment of prisoners. There was much in the law of arms which was simply ignored in the *Tree*, such as the obligations entailed by brotherhood-in-arms and the details of tournaments and jousts. The basic principles of the *Tree*, however, were antipathetic to those of the law of arms because where one was general the other was specific, and where one was concerned almost exclusively with the soldier in society the other dealt with the standing of the soldier within his own profession. When a military commander in the third quarter of the fifteenth century repeatedly enunciated the principle that 'ung bien particulier n'est pas à preferer à la chose publique',[39] the *Tree of Battles* had done its work, and the law of arms could look forward only to a marginal and threadbare existence.

For the fourteenth century, however, as Huizinga remarked, the *Tree of Battles* was only a theoretical treatise whose fine rules and generous exemptions were too rarely observed. If we look to the *Tree* for information concerning the actual conduct of war during the first half of the Hundred Years War, we are as likely to find it in the breach as in the observance of the *Tree*'s rules. We must, as the fifteenth-century herald advised his pupil,[40] read the *Tree of Battles*, but also 'follow the wars' in order to supplement the *Tree*'s theoretical principles with practical day-to-day details. To regard the *Tree*, as many have done, as an authority for the law of arms is likely to be an unfruitful exercise unless we appreciate that the conception of war which the *Tree* proposes 'was moving in a direction favourable to modern kingship':[41] a direction most unfavourable to the traditional law of arms. The *Tree* did not present a

39. Jean de Bueil, *Le Jouvencel*, ed. L. Lecestre and C. Favre (2 vols., S.H.F., 1887-9), ii. 12, 95 and 215.

40. See above, p. 13, n. 8.

41. P. Contamine, *Guerre, état et société à la fin du Moyen Âge. Études sur les armées des rois de France, 1337-1494* (Paris and The Hague, 1972), pp. 202-3.

codification of military practice but a programme of reform, and it became a practical treatise only when, during the fifteenth century, the
kings of France and of England created national 'chivalries' out of the
universal order of knighthood, and brought soldiers effectively under
their control.

3

Chivalry, Nobility,
and the Man-at-Arms

M. H. KEEN

There is a story told of the great English captain Sir John Hawkwood once being met at the gate of Montecchio by two friars who wished him peace. 'May the Lord take away your alms,' was his reply to their benediction, 'do you not know that I live by war and that peace would be my undoing.' 'So well did he manage his affairs', Sacchetti adds, 'that there was little peace in Italy in his day.'[1] This story and Hawkwood's own career illustrate eloquently an ambiguity in medieval attitudes towards war and the fighting man which had important social consequences. On the one hand, there was no doubt that Hawkwood and his kind were a scourge to the lands over which they campaigned. It was their activities that prompted the indignant cry of the lawyer Bartholomew of Saliceto: 'What shall I say of those companies of men-at-arms who overrun the territories of our cities? I reply that there is no doubt about their position, for they are robbers ... and therefore as robbers they should be punished for all the crimes that they have committed.'[2] But Hawkwood was not punished for his crimes: he thrived to be captain-general to the pope, Milan, and Florence, to marry Donnina, the natural daughter of Bernabo Visconti, lord of Milan, and to enjoy estates in the kingdom of Naples and at Poggibonsi in the Florentine *contado*. When he died in 1394 the grateful Florentines buried their ex-captain-general under an elaborate marble tomb in their cathedral. His own countrymen remembered him with pride; and he was one of those knights of the past whose noble deeds Caxton urged men of his own time to call to mind as models of chivalrous achievement.[3] Which was he then truly, knight or robber?

1. F. Sacchetti, *Novelle* (3 vols., Milan, 1804–5), iii. 91–93.
2. Bartholomew of Saliceto, Super VIII Cod. Tit. 51, l. 12.
3. W. Caxton, *The Book of the Ordre of Chyualry*, ed. A. T. P. Byles (E.E.T.S., 1926), p. 123.

Hawkwood was no isolated adventurer; he was only a spectacularly successful member of a class of soldiers whose advent brought devastation and social dislocation wherever they passed—dislocation that made the ravages of war a factor of social and economic importance at the very least comparable to the effect of plague in the later Middle Ages. The woeful comments of contemporaries make it clear how sharply aware they were of this impact of war. Jean de Bueil, picturing himself as a young man riding through the lands that had been wasted in the Anglo-French struggle of the fifteenth century, spoke of a country 'desolate and deserted', where the houses of the peasantry looked more like the lairs of wild beasts than the houses of men.[4] Thomas Basin's picture of the same scene is still more lugubrious:

I myself have seen the great plains of Champagne, of Beauce, of Brie, of the Gâtinais, of the country about Chartres and Dreux, of Maine, Perche, and the Vexin, French and Norman lands alike, of the Beauvaisis, of the *pays* of Caux, from the Seine to Amiens and Abbeville, the country around Senlis, the Soissonais and Valois as far as Laon and even in to Hainault, utterly deserted, uncultivated, abandoned, emptied of inhabitants, overgrown with thorns and brambles, or, where trees will grow, springing into forest.[5]

Little wonder that when Philippe de Mézières sought to draw his allegorical picture of Nimrod's 'horrible and perilous garden of war', he conceived it as a barren land, bringing forth leafless trees and infested by gigantic locusts.[6] Hawkwood and men of his stamp, and the companies that they led, did just what locusts do to the countryside: they stripped it bare—but with this difference, that in many places they proved to be no passing plague.

Soldiers such as these resembled locusts in another way, too; they could not have created the havoc that they did if there had not been swarms of them. One must of course guard against exaggerating their numbers unduly: it is easy nowadays to forget how, in the fourteenth or fifteenth century, a wide zone could be terrorized by a mere handful of determined and experienced men with a strong hill fort at their disposal as a headquarters. But it is clear that, at any rate by contemporary standards, the companies that operated in Italy under such leaders as Hawk-

4. Jean de Bueil, *Le Jouvencel*, ed. L. Lecestre and C. Favre, (2 vols., S.H.F., 1887–9), i. 19.
5. Thomas Basin, *Histoire de Charles VII*, ed. C. Samaran (rev. ed., 2 vols., Paris, 1964), i. 86.
6. See N. Jorga, *Philippe de Mézières et la croisade au XIVe siècle* (Paris, 1892; repr. London, 1973), p. 486. The quotation is from the 'Epistre au Roy Richart'.

wood and Bernardon de la Salle, and under their German predecessors, constituted substantial forces. The free soldiers who, confederated together, formed the famous Great Company that routed the French royal forces under King John's chamberlain the count of Tancarville in 1362, made a formidable army.[7] The size of the forces engaged in operations such as these—forces that were generated in the course of this or that dynastic or territorial quarrel, but which remained active for longer than the duration of the wars that had brought them into being —poses of itself a problem. How was it that the effect and scale of the activities of soldiers of fortune were permitted to get out of hand to the extent that they did in the later Middle Ages, and this despite the fact that contemporaries recognized these activities for the social bane that they were? The argument of this article is that the other side to the story of Hawkwood with which I began, the renown and honour which his 'noble deeds' earned him, gives the key to a part, though of course only a part, of the answer. That is to say that one reason for the failure of this age to keep the social problem of war within bounds lay, ironically, in the idealism of its attitude to war and to the soldier, in what we may call the ethic of chivalry.

Let us take, as a first illustration, the attitude of Honoré Bouvet, the late fourteenth-century canonist and prior of Selonnet, whose book, the *Tree of Battles*, is of particular relevance to any inquiry into chivalry, because it was widely read among knights and secular men and was regarded by many as an authoritative treatment of chivalry and war.[8] Bouvet could recognize clearly enough the contemporary evil consequences of war. 'In these days', he complained indignantly, 'all wars are directed against the poor labouring people . . . the man who does not know how to set places on fire, to rob churches and . . . to imprison the priests, is not fit to carry on war.'[9] But he did not dream of concluding from this that war in and for itself was to be condemned. 'I ask in what place war was first found', he wrote, 'and I disclose to you that it was in Heaven, when our Lord God drove out the wicked angels.'[10] Regarding war as cosmic and natural, at the human level a

7. On this battle and the operations preceding it, see also R. Delachenal, *Histoire de Charles V* (5 vols., Paris, 1909–31), ii. 315–22.

8. *The Tree of Battles of Honoré Bonet*, ed. and trans. G. W. Coopland (Liverpool, 1949) [henceforward *The Tree*]. For evidence of its widespread influence, see introduction, pp. 22–23; P. Contamine, *Guerre, état et société à la fin du Moyen Âge* (Paris and The Hague, 1972), pp. 202–4; and M. H. Keen, *The Laws of War in the Late Middle Ages* (London, 1965), p. 21.

9. *The Tree*, p. 189.   10. Ibid., p. 81.

reflection of the universal struggle against evil, he could not look on it as a condition that was bad *per se*. 'War is not an evil thing, but good and virtuous', he wrote, 'for war by its very nature seeks nothing other that to set wrong right.'[11]

About this view of Bouvet's, as I have quoted it so far, there was nothing very original: he was drawing on what was, in his time, a large and well-known *corpus* of received opinion, patristic and canonical, about the just war. Nor, indeed, is there anything specifically medieval about it, except its phraseology: the idea of the just war has proved by no means dead in the twentieth century. But certain extensions of Bouvet's view are more striking and cannot be made to sound modern. Logically, one might suppose that if participation in a war waged in a just cause was accepted to be a meritorious activity, to participate on the wrong side would be the opposite. That is not quite how Bouvet saw the issue. If men were wiser, he admitted, there would be greater tranquillity: nevertheless, he went on, 'I do not say that there is never war among wise men for just reason. For sometimes wars are begun by simple folk, or are undertaken foolishly, and then those that come after and know not the reasons make worthy war, for each *thinks* he is in the right.'[12] The prime question for Bouvet, therefore, was not whether the cause of war was just, but whether the individual combatant thought it was. The learned Italian canonist Angelus of Perusia put much the same point: if there was doubt as to which of the principals was in the right in a war it would be correct, he said, to 'regard the war as just on both sides'.[13] Both these doctors were less concerned about which side in a war had most right with it, than with the question of whether an individual might engage in it, on either side, without endangering his soul. There is clearly a very big difference between these two questions, and between the approaches to the problem of the just war that underlie them.

The answer that both men gave to this second question was, we see, an affirmative one, and that was what got across to the less learned men who read Bouvet's book. William Worcester, secretary to the great English soldier, Sir John Fastolf, had, we know, studied the *Tree of Battles*: 'Where', he asked in his *Boke of Noblesse*, 'is a holier, juster, or

---

11. Ibid., p. 125.   12. Ibid., p. 119.
13. Angelus of Perusia, *Disputatio, inc. Renovata Guerra* (Pavia, c. 1490, unpaginated): 'aut quilibet asseret se prius insultatum et se pro defensa sui juris facere dictam guerram, quo casu propter dubium ex utroque latere dicere possumus guerram justam'.

more perfect thing than to make war in your rightful title?'[14] Jean de Bueil, who had carefully read Christine de Pisan's *Livre des faits d'armes et de chevalerie* (which incorporates virtually the whole of Bouvet's writing about the laws of war),[15] put the same point even more elegantly: 'If God is willing', he wrote, 'we soldiers will win our salvation by the exercise of arms just as well as we could by living a life of contemplation on a diet of roots.'[16] I do not wish to overstress my point and suggest that Bouvet or Christine or the canonists from whom Bouvet drew his opinions were solely or directly responsible for the attitudes of such as Worcester and Jean de Bueil. The learning of the canonists, like that of most lawyers in most ages, simply gave legal expression to an accepted social outlook. Already in the fourteenth century, let alone the fifteenth, there was a very long history behind knightly confidence that participation in a just war (as opposed to a full-blooded crusade) was a holy activity. What the canonists' view did do that was important, in practical and social rather than theoretical terms, was to lend authoritative support to a view of the calling of arms which added lustre to that vocation, and so increased the difficulty of restraining men from responding to its appeal.

Let us turn from Bouvet's *Tree of Battles*, the work of a clerk, to a work written a couple of decades earlier by a genuine warrior, Geoffroy de Charny, John the Good's standard-bearer, knight of the Order of the Star, who died on the field of Poitiers. If anyone had a right to speak with authority about chivalry, clearly Charny had, and he called his book the *Livre de chevalerie*.[17] In this work, the winning of salvation by the exercise of arms supplies a dominant theme. For Charny, chivalry was an order, the highest and hardest among those that God had instituted and by means of which a man might save his soul. It was an

14. William Worcester, *The Boke of Noblesse*, ed. J. G. Nichols (Roxburghe Club, 1860; repr. New York, 1972), p. 22. On Worcester's use of *The Tree*, see K. B. McFarlane, 'William Worcester: A Preliminary Survey', *Studies presented to Sir Hilary Jenkinson*, ed. J. Conway Davies (London, 1957), pp. 210–11. It appears that most, if not all, of Worcester's knowledge of Bouvet's work came to him by way of Christine de Pisan's *Livre des fais d'armes et de chevalerie*.

15. See Coopland, introduction to *The Tree*, p. 22; and Caxton's translation of Christine de Pisan, *The Book of Fayttes of Armes and of Chyualrye*, ed. A. T. P. Byles (E.E.T.S., 1932), Appendix B, pp. 298–9. On Jean de Bueil's knowledge and use of Christine's work, see G. W. Coopland, '*Le Jouvencel* (Re-visited)', *Symposium*, v (1951), 137–86.

16. Jean de Bueil, *Le Jouvencel*, ii. 21

17. Printed, in part, in Froissart, *Oeuvres. Chroniques*, ed. K. de Lettenhove (29 vols., Brussels, 1870–7), i. pt. 2, 463–533.

order harder than that of the cloister, whose services were so ordered that monks had but to follow the 'points of their religion, without the need to arm themselves and go in peril of their bodies'.[18] It was a divine service quite as much as that of the priest: 'to the good man-at-arms it behoves to take arms and arm himself in his armour as dutifully and devoutly and with such an eye to his conscience as ever any priest who, to sing his mass, takes to robe himself the arms of our Saviour'.[19] For Charny, the model of knighthood was Judas Maccabeus, the Lord's warrior of the Bible: 'to whom God permits in his grace, as he did to this mightly *chevalier*, to gain honour in this world and in the end the saving of his soul in paradise; such a man can ask nothing more'.[20] The whole conception of the book is to explain how, by following chivalry—an order which has its own rules and ascetic exercises, its own rituals full of religious symbolism (such as the complicated rite for the creation of a knight)—a man-at-arms may win salvation. Appositely, it concludes with a combination of a prayer and war cry: 'Pray for him who made this book: Charny! Charny!'[21]

Throughout his book, Geoffroy de Charny looks on the man-at-arms as an individual called to the service of God in arms, rather than as a member of a host at the disposal of human authority. For him it is a knight's duty and honour to fight in his lord's war; that is perhaps as near to the idea of the service of the state as his mind, or that of the man-at-arms generally in the fourteenth century, was likely to reach. But, for Charny, a knight's duty does not end there. He must be ready to take up arms of his own accord 'where-ever he may find those who would take their honour or their heritage from the orphan, the helpless maid or widow, and who will not be deterred otherwise than by war or battle'.[22] And to fit himself for this service—of the injured and needy at large, as well as of his lord and of the church—the aspiring knight should exercise himself in tournaments and jousts when he is young, and in the wars where he may find them, especially in distant lands and amid unfamiliar hardships. One might expect that when Charny speaks of far-off lands, those which he would name would be Prussia, Spain, or the Holy Land, but they are not. The lands that he cites are 'Lombardy, Tuscany, Apulia, and other places where men-at-arms may find wages of war'.[23] These were the very lands into which the Free Companies, generated by

18. Charny, *Livre de Chevalerie*, p. 513.   19. Ibid., p. 521.
20. Ibid., p. 511.   21. Ibid., p. 533.   22. Ibid., p. 512.
23. Ibid., p. 468.

the war in France, poured in frightening numbers when, after the Treaty of Brétigny, fighting in the first stage of the Hundred Years War died down in France itself: and they brought with them their developed technique in wasting lands. Hawkwood was among the leaders of these men who were soon creating the same havoc in Lombardy that they had already wrought in Languedoc. The eye that Geoffroy de Charny cast towards Italy thus makes for us a very pointed connection between chivalry, in the full flight of its idealism, and the devastation and social distress which was everywhere in the late Middle Ages the accompaniment of the passage of men-at-arms.

Charny, when he talked of his ideal knight, Judas Maccabeus, stressed two things that in God's grace were given him; honour in this world and salvation in the next. The latter was of course explicitly the more important, but it is clear that the former was never far from Charny's mind. The desire for fame, for honour among men and for the love of woman, should be spurs to the courage of the young knight and encourage him in his quest for martial experience. There is an extension of this theme, of chivalry as the source of worldly honour, which is not explicit in Charny's book but which is made very clear in other books of chivalry, and which is apposite to our purpose. Perhaps it was best put by Ramon Lull in his work *The Order of Chivalry*, another widely read and influential treatment and one which Caxton was to translate into English. 'So high and noble is the order of chivalry', Lull wrote, 'that it sufficeth not that there be made knights of the most noble persons or that there should be given them the most noble beasts and the best, the most noble arms and the best; but it behoveth that he be made lord of many men, for in seignory is much nobleness . . . and it behoveth also that the common people labour the lands to bring forth fruits and goods whereof the knight and his beasts have their living.'[24] We could still, on the basis of this last sentence of Lull's, continue the comparison that Charny made between the order of chivalry and a monastic order, for common men laboured to sustain monks as well as knights. The overtones of the comparison have by this stage altered significantly though: they no longer concern the service of God so directly as they do the right to the service of man.

An association between noble status and the calling of arms was, in the later Middle Ages, an accepted social attitude with a long history

---

24. Caxton, *Book of the Ordre of Chyualry*, pp. 18–20 (Caxton's translation of Lull).

behind it. 'We poor soldiers', wrote Jean de Bueil, 'are for the most part noble by birth, and those who are not are noble by the exercise of arms, for the *métier* of arms is noble of itself.'[25] Even in France, where the nobility early emerged as a legally defined estate, we find that the notion that proven service as a man-at-arms could of itself constitute a claim to noble status was sufficiently current to be advanced in legal proceedings. ' Quant aucun est passé deux fois en monstres, est deinceps reputé noble': so argued one advocate in the *Parlement* of Paris in 1426.[26] In England, although she knew no legally defined status of nobility such as France did, traces of a similar attitude are none the less found. When those commissioned to take evidence in the dispute pending in the Constable's Court of Chivalry between Sir Richard Scrope and Sir Robert Grosvenor set about their business, much emphasis was laid on the fact that they were seeking the testimony of men who were *generosi*;[27] and they made sure of this by noting in the case of each witness how long he had been armed and where he was first armed. To live nobly was understood to mean to live by following, or at least on occasion to have followed, the profession of arms.

There is a difference between regarding the profession of arms as honourable, as Geoffroy de Charny did, because it is dangerous, calling for courage, endurance, and a constant readiness for the sacrifice of life itself, and accepting the fact that a man has served in arms as title to social status. Yet the second view is really no more than the first formalized in social and perhaps legal terms, a short step, but a very important one, taking us out of the world of religious and moral justification into that of social competition. Something of the idealistic justification, of course, remains after this step has been taken; the man-at-arms, it can still be argued, deserves esteem because his way of life is perilous and hardy. All the same, to accord him honour in the formal sense of rank, as well as in an informal way, clearly added very noticeably to the allure of his profession, both psychologically and in hard, practical terms. For here we see the canonist's verdict, that a man may save his soul by service in arms, being dangerously extended; he may not only save his soul

25. Jean de Bueil, *Le Jouvencel*, ii. 80.
26. Arch. Nat., X¹ᵃ 4794, fos. 261 ff.; quoted by A. Bossuat, *Perrinet Gressart et François de Surienne, agents de l'Angleterre* (Paris, 1936), p. 2. Cf. the cases discussed by Contamine, *Guerre, état et société*, pp. 238 and 474–5.
27. *The Scrope and Grosvenor Controversy*, ed. N. H. Nicolas (2 vols., London, 1832). For explicit references to the status of witnesses as *generosi*, see i. 248–51. Interestingly, these references concern the examination of witnesses for Grosvenor, men who were generally of much lesser estate than were the Scrope witnesses.

but win as well things that are, to most men, very desirable in this world, social identity, privilege, and recognition among his own kind.

There is a good deal of evidence, from the fourteenth and fifteenth centuries, of what one must call a social mystique associated with the conduct of war; ceremonial knightings before battles, the formal ennoblement of common men who had distinguished themselves by acts of courage,[28] and so on. Significantly some evidence, in its nature fragmentary and impressionistic but still impressive, suggests that this social mystique was of considerable importance not just to the aristocratic upper class of the chivalrous world but also, perhaps particularly, to those upon the least secure fringes of the profession of arms, the men of the Free Companies and the *condottieri*, whom their social superiors often liked to regard as intruders into the aristocratic military world: 'people of small estate and sometimes even labourers and artisans, who, some by their hardiness and others merely by pillaging, have made themselves into men-at-arms'.[29] Thus we find the companies of foreign *condottieri* in Italy in the 1360s coining for themselves extravagant titles, such as the companies of the Flower, of the Star, and of St. George: these seem the sort of names that one might expect to be associated not with bands of common *routiers* but with seigneurial orders of chivalry. We find Geoffroy Tête-Noire, in the eyes of many the blackest of all the free captains in southern France in the 1370s and 1380s, styling himself in his safe conducts 'Duke of Ventadour, count of Limousin, and sovereign lord of all the captains of Auvergne, Rouergue and Limousin'.[30] His sword apart, he had no claim to any title of dignity, but he played the act to the finish, bequeathing in fine style on his death bed 1,500 francs of his booty to enlarge and beautify 'our Chapel of St. George in the castle of Ventadour'.[31] We find Anjou King of Arms complaining that every petty captain had his own herald or pursuivant dressed in his arms (wherever he may have got *these* from) whose conduct, not surprisingly, the King of Arms considered to fall short of the high standards of the true and ancient order of heralds.[32] We even find the Free Companies proposing a great tournament against the

28. For an example of ennoblement for courage, see Jean de Waurin, *Recueil des croniques et anchiennes istories de la Grant Bretaigne*, ed. W. and E. L. C. P. Hardy (5 vols., R.S., 1864–91), iv. 345–6.
29. Philippe de Mézières, *Le Songe du Vieil Pèlerin*, ed. G. W. Coopland (2 vols., Cambridge, 1969), i. 530; quoted by Contamine, *Guerre, état et société*, p. 150.
30. Froissart, *Chroniques*, xii. 352.   31. Ibid. xiii. 289.
32. Bodleian Library, Oxford, Rawlinson MS. C 399, fo. 76ᵛ.

combined chivalry of Burgundy and Savoy in 1365. It was not the
unwillingness of their knightly adversaries that prevented the challenge
being taken up, it should be added, but rather, it seems, the prohibition
of the event by Pope Urban V.[33]

There were, of course, more tangible attractions about the service of
a Geoffroy Tête-Noire—or a Mérigot Marchès or a Seguin de Badefol,
or of any of the others of their ilk whose raiding and pillaging Froissart
records in the language of chivalry—than a rather shaky claim to some
sort of professionally acquired social esteem. Loot, in the form of
straight booty and of ransoms, was the mainstay of the lives of men of
this stamp—and it also made the chances of war alluring to men of much
more secure social status than they. No English historian should need to
be reminded of the significance of gains of war for English social history
in the age of the Hundred Years War, a subject which has been so
tellingly illuminated by the late K. B. McFarlane.[34] But even this quest
for financial gain does not quite take us outside the idealistic world of
chivalry. Theoretical and idealistic justification could be offered in
defence of the right of men-at-arms to keep what they won in war. Out
of the spoils of war the prince must allow his soldiers their portion,
wrote Christine de Pisan 'the which grace to say well and largely behoves him, as to them that set in adventure so dear a chattel as is the
blood, the limbs, and the life'.[35] There was, moreover, a *cachet* that
attached to such winnings that gave them a meaning over and above
their pure monetary value, because they had been won—in theory at any
rate—amid the glorious hazards of the battlefield. The social mystique
attaching to arms ran right through the contemporary attitude to military life and its incidents.

What I am suggesting here about a mystique colouring the whole
way of life of the man-at-arms is probably best illustrated by example.
Let me quote the story of his life, as it was told to Froissart by an old
soldier, Bascot de Mauléon, at the count of Foix's castle at Orthez 'as we
were sitting round the fire, chatting and waiting for midnight, which
was the hour when the count supped':

The first time that I bore arms, [Bascot told Froissart], was under the Captal de
Buch at Poitiers: and by good luck I made that day three prisoners, who paid me,

33. *Lettres secrètes et curiales du Pape Urbain V*, ed. P. Lecacheux and G. Mollat
(Paris, 1902), nos. 2069 and 2070.

34. K. B. McFarlane, *The Nobility of Later Medieval England* (Oxford, 1973),
especially ch. ii.

35. Christine de Pisan, *Book of Fayttes of Armes and of Chyualrye*, pp. 219–20.

one with the other, four thousand francs of ransom. . . . Later I was in Brittany at the battle of Auray, where I served under Sir Hugh Calveley . . . the day was ours and I made such good prisoners that they paid me two thousand francs; I accompanied Sir Hugh with ten lances into Spain when we drove from thence Don Pedro . . . and when the treaty was made between Don Pedro and the Prince of Wales, I returned with Sir Hugh to Aquitaine. That was when the war was renewed between the King of France and the Prince, and we had enough to do, for the fighting was stern; great numbers of the English and Gascon captains lost their lives; however, thanks to God I live. . . . At times, I have been so miserably poor that I have not had horse to mount; at others, rich enough, just as fortune befell me. Raymonnet de l'Espée and I were one time companions and held the castles of Mauvoisin, Trigallet and Nantilleux in the Toulousain . . . when the Duke of Anjou came to attack them with his army, Raymonnet turned to the French: but I have remained true to the English and shall be so for as long as I live.[36]

Bascot de Mauléon appears to have been a member of a poor but noble southern French family, a man of the same sort of status as were Mérigot Marchès, Raymonnet de l'Espée, Perrot le Béarnois, Seguin de Badefol—and many of the same type whose names are familiar from Froissart. His long career in arms finally achieved for him, it would seem, a niche in the service of the count of Foix, but it did not advance him or his kinsmen in any very marked degree. It does not appear that, when he talked to the famous chronicler, there was very much left of the great prizes that he had won at Poitiers and Auray. He does not tell us how his winnings were wasted, as likely as not diced and drunk away; nor does he tell us any details of the means by which he survived hard times. About that, however, there is not much problem: Bascot de Mauléon's world was that of the free soldier, and there is no reason to doubt that in the Toulousain he, like others, sustained himself largely by terrorizing the country folk into paying him protection money. The main impression one has of his story, as Froissart recounts it, is of a life that he could feel had been lived in style. He had seen famous fields; he had run great risks and won prizes; when the going was good, he had been able to live like a lord, but he had had the strength to endure hard times, too, and had proved faithful to old masters. Without in any way approaching, say, the ideal proposed by Geoffroy de Charny, he is still, as the chronicler portrays him, the kind of veteran to whom Geoffroy encouraged every young knight to listen with respect.[37] At the same time, when one considers the havoc that he and his kind wrought over

36. Froissart, *Chroniques*, xi. 108–20.
37. Charny, *Livre de Chevalerie*, pp. 467 and 475–8.

wide areas of southern France, it is hard to regard him, or them, as anything but parasites upon society.

Chivalry was an essentially upper-class mystique, and for just that reason its trappings and the chivalrous calling of arms had a particular significance and attraction for those at the fringes of nobility, heirs of insufficient estate, cadets, bastards. Philippe de Mézières, in the introduction to the statutes of his crusading Order of the Passion (through which he hoped to turn arms that had been hitherto misused back to holy purposes), put his finger very aptly on the dilemma of men such as Bascot. It was the dilemma of:

the second and third born sons, and others, who by the custom of the land have little or no portion in the inheritance of their fathers, and who by poverty are often constrained to follow wars that are unjust and tyrannical so as to sustain their estate of *noblesse*, since they know no other calling but arms; and therein they commit so much ill that it would be frightening to tell of all the pillaging and crimes with which they oppress the poor people.[38]

The second and third sons of the nobility, says Philippe, generalizing for the type. It is not easy to test his assertion, since the evidence on which a social profile of the Free Companies could be constructed is not easy to come by. Nevertheless, there is some evidence that supports his suggestion. Schäfer, in his great work on the German companies in Italy in the fourteenth century, undertook a major programme of research into the origins of the men-at-arms listed in the contracts of employment that the companies made with Italian princely and city governments. Of those whose origins seemed to him to be traceable, a very large number were drawn from the ranks of the lower nobility and in particular from ministerial families—among the simple men-at-arms, that is; among the captains and constables, he found a leavening of the higher aristocracy.[39] No one has yet attempted a comparable study of the composition of the French and English companies in Italy, and there is not, I think, sufficient evidence from which to study the composition of the Free Companies that operated exclusively in France. It is however significant that most of the captains whom Froissart singled out for mention seem to have been of noble birth. The famous Mérigot Marchès, for instance, would fit very well into Mézières's picture; his father held the castle of Baudeduit of the

38. Bodleian Library, Oxford, MS. Ashmole 865, fo. 423.

39. K. H. Shäfer, *Deutsche Ritter und Edelknechte in Italien während des 14 Jahrhunderts* (4 vols., Paderborn, 1911–40). See in particular, i. 110 ff.

bishop of Limoges, but the estate had fallen on evil days and the castle into disrepair,[40] and that is why the young man was placed in the service of an 'English' squire, Thomas de Roux (? Roos). His interpretation of his rôle when he rose to be a captain also tallies well with what Mézières says. To use Mérigot's own words, he did 'all those things which a man can and ought to do in a just war, as taking Frenchmen and putting them to ransom, living on the country and despoiling it, and leading the company under his command about the realm of France, and burning and firing places in it'.[41]

Of course, there were to be found among the free soldiers of the late Middle Ages plenty of sheer adventurers, like the labourers and artisans of whom Mézières elsewhere complains, who by 'hardiness or pillaging make themselves men-at-arms'.[42] The ranks of the companies must have been socially very heterogeneous. But even for the adventurers, gain was clearly not the sole lure of war; that is not what adventure means. There was enough glamour in the tightrope existence that the military calling could very easily be, in the privilege of being able at least to dice and drink away fortunes and windfalls in style, to make it attractive alike to men who had started in a rank of society generally esteemed lowlier than that of the man-at-arms, and to those whose self-esteem as being of gentle or near gentle birth was put at risk by social and economic pressures. That was just what the problem was, that its appeal was so wide. In an age that did not question the right of all sorts of authorities —dukes, counts, noblemen and cities, as well as kings and kingdoms— to use arms to settle territorial and dynastic quarrels, there was no lack of occupation for such people. One party to a quarrel could hardly abstain from employing them unless it could trust the adversary to abstain too, which it clearly could not. So the supply of armed men generated what one might call a kind of spurious demand; so their numbers swelled, and their quest for continuing martial employment uprooted them from their homelands and strengthened their dependence on pillaging for survival. But still the tinsel glint of chivalry clung about their calling, and helped to draw yet more into their parasitic ranks.

Chivalry made the special problem created by the existence of large companies of men-at-arms intractable in another way, too. Because of its underlying religious and idealistic justification, it made it difficult for

40. H. Duplès-Agier, *Registre criminel du Châtelet de Paris du 6 septembre 1389 au 18 mai 1392* (2 vols., Paris, 1861–4), ii. 184.
41. Ibid. ii. 187–8.   42. *Songe du Vieil Pèlerin*, i. 530.

men to look squarely at the parasitic activities of soldiers and to recognize them for what they were. In this article I have laboured the dark side of chivalry, but it would not have been the potent force which it was if there had not been another side. I have said nothing about the men who went to war in Prussia, in Livonia, and in Granada against the pagans, of those who wrested Satalia from the Turks or of those who, under King Peter of Cyprus, captured Alexandria in 1365. Many of them were men not very different, if different at all, from those whose activities we have been examining; Bascot de Mauléon, for instance, had been on crusade to Prussia and with the Great Company at the battle of Brignais in 1362 when the free companions routed Tancarville's soldiers, as well as serving at Poitiers, at Auray, and in Spain. He is a useful reminder of the difficulty of applying any touchstone in order to distinguish the gold from the base metal in chivalry. The good and ill in its ethic were alike products of a single framework of ideas. For that reason men thought of the cure for the latter too often in terms of the former. Philippe de Mézières could not see that the dream of recruiting the men who had laid waste France to the service of a new crusading order was no answer, and that, by appealing to chivalrous aspirations, he was emphasizing the very attitudes that were, in an important part, the cause of the distress and disorder that he deplored. What was needed was a new synthesis, a new concept of the role of the man-at-arms and indeed of nobility, and that was something that could only come very slowly, as it did, with the growth of the idea of the soldier not as a knight errant, but as the state's servant, not called to seek wars by birth and vocation, but licensed to fight them by his sovereign. Chivalry, with its idealization of the freelance fighting man, could not be a force effective in limiting the horrors of war: by prompting men to seek wars and praising those who did so, its tendency, for all its idealism and because of it, was rather to help to make those horrors endemic.

4

Sir John Fastolf
and the Law of Arms

C. A. J. ARMSTRONG

On 2 January 1433 Sir John Fastolf received a grant from John, duke of Bedford, acting as regent for Henry (VI) of Windsor as the Lancastrian king of France. The grant conferred on Fastolf was noteworthy not only for its exceptional generosity but also for its unusually abundant historical detail recapitulated in the royal letters justifying Fastolf's right to such munificent treatment at the hands of the Lancastrian crown in France.

The *lettres royaux* of the French crown, when conferring a favour, normally began by employing (with the consequential syntactical changes) the form of words used by the beneficiary in his original petition (*requête*) soliciting the crown's clemency or generosity. This fact was regularly announced at the start of the preamble to grants: 'Nous avons receu l'humble supplicacion de . . .', whereafter followed the name and status of the grantee. Fastolf being a person of conse-quence, the grant to him in 1433 was couched in ceremonious terms: 'l'humble supplicacion *etc* de nostre amé et féal conseiller Jehan Fastolf, chevalier, grant maistre d'ostel de nostre très chier et très amé oncle Jehan duc de Bedford, gouverneur et régent de France'.[1]

The preamble then proceeded to set out, in remarkable detail as already noted, Fastolf's personal reasons for requesting a royal grant of lands deemed to be worth 1,560 *saluts d'or* per annum by the rent-rolls of 1421 ('eu regard au temps de l'an 1421'). Fastolf's petition was not legalistic but military and highly personal. Like most Fastolf papers relating either to English or French affairs, it is marked by the avidity

---

1. Arch. Nat., JJ 175, fos. 66–67. 'Donné à Paris le second jour de janvier MCCCCXXXij [o.s.] et de nostre règne le XIème. Ainsi signé par le Roy à la relacion de Monseigneur le Gouverneur et Régent de France duc de Bedford. J. de Rinel.' Complete references to Rinel in J. Ferguson, *English Diplomacy 1422–1461* (Oxford, 1972), pp. 182 and 260.

and clarity which characterized him.[2] He must have dictated his own petition to a secretary, although the final portion containing the extremely detailed conditions according to which the crown was to alienate land to him would have been the work of a legal adviser, such as Maître Jean de Paris,[3] who, in 1433 had been looking after Fastolf's litigation for the past decade or so.

Fastolf's narrative unrolled as follows. In 1423, upon the orders of the regent, Bedford, and at the insistence of the *prévôt des marchands* and burgesses of Paris, Sir John had taken command of a force to recover strongholds within the county of Valois ('à l'environ de nostre bonne ville de Paris') held by the enemy, the so-called Dauphinists claiming to fight for Charles VII. One such stronghold, Passy-en-Valois,[4] Fastolf reduced 'en quelques jours' and its commander, Guillaume Remon, popularly known as 'Marjolaine', surrendered to Fastolf, undertaking to pay him a ransom of 20,000 *saluts d'or*, in addition to an increment of 20 per cent commonly known as 'les marcs'. Remon was sent into custody at the castle of Rouen, where he lay captive at Fastolf's expense. While Remon was thus imprisoned, Sir John went off to the county of Maine, where, as his petition recalled, he participated notably in the capture of Beaumont-le-Vicomte.[5] In the meantime (on the night of 30 November–1 December 1423), Compiègne, a much more important place than Passy-en-Valois on the north-eastern approach to Paris, was retaken by the Dauphinist enemy;[6] and, as Fastolf's petition reminded him, the regent, in consternation at the military and economic effects of its loss, assembled a large force for its recovery.[7]

However, as the preamble to the royal letters of 1433, quite accurately stated, the siege of Compiègne dragged on and expenses mounted, while the troops deserted for lack of pay. Foreseeing that the siege would have to be broken up, the regent—though not expressly named in the *lettres*

2. K. B. McFarlane, 'The Investment of Sir John Fastolf's Profits of War', *T.R.Hist.S.*, 5th ser., vii (1957), 91–116.

3. Probably the most sought-after *procureur* in the *Parlement* between 1420 and 1435; see the index to *Journal de Clément de Fauquembergue*, ed. A. Tuetey (3 vols., S.H.F., 1903–15), i. 36 and iii. 191.

4. Aisne, arrond. Château-Thierry, canton Neuilly-Saint-Front.

5. Now Beaumont-sur-Sarthe, Sarthe, arrond. Mamers. R. Charles (*L'Invasion anglaise dans le Maine de 1417 à 1428* (Mamers, 1889)) had not much to say about the campaigns of 1423–4, nor had M. Passe (*Notice historique sur Beaumont-le-Vicomte et ses seigneurs* (Mamers, 1891)).

6. *Mémoires de Pierre de Fenin*, ed. Mlle Dupont (S.H.F., 1837), p. 210.

7. Ibid., p. 211; *La Chronique d'Enguerrand de Monstrelet*, ed. L. Douët-d'Arcq (6 vols., S.H.F., 1857–62), iv. 176.

royaux—saw to it that means were found ('furent trouvées manières') to regain Compiègne by the full release of Remon in return for the submission of the town.

The point insisted upon by Fastolf was that, without his knowledge or consent, his prisoner had been released and relieved of any obligation to pay ransom. This annulment of Remon's liability was also expressly extended to cover the release of other notable prisoners of Fastolf's, the lord of Passy-en-Valois[8] (captured in the first instance by Remon with the stronghold) and the lord of neighbouring Roye. These, and others unnamed, had been freed, together with their own captor, Remon, to enable the regent to recover Compiègne. Had they not been so released, Fastolf could have expected 'grosses finances' from all of them.

At the date of his grant from the crown (2 January 1433), Fastolf was to claim that he had received no satisfaction, whether from Remon himself[9] or from Remon's captives, all of whose ransoms should have been payable to him, Fastolf, as the captor of Remon. Moreover, although the regent had promised Fastolf compensation for these grave financial losses,[10] Sir John had received nothing. It was, then, under these circumstances that Fastolf was accorded the lavish grants in land to which reference has already been made, since, as the royal letters patent candidly admitted, the precarious state of the crown's finances precluded any possibility of an equivalent compensation being paid to him in hard cash.

The facts alleged on Fastolf's behalf were correct, even if they require some amplification. The crux was, of course, the regent's release of Remon. There can be little doubt that Bedford was entitled to do this, considering that he was the Lancastrian 'governor' of France and that Fastolf was his *grand maître d'hôtel*, a domestic, albeit an exalted one. Needless to say, therefore, the grant of 1433 never called into question the regent's right to dispose of Fastolf's prisoners. Whether this could be done without compensation however, was another matter. This was

---

8. According to the Abbé Poquet ('Passy-en-Valois, ses seigneurs, son château, son église, ses inscriptions funéraires', *Bull. soc. archéologique et historique de Soissons*, 2° sér., xiv (1883), 66–67), Louis, lord of Passy, was captured by Armagnacs in 1420 and released for 100 *saluts d'or* in 1425. He attended the French coronation of Henry VI (*Chronique de Monstrelet*, ed. Douët-d'Arcq, v. 2).

9. He had fallen at Verneuil on 17 August 1424 (*Chronique de Monstrelet*, ed. Douët-d'Arcq, iv. 196).

10. The regent probably owed Fastolf a balance of 4,000 marks for the capture of the duke of Alençon at Verneuil (McFarlane, 'The Investment of Sir John Fastolf's Profits of War', p. 95, n. 2).

the issue on which a lord's duty to his feed man and the convention of the law of arms coincided. The grant of 1433 to Fastolf admitted as much.[11]

Some amplification of the circumstances under which the regent recovered Compiègne is necessary. The royal letters, reproducing Sir John's petition, were discreet; for the real facts of the surrender were too grim to be suitably included in *lettres royaux*. These facts have for long been known from Hall's *Chronicle*. Under the walls of the besieged Compiègne, Guillaume Remon was paraded in full view of the defenders with a halter around his neck, and threatened with instant hanging if the town were not immediately given up. The garrison, largely composed of men whom Remon had commanded, submitted to save the life of their former captain. Thus Compiègne returned to the Lancastrian obedience.[12]

This sensational episode unbecoming to an official grant was, however, recorded elsewhere, thanks to Fastolf's exceptional concern with documentation which could support his own claims. Fastolf's secretary, William Worcester, copied for him extracts from a narrative of the Wars of the English in France, which may be designated as 'the Basset Fragment', although Lucas Nantron was probably the composer of the chronicle from which the passages useful to Fastolf as narrative *pièces justificatives* about his activities in France were drawn.[13] Edward Hall seems to have used this manuscript, which Worcester transcribed for Fastolf; and certainly the more interesting information which Hall's Chronicle has to give about the war in France can be traced to it.

The lords of Passy and Roye avoided prosecution by Fastolf for the

11. Prisoners' ransoms have received much attention since the importance of the subject was emphasized by A. Bossuat, 'Les Prisonniers de guerre au XVᵉ siècle: la rançon de Guillaume de Châteauvillain', *Annales de Bourgogne*, xxiii (1951), 7–35, and 'La Rançon de Jean seigneur de Rodemack', *Annales de l'Est* (1951), 145–62. D. Hay ('The Division of the Spoils of War in Fourteenth-Century England', *T.R.Hist.S.*, 5th ser., iv (1954), 91–109) gives the best summary for the earlier literature including the fourteenth century. Of great importance, too, is M. H. Keen, *The Laws of War in the Late Middle Ages* (London, 1965), ch. x, 'The Law of Ransom'. For the latest from the French side, see P. Contamine, *Guerre, état et société à la fin du Moyen Âge* (The Hague and Paris, 1972), the analytical index under *prisonniers* and *rançons*.

12. *Hall's Chronicle*, ed. H. Ellis (London, 1809), p. 120. On 4 April 1424 the regent pardoned Compiègne for negligence in defending itself against the enemy (Arch. Nat., JJ 172, fo. 256ᵛ).

13. College of Arms, MS. M 9, analysed by Miss B. J. H. Rowe, 'A Contemporary Account of the Hundred Years War from 1415 to 1429', *E.H.R.* xli (1926), 504–13. On Lucas, or Luket, Nantron 'natus de Parys unus de clericis Iohannis Fastolf', see K. B. McFarlane, 'William Worcester: A Preliminary Survey', *Studies presented to Sir Hilary Jenkinson*, ed. J. Davies (London, 1957), p. 208.

recovery of the ransom, which they had undertaken to pay Guillaume Remon because they, together with their captor Remon, had been released *gratis* by the regent in exchange for the submission of Compiègne. Others were less lucky. Ironically, those from whom Fastolf sought to extort ransoms by litigation for his own profit were foreign merchants. They had merely been so unfortunate as to let themselves be captured by Remon while engaged in bringing food to Paris[14] from the southern Netherlands. The purpose of the military enterprise entrusted to Fastolf in the spring of 1423 had been to open this supply route into Paris; but the merchant prisoners who passed from the hands of Remon into those of Fastolf were now required to pay an equal, or possibly larger, ransom to their deliverer, namely Fastolf. They had been 'liberated' to use the word in its pejorative 1944 sense.

The whole disagreeable story revealed itself in legal proceedings narrated in considerable detail in the records of the *Parlement* of Paris. The defenders of Passy, Remon and company, learning that the place was about to be assaulted, sent their valuable merchant captives for safekeeping to La Folie, a neighbouring fortress under their control.[15] In the course of the subsequent proceedings both parties agreed that the merchants had, immediately on their transfer to La Folie, entered into negotiations with Fastolf for their release. Although the merchants later maintained that they had settled with the garrison of La Folie for a ransom of about 100 *écus* ('que ont esté paiez pour ung roncin'), Fastolf asserted that they had covenanted to pay him 500 *écus* as the price of their liberty. On this understanding Fastolf claimed that he agreed to set free the captive merchants on the capitulation of La Folie, the surrender of which had been included in the terms of submission for the major fortress, Passy-en-Valois.[16]

Two of the foreign merchants had offered themselves as sureties for payment of the combined ransom. They were Henry de Lidam and Denis Sauvage. Lidam was the wealthier and more influential. He was said to understand English and to be acquainted with Fastolf and other members of the regent's household.[17] He was probably Dutch. None the less, while the preliminary discussions with Fastolf for setting free

---

14. Denis Sauvage declared that he was 'acoustume d'amener vivres en la ville de Paris' (Arch. Nat., X^{1a} 4793, fo. 384^v).

15. 'Et furent les marchans prins par la garnison de Pacy et depuis furent transportes a la Folie quant on veult mettre le siege a Pacy' (ibid.).

16. Facts laid before the court on 28 February 1424 (ibid., fos. 384^v-5).

17. Arch. Nat., X^{1a} 64, fo. 227.

the entire company of merchants were still proceeding, Lidam was imprisoned in the Bastille, where Fastolf himself was in command,[18] while Sauvage was sent to the Châtelet, the prison of the *prévôt* of Paris.[19]

The matter came before the *Parlement* because Fastolf, endeavouring to bring into his own custody Denis Sauvage as well as Henry de Lidam, had instructed his attorney (*procureur*) to require the *prévôt* of Paris to hand over Sauvage to Fastolf as his private prisoner of war, or to send him before the marshals of France to be heard under their military jurisdiction. While refusing to give up Sauvage to Fastolf, the *prévôt* agreed to send him to the marshals' court because the case arose out of military action. Faced with this prospect, Sauvage preferred to appeal to the *Parlement*, which, on 28 February 1424, heard his appeal against Fastolf, who was represented by his *procureur*, Jean Sac, an Italian merchant-banker closely associated with Fastolf's business interests.[20]

It was accepted that the duke of Bedford had intervened ('si y a mis la main le duc de Bedford par sa sentence') by adjudging Sauvage to be a prisoner of war whose case should be taken to the marshals' court. This notwithstanding, the *Parlement* accepted the appeal of Sauvage, and handed the suit over to be heard before the *conseil*, the highest chamber within the *Parlement*, by Jean Aguenin, the court's second president. Both parties were told to submit their evidence on the same day, 28 February 1424, an unusually swift procedure, but followed by the traditional laconic note, that boded delay: 'et la court verra'.[21]

Fastolf was in a strong position, because each of the merchants admitted that he owed Fastolf a ransom, although the amount might be a debatable question, but both Sauvage and Lidam alleged that the other had incurred the major liability to discharge this debt to Fastolf on behalf of their companions.

Accordingly, on 6 March 1424 Lidam submitted to the *Parlement* a *requeste par escript*, the strictest form of appeal, against Sauvage.[22] Being himself a prisoner in the Bastille, Lidam not unnaturally opposed the request of Sauvage to be released from the Conciergerie to which the *Parlement* had assigned him. Lidam also claimed to have a signed bond

18. He had been appointed keeper of the Bastille by Henry V on 21 January 1421 (McFarlane, 'The Investment of Sir John Fastolf's Profits of War', p. 103, n. 6).

19. Arch. Nat., XI[a] 4793, fo. 384[v].

20. Ibid. Sacco.: Fransac.: de Fransechis was an expert who had estimated the value of the treasure of Saint-Denis for the *Parlement*. (Ibid., fos. 346[v], 379[v], and 380[v] (17 and 21 February 1424).) McFarlane ('The Investment of Sir John Fastolf's Profits of War', pp. 96 and 100) underestimated his importance.

21. Arch. Nat., XI[a] 4793, fo. 385.   22. Ibid., fo. 390.

in which Sauvage promised to pay him 400 *écus* to be passed on to Fastolf to settle the ransom of the entire party of merchants. On 9 March, however, the *Parlement* released Sauvage from the Conciergerie on bail of 400 *écus* underwritten by two Parisian merchants,[23] and on 13 March granted him a safeguard,[24] which enabled him to move about Paris without danger of arrest on condition that he submitted to the court an acceptable official address, for which he chose the house of Maître Jean Bailli, his *procureur*, a member of the Parisian bar.[25]

Throughout May, June, and July 1424 the case before the *Parlement* proceeded without noticeably progressing, save that Lidam was released from the Bastille on 16 May on bail in the sum of 400 *écus*, the same amount as had been required for Sauvage. During the summer of 1424 Fastolf's plea of absence from Paris was no mere procedural excuse, as he was campaigning with his master, the regent, whom he accompanied on the battlefield of Verneuil (17 August), where he collected a fortune in prisoners' ransoms. All the while Fastolf's interests were being watched by his *procureur* in the *Parlement*, one of the most redoubtable practitioners of the time, Maître Jean de Paris. The fact that Fastolf had changed his *procureur* from the merchant, Jean Sac, to an expert jurist, suggests that he foresaw a long and tricky lawsuit.[26]

As the case dragged on from the late summer of 1424 into the next session of the *Parlement* in the autumn of that year, and through into the winter of 1424-5, it grew progressively more embarrassing for the regent. In the first place, the *Parlement* had rebuffed Bedford in receiving the appeal of Sauvage, since he, the regent, had ruled that Sauvage should be sent before the tribunal of the marshals. It was another move on the part of the *Parlement* against the regent in the game of legal backgammon which the two were engaged in playing against each other. For the regent the most tiresome aspect was the diplomatic one, for Lidam and Sauvage were, like the rest of their company, not subjects of the French crown, but strangers from outside the kingdom and natives of the county of Hainault, an imperial, not a French, fief.[27] The fact was not questioned by either Fastolf or the *Parlement*. On the contrary, it was admitted in court that the towns of Brabant and Hainault had

23. Arch. Nat., X¹ª 4793, fo. 394ᵛ.

24. Ibid., fo. 397; and again on 14 March (fo. 398).   25. Ibid., fo. 395.

26. Ibid., fos. 417 (4 May 1424), 421 (11 May), 424ᵛ (16 May), 432 (2 June), 442 (26 June), 453ᵛ (17 July), and 478ᵛ (6 September).

27. Ibid., fo. 385: 'l'appelant [Denis Sauvage] dist qu'il est bon marchant du pais de Henault et les autres aussi et sont estrangiers et leur doit on administrer bonne justice'.

written to the regent expostulating at the incarceration of Lidam and Sauvage.[28] Both Brabant and Hainault were areas fraught with risk for a Lancastrian government, since, notwithstanding the fact that both territories were acknowledged to lie within the Burgundian sphere of interest, the regent's brother, Humphrey, duke of Gloucester, in November 1424 carried out his longstanding threat to invade Hainault, claiming to hold it by right of his wife Jacqueline, the heiress of the county. Humphrey's action imperilled the Anglo-Burgundian alliance upon which the regent relied for the preservation of Lancastrian rule in France; and Fastolf's claim on the merchants constituted a further, if minor, aggravation of an awkward situation.

Having deprived Fastolf of his wealthiest prisoner, Remon, and those freed with him, the regent was under an obligation to co-operate with his *grand maître d'hôtel*. When the *Parlement* reopened after Martinmas (11 November 1424) the case between Lidam and Sauvage was resumed over the issue of which of the two was ultimately responsible for the general ransom of not less than 400 *écus* demanded by Fastolf as the ransom of the whole company of merchants. Fastolf still hoped to have Lidam, whom he must have come to consider as the wealthier of his two captives, tried before the regent, but whether in Bedford's personal capacity as Fastolf's lord or in his official right as head of the *Grand Conseil* is by no means clear.[29]

Since Fastolf was grand master of his household, the duke of Bedford must have known something in advance of the method by which Fastolf planned to cite Lidam before him as judge in the matter. One evening, probably 27 November 1424,[30] a sergeant of the *Parlement*, Chrétien Colart, called Biscaye (like a pursuivant), was sent by Fastolf to arrest Lidam and to cite him before the regent. Lidam was fortunate to be out when 'Biscaye' called; but the sergeant seized his horse and told the hostess of the inn where Lidam lodged that he had taken it for the purpose of constraining Lidam to appear before the regent.

The incident caused a sensation on 28 November 1424 when brought to the attention of the *Parlement*. Business was interrupted, and 'Biscaye' was hauled before the court for interrogation. The *Parlement* felt aggrieved, since it had repeatedly issued releases from prison and

28. Ibid., fo. 384ᵛ: 'lesdis marchans ont obtenu des bonnes villes de Henault ou Brabant lettres adrecans au duc de Bedford'.

29. Arch. Nat., X¹ᵃ 4794, fo. 3 (20 November 1424) and fo. 6ᵛ (27 November).

30. Had the incident happened before 27 November, the proceedings would have been broken off that day when the case came up.

safeguards to Lidam, whose freedom to move about Paris had been guaranteed by the court and vouched for to the sum of 400 *écus* by nine merchants. The court bound over Fastolf, his *procureur* Maître Jean de Paris, who, like the regent, must have known something about this illegal enterprise, and the sergeant to refrain from disregarding the safeguard accorded by the court to Lidam on pain of a fine of 2,000 *livres parisis*.[31]

How much cash Fastolf succeeded in extracting from each of his prisoners it now seems impossible to assess. Henry de Lidam was lucky since he won his case against Denis Sauvage. On 20 January 1425 a judgement of the *Parlement* (*judicatum: jugé*) relieved him of all liability for the ransom demanded by Fastolf from Sauvage and the others, and costs were awarded to Lidam against Sauvage.[32] Probably Fastolf's demands for ransom money were now at least partially satisfied at the expense of the unhappy Denis Sauvage. The reason for supposing so is that the whole affair disappears for the next twenty-three months from the records of the *Parlement*.

Evidently, however, Sauvage had not discharged the full amount claimed by Fastolf by December 1426, for in that month Lidam submitted to the *Parlement* a written appeal against Fastolf, who refused to restore any caution money until he had been fully satisfied by Sauvage. At the same time Lidam sued Sauvage for losses incurred while acting as his surety towards Fastolf. The court adjourned Lidam's appeal on the score of reviewing, once more, the written evidence.[33] On 6 February 1427[34] the hearing was again adjourned because of Fastolf's absence from Paris; but on 10 February the court was informed on his behalf that Lidam should not be released from his bond until Sauvage had paid up in full—'*quia interest creditoris plures habere debitores*'.[35] In April 1427 Lidam renewed his appeal, but the court deferred the case until after La Madeleine (22 July).[36]

In fact, it was not until November 1427, after the annual opening of the court, that Lidam reintroduced his case;[37] and by then even Fastolf would appear to have lost interest. Perhaps he had got all he ever expected to get from Sauvage. At any rate, Maître Jean de Paris told the

31. Arch. Nat., X^{1a} 4794, fo. 7^v (28 November 1424). The same was reiterated 'sub magnis poenis' on 4 December (fo. 9).
32. Arch. Nat., X^{1a} 64, fos. 226^v–7.
33. Arch. Nat., X^{1a} 4795, fo. 15^v (17 December 1426).
34. Ibid., fo. 39^v.   35. Ibid., fo. 42.   36. Ibid., fo. 89^v (29 April 1427).
37. Ibid., fo. 173^v (25 November 1427).

court that 'Fastolf est prest d'entendre à l'avancement du procès et veult bien prendre droit par l'enqueste de tesmoins viels valitud[inaires] qui sont trespassés'.[38]

The end of the case was at last in sight, though the *Parlement* regularly heard longer and equally unedifying suits. On 1 December 1427 the parties, Fastolf, Lidam, and Sauvage, though not in full accord one with another, were at least in sufficient agreement to have the whole issue submitted to the *conseil*, for judgement;[39] and on 31 January 1428, the second president, Jean Aguenin, who had first taken the case in hand in 1424, gave sentence (*arrestum: arrêt*) which pronounced Henry de Lidam and his sureties free from all liability toward Fastolf.[40] The judgement reflected, perhaps unintentionally, the deep-seated dislike, which the *Parlement* nursed towards the Law of Arms,[41] and was intended, probably, to score off the regent by rejecting the extravagant claims of his *grand maître d'hôtel*.

How much Fastolf succeeded in extorting from Lidam, Sauvage, and their associates is scarcely ascertainable from the archives of the *Parlement*; but the history of the case, as recorded, suggests that it was profitable to him, even if he got less than he had hoped for.

There was nothing unusual in Fastolf's demands upon his prisoners. The records of the *Parlement* abound in cases arising from similar circumstances. In January 1421 Girard Rolin, captain of Lagny, sued the municipality of Paris and three brothers whom the city had sent forth on a military expedition to safeguard food supplies coming into Paris. Rolin took prisoner a certain Lespinasse, a member of the enemy garrison at Meaux, whose men shortly afterwards made prisoner the three brothers, who at first recognized, but subsequently questioned, their obligation to pay Girard Rolin the same ransom, which they had undertaken to pay Lespinasse.[42]

An even closer analogy with the merchants held by Fastolf occurs in a case heard before the *Parlement* arising out of the capture by Thomas,

---

38. Ibid., fo. 174 (27 November 1427).

39. Ibid., fo. 176[v]: 'Au conseil [Philippe de]Morvillier. Appointé que la court verra la requeste [de Lidam] et l'appointement [avec Fastolf] et fera droit au conseil.'

40. Arch. Nat., X[1a] 1480, fo. 393: 'A conseiller l'arrest ou appointment d'entre Henry de Lidam d'une part et Messire J. Fastolf et Denis Sauvage d'autre part.' The *arrêt* was pronounced on the same day (Arch. Nat., X[1a] 66, fos. 61[v]–62).

41. For example, the famous case of the duke of Burgundy and Sir Louis Bournel versus Sir John Dedham (Arch. Nat., X[1a] 4796, fos. 298[v] and 301[v] (14 and 21 January 1432)).

42. Arch. Nat., X[1a] 4793, fos. 10 (13 January 1421) and 13 (26 January).

Lord Scales, of the castle of Gaillon.[43] In this instance the merchants had previously been taken by the garrison of Gaillon; and the case turned on the question of whether or not they were prisoners of war.[44] Scales, belonging to an English noble family, was more merciful than Fastolf (descended from a Danish immigrant) and was prepared to keep his principal hostage Jean Peron in his own household. An exceptionally cruel case of the treatment of captive hostages, some of whom died of maltreatment in passing from one captor's hands into those of another, is associated with the ransom of Guillaume de Châteauvillain.[45] Happily, a reaction against this mercenary form of chivalry was already under way. The criticism of Fastolf for his conduct on the field of Patay by the chronicler Monstrelet[46] was a pointer in this direction; and the statutes of the Order of the Golden Fleece were drafted to encourage personal valour rather than private profit.

43. Eure, arrond. Les Andelys.
44. Arch Nat., X¹ᵃ 4794, fos. 83ᵛ (15 May 1425), 284 (18 July 1426), and 286 (24 July 1426).
45. Bossuat, 'Les Prisonniers de guerre au XVᵉ siècle', p. 24.
46. *Chronique*, ed. Douët-d'Arcq, iv. 331–2; *Proceedings and Ordinances of the Privy Council of England*, ed. N. H. Nicolas (7 vols., London 1834–7), v. 169.

5

New Techniques and Old Ideals:
The Impact of Artillery on War
and Chivalry at the End of the
Hundred Years War

M. G. A. VALE

Blessed be those happy ages that were strangers to the dreadful fury of these devilish instruments of artillery, whose inventor I am satisfied is now in Hell, receiving the reward of his cursed invention, which is the cause that very often a cowardly base hand takes away the life of the bravest gentleman; and that in the midst of that vigour and resolution which animates and inflames the bold, a chance bullet (shot perhaps by one who fled, and was frighted by the very flash the mischievous piece gave, when it went off) coming nobody knows how, or from where, in a moment puts a period to the brave designs and the life of one that deserved to have survived many years.[1]

Don Quixote's lament for the passing of those 'happy ages' which knew no firearms is celebrated. War had become impersonal and mechanical. 'The indiscriminate death dealt by shot and ball', observes Professor Hale, 'ruined war as a finishing school for knightly character.'[2] It is normally assumed that the introduction of the arquebus in the sixteenth century lay at the root of Cervantes's complaint. But the beginnings of that process whereby the knightly ideal was undermined might be sought at an earlier period. It is the purpose of this article to examine the impact of artillery on the practice of war, and on chivalrous ideals, during the later stages of the Hundred Years War. It will be argued that the first effective small-arms, charged with gunpowder, developed as a result of the introduction of effective siege-guns. Offensive techniques provoked a defensive reaction. It is therefore essential to begin by considering the nature of later medieval innovations in the techniques of attack.

1. Miguel de Cervantes Saavedra, *Don Quixote* (Bohn ed., London, 1925), i. 402.
2. J. R. Hale, 'Fifteenth- and Sixteenth-Century Public Opinion and War', *Past and Present*, xxii (1962), 23.

In siege warfare, the patterns of attack and defence had remained largely static during the early Middle Ages. In the early fourteenth century, the advantage still tended to lie with the defenders of a fortified place, who relied upon the height and thickness of their walls and their ability to withstand starvation and undermining by the enemy. In attack, little movement was made to improve upon the siege-engines and catapults described by the Roman theorist Vegetius. By the late fourteenth and early fifteenth centuries, however, it is common knowledge that techniques had been developed so that large cannon of vast calibre could be manufactured and utilized.[3] Yet the effectiveness of this new artillery has been disputed. The liability of these guns to fracture and burst, to roll off their carriages, to become bogged down, and to provoke crippling transport problems has often been pointed out. 'Artillery', it has been argued, 'had little effect on the fortunes of campaigns as a whole or on the balance of political power' at this time.[4] Fire-arms exerted 'no serious influence on the issues of battles before the late fifteenth century', and it has been concluded that 'gunpowder . . . revolutionized the conduct, but not the outcome, of wars'.[5] How far are these observations, made in the context of Italian Renaissance warfare, valid for the later stages of the Hundred Years War?

When discussing Henry V's bombardment of Harfleur in 1415, J. H. Wylie remarked 'it would be a mistake to suppose that much change had been introduced into siege methods by the introduction of gunpowder'.[6] Sir Charles Oman was of the opinion that 'we may almost say that the triumph of artillery only commences in the middle years of the fifteenth century'.[7] Before agreeing with either of these conclusions, we must look at the surviving evidence a little more closely. In south-west France, the constant state of war or truce between areas in English and French obedience gave rise to a kind of arms race. At Bordeaux, the

3. For recent surveys see C. M. Cipolla, *Guns and Sails* (London, 1965), pp. 21–30; J.-F. Finó, *Forteresses de la France médiévale* (Paris, 1967), pp. 273–98; B. J. St. J. O'Neil, *Castles and Cannon* (Oxford, 1960), pp. xiii–xvii and 1–21; and, for older but still valuable accounts, T. F. Tout, 'Firearms in England in the Fourteenth Century', *E.H.R.* xxvi (1911), 666–88 and R. C. Clephan, 'The Ordnance of the Fourteenth and Fifteenth Centuries', *Archaeological Journal*, lxviii (1911), 49–64.

4. J. R. Hale, 'Gunpowder and the Renaissance', *From Renaissance to Counter-Reformation*, ed. C. H. Carter (London, 1966), p. 114.

5. J. U. Nef, *War and Human Progress, c. 1494–1640* (London, 1950), p. 29; and Hale, 'Gunpowder and the Renaissance', p. 115.

6. J. H. Wylie, *The Reign of Henry the Fifth* (3 vols., Cambridge, 1914–29), ii. 33.

7. C. Oman, *A History of the Art of War in the Middle Ages* (2 vols., London, 1924), ii. 226.

capital of English Gascony, the probable effectiveness of the communal artillery in the 1420s can be assessed by comparing the ballistic force of its cannon, for which detailed figures survive, with others derived from the accounts and inventories of other European towns. In August 1420, reference was made in the registers of the town council to a large cannon, which would throw a stone weighing 7 hundredweights (784 pounds).[8] Later in that year, the town gun-founder was commissioned to make another cannon, which would fire stones of 5 hundredweights (560 pounds), or 5¼ hundredweights (588 pounds).[9] In comparison with the pieces recorded at Nuremburg in 1427, which fired projectiles weighing 200 pounds, and at Munich in the 1450s, which fired projectiles weighing 392, 224, and 25 pounds, the Bordeaux guns of 1420 might leave little doubt about the potential damage which they could inflict.[10]

With the introduction and development of artillery, sieges and siege-craft became more complex. Broadly speaking, the use of guns meant that sieges could be brought to a conclusion much more quickly. In Gascony, as in other regions of France, castles and fortified towns studded the frontiers. To reduce an area successfully the invader had to take such strongpoints. They would serve to hold down the surrounding area, and provide a secure centre from which raids could be conducted and the reduction of a whole region begun. If a frontier outpost were not taken, the risk of a rearguard action was high. The castles and fortified towns of Gascony also commanded routes of communication and supply, especially when they were sited, like Fronsac, Beynac, Domme, or Clermont-Dessus, on the rivers. For the defender, the stubborn resistance of his forts meant that the enemy's manpower would be immobilized and absorbed for many months. In the autumn and winter of 1442, for instance, the refusal of the English garrison at La Réole on the Garonne to surrender saved Bordeaux from being besieged by the French.[11] The English garrisons knew that they could both disperse and

---

8. *A.M.B.*, ed. H. Barckhausen, iv (Bordeaux, 1883), 426.
9. Ibid. iv. 478 (14 December 1420).
10. See Clephan, 'Ordnance', pp. 102–4.
11. See Thomas Bekynton, *Official Correspondence*, ed. G. Williams (2 vols., R.S., 1872), ii. 213 and 238; Arch. Nat., JJ 182, no. 1; *Histoire de Gaston IV, comte de Foix, par Guillaume Leseur*, ed. H. Courteault (2 vols., S.H.F., 1893–6), i. 22. Fortunately for the defenders, a 'grete gunne' which the French had before the castle of La Réole was fractured on 29 October, and the siege ended on 7 December, having lasted two months. See Bekynton, *Correspondence*, ii. 219 and 247–8; P.R.O., E.364/84; and P.R.O., E.101/650, no. 285 (8 December 1442).

delay the concentration of French forces at the decisive point—Bordeaux—by holding out for as long as they could. What then were the effects of the use of artillery on the pattern of war in this much-contested area of France?

With the introduction of effective siege-guns, the advantages of attack over defence became apparent. The speedy recovery of seven strongpoints from the French by the troops of Bordeaux between April 1420 and October 1421 owed much of its success to the communal artillery.[12] The guns were carried from siege to siege by water, thereby reducing the difficulties and chronic delays of overland carriage.[13] But by the later 1430s the English were being thrown on to the defensive by a series of French invasions of their duchy. In 1442, English superiority in the use of siege artillery received a serious challenge from the French. It is to the measures taken by the English administration in Gascony to meet the attacks of 1437–8, 1442–3, and 1449–53 that we can turn to assess the extent to which the situation had changed.[14]

There is a good deal of evidence for an extensive use of cannon by the French armies launched against English Gascony after about 1439. Towns such as Montréal-du-Gers, which gave their loyalty to Charles VII, offered their metallurgical and technical resources to the royal cause. They supplied raw materials to the master of the king's artillery and received culverins (that is, light cannon) from the dauphin in return.[15] Not only did the companies of *ordonnance* gain the help of the royal siege-train, but also the great magnates of the south-west maintained their own cannon. In 1450, Gaston IV, count of Foix, marched through the English area of Labourt with seven 'great culverins of metal', before returning to Béarn to refresh his troops and repair, re-stock, and refurbish his artillery.[16] Similarly, in 1443, Charles II, lord of Albret, was negotiating with the town council of Montréal-du-Gers for the provision of 4 hundredweights of metal with which to cast bombards and cannon.[17] In France, the manufacture and use of artillery was

12. *A.M.B.* iv. 363–596.

13. Ibid. iv. 434 and 520. See P.R.O., E.101/189/12, fos. 40ᵛ and 61ᵛ for the use of river transport for artillery at the siege of Marmande by the English in March 1428.

14. For an account of these campaigns, see *Histoire de Bordeaux*, iii, ed. Y. Renouard (Bordeaux, 1965), 505–21; and M. G. A. Vale, 'The Last Years of English Gascony, 1451–1453', *T.R.Hist.S.*, 5th ser., xix (1969), 119–38.

15. See 'Comptes des consuls de Montréal-du-Gers', ed. A. Breuils, *A.H.G.* (58 vols., Bordeaux, 1859–1932), xxix. 26 and xxxii. 4, 9, and 33.

16. *Histoire de Gaston IV*, i. 99 and 106–7.

17. *A.H.G.* ii. 33, 35, and 43.

in no sense a royal monopoly during the fifteenth century. Charles VII was on the whole well served by the possessors of private siege-trains, but his son was often to be cruelly harassed by them.

It is often difficult to ascertain precisely where the hand of the gunner was responsible for the speedy conclusion of a siege or for the dilapidation of town and castle walls. But in at least two cases, the evidence from Gascony seems quite specific. In a grant by letters patent of Henry VI on 22 March 1437, the castle of Castelnau-de-Cernès, which had been recently recaptured from the French, was assigned to a loyal supporter of the English.[18] It was said that the place had been 'broken down during the said siege by cannon and engines, and a great part of the walls of the same thrown to the ground, so that it was in no way defensible against the king's enemies'.[19] Similarly, in July 1453, the manner in which the French entered the town of Castillon was said to be 'through the breaches made by the artillery', and by means of a 'collapsed tower'.[20] To meet such threats to fortifications which had previously been considered impregnable a number of measures could be taken. At the seigneurial castle of Blanquefort, near Bordeaux, modifications were made between 1380 and 1420 to existing structures.[21] Gun-emplacements were built in the outer concentric wall and a specially strengthened tower, to provide flanking fire, was added to the more exposed portion of the defences. At Bordeaux, in the summer of 1442, when preparations were being made to meet an expected French invading force, earthworks described as *boulevards* were thrown up before the principal gates of the city,[22] and stocked with defensive artillery. A similar concentration on the outer defences of a fortress or town—barbicans and *boulevards*—is found in the repairs which were in progress at Langon, Saint-Macaire, and Bordeaux from 1432 to 1434.[23] At Dax,

18. P.R.O., C.61/127, m. 9.   19. Ibid.
20. B.N., MS. Duchesne 108, fos. 35 ᵛ, 40, and 41.
21. See L. Drouyn, *La Guienne militaire* (Bordeaux and Paris, 1865), pp. 53–65 and plate 72.
22. J. Bernard and F. Giteau, 'Compte du trésorier de la ville de Bordeaux pour 1442 (février-août)', *Bulletin philologique et historique du comité des travaux historiques et scientifiques*, 1961 (1963), p. 200. For the etymology of *boulevard*, deriving from the German *bolwerk* and Dutch *bolwerc*, meaning a fortification made of earth and timber, see O. Bloch and W. von Wartburg, *Dictionnaire étymologique de la langue française* (2 vols., Paris, 1932), i. 93. The date of its first appearance is given as 1435.
23. See P.R.O., E.101/191/5 and 191/7, nos. 7 and 8. In January 1446, John Clement, lieutenant of Sir Edward Hull, constable of Bordeaux, was paid for going with carpenters to Bourg to survey the construction of 'the walls of *Bollewerk*' there (P.R.O., E.364/84). For three 'bolvers de bois' at the Burgundian castle of Le Crotoy in May 1469, see B.N., MS. fr. 26092, no. 810.

Guissen, and Cadillac, in 1449 and 1451, the French encountered heavy resistance from outer works which the defenders had constructed.[24] But as far as surviving architectural and documentary evidence permits generalization, there was as yet little attempt to build new permanent defences designed both to resist and house artillery. It is only at the seigneurial castle of Bonaguil, rebuilt by the Roquefeuil family from 1445 onwards, that an approach towards such sophistication was made.[25]

In English Gascony, the administration at Bordeaux had always provided defensive artillery for the garrisons which lay in the path of invading armies. From Easter 1437 to Easter 1438, for instance, when the French were converging on Bordeaux, the constable of Bordeaux disbursed at least 224 pounds of gunpowder at $7\frac{1}{2}d.$ and 8d. sterling per pound.[26] This figure represents a significant fall in price since the early years of the fifteenth century, when gunpowder stood at 1s. per pound.[27] Between March and December 1437, two cannon were sent by the constable to the frontier of war.[28] One of these had three detachable breech-blocks or 'chambers' whereby it could be loaded. But the most common defensive fire-arm bought by the constable at this time was the culverin, of which eleven were dispatched. Figures computed from his accounts suggest that these were probably handguns, for large steel crossbows cost twice as much, and cranking devices for the crossbow were equal in price to them.[29] That the culverin, at least in its smaller calibres, was a portable fire-arm seems evident from the appearance of references to *couleuvrines enfustées en bastons* in an account of 1431.[30] The inventory of the artillery found in the castle of Rouen on the death of John, duke of Bedford, in 1435 also lists many 'small culverins',

24. *Histoire de Gaston IV*, i. 5–14 and 71–73; and ii. 24, where the French met fierce opposition from the 'portal du boulevert que les Angloys avoient tousjours jusques alors tres bien . . . defendu' at Cadillac in 1451.

25. R. Ritter, *Châteaux, donjons et places fortes* (Paris, 1953), pp. 131–3; P. Lauzun, *Le Château de Bonaguil* (Agen, 1897), *passim*.

26. P.R.O., E.101/192/9, nos. 14 and 27 (1 October 1437 and 18 April 1438).

27. See P.R.O., E.101/404/6, m.1 (Privy Wardrobe account, 5 November 1399–5 November 1401). The price of gunpowder in English Gascony also stood at 1s. sterling in March 1415 (*A.M.B.* iv. 123).

28. P.R.O., E.101/192/9, no. 28.

29. Ibid., nos. 14 and 28; E.101/193/15, no. 24. For *couleuvrine* (Lat. *colubrina*) deriving from Latin *colubra, colobra*, a serpent, see Bloch and Wartburg, *Dictionnaire étymologique*, i. 183.

30. Napoleon III and I. Favé, *Études sur le passé et l'avenir de l'artillerie* (6 vols., Paris, 1846–71), iii. 134–5; and Clephan, 'Ordnance', p. 93. For early references to handguns in fourteenth-century England, see Tout, 'Firearms in England', pp. 678–87.

including no less than twenty-nine which were said to be *ad manum*.[31] Tripods and other stands for these small guns were also listed. A distinction was made between gunpowder intended for culverins and for cannon—the former being twice as expensive. These guns fired lead shot, and, with their long wooden stocks, could be mounted on battlements or parapets for use against the personnel of a besieging force.[32] Although still outnumbered by the crossbow in such sources, the increasingly frequent occurrence of such entries suggests that a cheap manual fire-arm, possessing some degree of accuracy and effectiveness, had been devised. The arquebus did not finally oust the crossbow from French armies until 1567. But the introduction of the handgun meant that it now had a potentially dangerous rival.

It is from the second quarter of the fifteenth century that examples of death or mutilation by gunfire become more numerous. There were others besides Thomas Montagu, earl of Salisbury, who owed their deaths to artillery fire.[33] In November 1442, John Payntour, an English esquire, was killed by a culverin shot at La Réole.[34] Four years previously, Don Pedro, brother of the king of Castile, had been decapitated by a gunshot during the siege of the castle of Capuana at Naples.[35] The death of Prégent de Coëtivy, lord of Rais, admiral of France and bibliophile, was due to a cannon shot while he was directing trenching operations at the siege of Cherbourg in August 1450. With him perished Tudal le Bourgeois, *bailli* of Troyes, who was killed by a culverin.[36] Others were fortunate to escape death, although they were badly wounded by gunfire. In April 1422, one Michel Bouyer, esquire, was

31. *Letters and Papers Illustrative of the Wars of the English in France during the Reign of Henry VI*, ed. J. Stevenson (2 vols. in 3, R.S., 1861–4), ii. 567. They were distinguished in the inventory from the *magnae columbrinae*, the smallest of which fired a lead shot weighing half a pound.

32. Ibid. ii. 567–8. For a description of the earliest culverins, appearing in the late fourteenth century, see Finó, *Forteresses*, pp. 278–9. For an illustration of an early fifteenth-century handgun (*bâton à feu*), see ibid., fig. 71. For an illustration from the *Bellifortis* of Konrad Kyeser (c. 1400), see B. Gille, *Les Ingénieurs de la Renaissance* (Paris, 1964), p. 53.

33. Thomas Basin (*Histoire de Charles VII*, ed. C. Samaran (rev. ed., 2 vols., Paris, 1964), i. 118 and 120) said that the earl of Salisbury was killed by a stone cannonball fired from a bombard. The ball shattered as it hit the window, and the earl was mortally wounded in the head by a fragment (24 October 1428). It was also reported that Thomas Fitzalan, earl of Arundel, was killed by a culverin shot at Beauvais in 1434. See Napoleon III and Favé, *Études*, ii. 101.

34. Bekynton, *Correspondence*, ii. 223 and 228.

35. J. Nève, *Antoine de la Salle: sa vie et ses ouvrages* (Paris and Brussels, 1903), pp. 40 and 226–31.

36. Jean Chartier, *Chronique*, ed. V. de Viriville (3 vols., Paris, 1858), ii. 231–2.

languishing in prison at Meaux, 'gravely ill and mutilated in one of his legs by a cannon shot, in such a way that he cannot aid himself'.[37] In August 1451, at the siege of Bayonne by the French, Bernard de Béarn was struck in the leg by a culverin ball, but recovered, it was said, through the skill of his surgeons.[38] On the same occasion, a French esquire, Philippe Charrapon, lost one of his feet through being hit by a cannon shot, but apparently lived on as a war pensioner.[39] The gun dealt perhaps its cruellest blow to that paragon of chivalry, the *bon chevalier* Jacques de Lalaing, jouster and knight-errant, who was killed by a cannon shot in Philip the Good's army outside the castle of Pouques, near Ghent, in June 1453.[40] It was becoming patently obvious that the gun could not only batter down fortifications, but could kill, and kill selectively, from afar.

Yet the crossbow had done so since the twelfth century. It is, perhaps, hardly surprising that there was no 'chorus of disapproval' directed at the gun during the fifteenth century.[41] Its alleged association with the devil did not deter Christian princes from using it.[42] The risk of death at the hands of a 'cowardly', plebeian crossbowman was merely augmented by that of death by gunfire. Yet the greater range and penetrating power of the culverin and handgun was coming to be acknowledged. Pope Pius II could write that 'no armour can withstand the blow of this torment, and oaks are even penetrated by it'.[43] Death was, above all, meted out indiscriminately by an unseen hand, which sheltered behind the smoke created by its cowardly weapon. There is some evidence of social prejudice against the operators of such weapons in the fifteenth century. At Naples in 1438, Antoine de la Salle commented that Don Pedro had been killed by men who were 'only artisans by trade'.[44] But this notion does not appear to have penetrated north of the Alps. La Salle's account is, moreover, slightly ambiguous in its attitude to the gunners concerned. The soldier who brought Don

---

37. *Choix de pièces inédites relatives au règne de Charles VI*, ed. L. Douët d'Arcq (2 vols., S.H.F., 1863–4), ii. 86.
38. Gilles le Bouvier, Berry Herald, *Chronique*, in *Histoire de Charles VII*, ed. D. Godefroy, (Paris, 1661), p. 464.
39. B.N., MS. fr. 32511, fo. 146.
40. Basin, *Histoire de Charles VII*, ii. 212; Georges Chastellain, *Chronique*, in *Oeuvres*, ed. K. de Lettenhove (7 vols., Brussels, 1863–5), ii. 360–4.
41. See Hale, 'Gunpowder and the Renaissance', p. 134.
42. 'Instrumento illo bellico sive diabolico quod vulgariter dicitur gonne' as it is described in John Mirfield's treatise of 1390 (B.L., MS. Harley 3261).
43. Quoted by G. L. Tomasi, *Ritratto del Condottiero* (Turin, 1967), p. 234.
44. Nève, *Antoine de la Salle*, p. 228.

Pedro's severed head to the Angevins within the castle of Capuana was given a reward of six ducats by Isabella of Lorraine, René of Anjou's queen.[45] The story was also used by La Salle to demonstrate that sacrilege does not pay: the besiegers had mounted some of their artillery in a church, and thus earned their just deserts.[46] There seems to be no evidence from France at this time that captured gunners were executed or maltreated in the manner which was allegedly common in Italy.[47] In the chronicles, the potentially dangerous and socially disruptive implications of using the culverin and handgun were simply not considered.

The increasing accuracy and range of the culverin was paralleled by improvements in the larger siege cannon. In English Gascony, the leisurely pace of siege warfare was quickened, as it was in Normandy, by Charles VII's artillery under the Bureau brothers. During the spring and summer of 1346, for instance, the French spent four months besieging Aiguillon.[48] In August 1442, Charles VII took Dax, after an artillery bombardment, in three weeks, and Saint-Sever fell in less than a month.[49] At Bourg, in June 1451, the town surrendered in less than six days, after the heavy artillery of the French had been brought up, without firing a shot.[50] Castillon capitulated to them in July 1453 after a bombardment by the siege-guns.[51] At Cadillac, a section of the town walls was rapidly demolished by the French guns.[52] But the inhabitants of many towns preferred to come to terms with their besiegers. It was often in the best interests of those besiegers, moreover, to withhold their siege artillery and press for an agreement to surrender, as the French did at Bergerac in November 1450 and at Fronsac in June 1451.[53] By withholding their guns, they gained not only an undamaged fortress,

45. Ibid., p. 231. 46. Ibid., pp. 231–2.
47. See Tomasi, *Ritratto del Condottiero*, pp. 234–5. But cf. Hale, 'Gunpowder and the Renaissance', p. 125, for evidence to the contrary.
48. E. C. Lodge, *Gascony under English Rule* (London, 1926), p. 82; and K. A. Fowler, *The King's Lieutenant: Henry of Grosmont, first Duke of Lancaster* (London, 1969), pp. 213–14.
49. Bekynton, *Correspondence*, ii. 187, 196 and 213–14; P.R.O., E.364/84, m. 5; *Histoire de Gaston IV*, i. 28–41.
50. Enguerrand de Monstrelet, *Chroniques*, ed. J.-A. Buchon (15 vols., Paris, 1826–7), xii. 93.
51. *Histoire de Gaston IV*, ii. 19; B.N., MS. Duchesne 108, fos. 35–42; MS. fr. 18442, fos. 46–47ᵛ (24–29 July 1453). The town was said to have capitulated on 20 July, three days after the battle in which Talbot was killed.
52. *Histoire de Gaston IV*, ii. 21–25. The *grosses couleuvrines* of the French were trained so as to 'batre tout du long de ce pan de mur'. See also Drouyn, *La Guienne militaire*, pp. 258–9.
53. See *Ordonnances des Rois de France de la troisième race* (21 vols., Paris, 1723–1849), xiv. 109; Chartier, *Chronique*, ii. 268–77.

but also, under the laws of war, the sum total of all heavy artillery which could not be carried out on horseback or foot by the defeated garrison.[54] In July 1453 Roger, lord Camoys, told the Three Estates of the Bordelais that Charles VII possessed 'marvellous artillery'.[55] Such scanty evidence as is found in other sources seems to bear out his words.

Throughout the campaigns of 1449–53 in Normandy and Gascony, however, little approach was made towards the development of field artillery. There was no part for it to play in a war of attrition conducted almost entirely by means of sieges. Technical improvements were introduced into Charles VII's siege-guns under the pressure of events. During the conquest of Normandy, between August 1449 and February 1450, the Genoese Louis Giribault, the king's gunner, was experimenting with a design for a new gun-carriage,[56] a model of which was sent to the king during the campaign. The object of the experiment was to create a gun-carriage which was not drawn by horses. The siege-train might then be drawn by other means, but whether that required oxen or men is not clear. Perhaps the detrimental effects of requisitioning horses from those who lived in the path of the armies of reconquest might be somewhat mitigated.[57] If horses were less in demand, other 'necessities' for the artillery were not. The abbot and monks of Saint-André-le-Gouffier, near Falaise, were recompensed for the loss of timber taken from their woods by the king's artillerymen for the siege of Falaise.[58] Others were paid for their services. On 24 May 1450, sixteen local masons were paid by Robin Fontaine, *commis* for the payment of pioneers and siege-works at Bayeux, for making gun-stones to be fired by the king's cannon and bombards during the siege.[59] They had worked for sixteen weeks on their task. Three months later, Cherbourg fell after a bombardment by guns mounted in batteries on the sea-shore.[60] These were covered with greased skins at high tide and,

54. Chartier, *Chronique*, ii. 273. 55. B.N., MS. Duchesne 108, fo. 31ᵛ.

56. 'Recueil de pièces pour servir de preuves à la Chronique de Mathieu d'Escouchy', *Chronique de Mathieu d'Escouchy*, ed. G. du Fresne de Beaucourt (3 vols., S.H.F., 1863–4), iii. 381–2.

57. For the requisitioning of horses and carters for the Guyenne expedition of 1453, see P. Contamine, *Guerre, état et société à la fin du Moyen Âge* (Paris and The Hague, 1972), p. 311.

58. Beaucourt, 'Recueil de pièces', p. 390.

59. B.L., Add. Ch. 4066 (24 May 1450). See Chartier, *Chronique*, ii. 204–11 for an account of the siege and surrender of Bayeux. During the siege, which lasted 'fifteen or sixteen days', many men were killed by bowshots or culverin fire (ibid. ii. 205).

60. Ibid. ii. 232–3.

according to the chroniclers, the powder with which they were charged remained dry. But three bombards and one cannon were fractured during the bombardment, and the town surrendered by agreement.

The climate of war was not such as to nurture any species of artillery besides the bombard and the culverin. Even on the field of Castillon (17 July 1453) where the heavy and light guns of the French horrifically demonstrated the murderous effects of enfilading on infantry advancing in close order, no field-guns were used. Siege-guns and culverins were placed in an earthwork camp dug by the French pioneers. Talbot's dismounted men-at-arms and foot, who were attempting to storm the camp, were mowed down by this hail of gunfire. There is no need, as some have done, to look for deep-seated strategic principles behind this 'curiously defensive step'.[61] It had become normal practice by the 1440s for besiegers to construct an entrenched park for their artillery out of the range of the defenders' guns, from which trenches might be dug as far as the battery positions.[62] The principle had been put to the test at Dax in 1442,[63] and at Mauléon and Guissen in 1449. During the siege of Guissen, near Bayonne, Gaston IV of Foix prepared a large fortified earthwork with which to repel an Anglo-Gascon relieving force. It was defended by 'great culverins of metal . . . and great serpentines'.[64] At the second taking of Dax in 1451, according to Guillaume Leseur, it was possible to 'go safely from one extremity of the siege to the other' by way of the network of supply trenches dug by pioneers during the night.[65] The principles of cross-fire and its terrible effects were already appreciated, and the distribution of gun-ports in Gascon strongholds suggests that it had been applied to their defence. At Mauléon and Guissen in 1449 the defenders seem to have enfiladed the French from their outworks. At Guissen the English had 'a strong fort which they had built and fortified at the foot of their castle', and met the French assault with fire which was 'so vigorous and accurate where they saw the press of our men that they galled them with it'.[66] The culverin and the earthwork *boulevard*, it could be argued, represented the first positive reaction to the great improvements which had been made in the techniques of attack. Experiments, which were to result in the development

---

61. A. H. Burne, *The Agincourt War* (London, 1956), p. 334.
62. See Napoleon III and Favé, *Études*, ii. 97–100.
63. *Histoire de Gaston IV*, i. 11–12.
64. Ibid. i. 85. For the siege of Mauléon, see i. 52.
65. Ibid. i. 119. See Napoleon III and Favé, *Études*, ii. 97–98 for other instances.
66. *Histoire de Gaston IV*, i. 73.

of the permanent angle bastion and gun platform, had already begun in France by the 1440s.[67]

In theory, as well as in practice, soldiers were putting their minds to the problems of the most effective use of artillery. No objections were raised to the cannon, least of all by the church, which gave gunners a patron saint—St. Barbara.[68] There was no room in fifteenth-century France for a Cervantes to deliver a tirade against 'those devilish instruments'. The gun, like the standing army, had come to stay. Jean de Bueil could advocate the siting of a besieger's camp before a beleaguered fortress on the model of the fortified entrenchments dug at Mauléon, Guissen, Cherbourg, Dax, and Castillon fifteen years before.[69] Trenches, he wrote, were to be dug from one part of the siege to another, covered by hoardings. Ease of contact and movement between the units of the encircling force could thus be ensured. The gunners themselves were to be shielded by wooden mantlets. From the trenches, the enemies' gunports and arrow-loops could be effectively damaged, while the besiegers were sheltered from their artillery fire.[70] In the accounts of the Norman and Gascon campaigns of 1449–53 by Jean Chartier, Gilles le Bouvier, and Mathieu d'Escouchy, the French seem to have gone about their task of reducing strong-points in just this manner.[71] Louis XI put the reverse principle into practice when resisting the forces of Charles of Burgundy, who was besieging Paris in August and September 1465.[72] A trench was dug from the city at a crucial point towards the enemies' positions. A *boulevard* of earth and wood was thrown up at the furthest extremity of the trench and the royal artillery opened fire on the troops of Duke John of Calabria from this vantage point. Commynes, in an engaging passage,

67. For Italian developments at this period, see J. R. Hale, 'The Early Development of the Bastion: An Italian Chronology, c. 1450–c. 1534', *Europe in the Late Middle Ages*, ed. J. R. Hale, J. R. L. Highfield, and B. Smalley (London, 1965), pp. 466–94.

68. J. R. Hale, 'War and Public Opinion in Renaissance Italy', *Italian Renaissance Studies*, ed. E. F. Jacob (London, 1960), p. 102. For St. Barbara, see *Bibliotheca Hagiographica Latina* (Brussels, 1898–9) pp. 142–6; and for her patronage of gunners, see S. Peine, *St. Barbara, die Schützheiliger der Bergleute und der Artillerie, und ihre Darstellung in der Kunst* (Freiburg, 1896), pp. 10–14.

69. Jean de Bueil, *Le Jouvencel*, ed. L. Lecestre and C. Favre (2 vols., S.H.F., 1887–9), i. 164–9.

70. Ibid. ii. 41.

71. See for example, Chartier, *Chronique*, ii. 237–8., where he wrote: 'c'estoit merveilleuse chose à veoir les boulevers, approuchemens, fossez, trenchées et mines que les dessus dits [Jean et Gaspard Bureau] faisoient faire devant les villes et chasteaux qui furent assiégez durant icelle guerre . . .'. He reckoned that all those places taken by agreement to surrender could easily have been taken by assault.

72. Philippe de Commynes, *Mémoires*, ed. J. Calmette and G. Durville (3 vols., Paris, 1924–5), i. 60–61.

wrote of the panic inspired in the besieging army, especially when two cannon balls were shot into the upper room where Charles was dining. One of his servants was killed instantly, and the count, fearing the worst, uncharacteristically retired to the ground floor and 'decided not to budge'.[73] The principle of contravallation by the defender, as well as circumvallation by the besieger, was obviously appreciated at this time. Although such outworks were generally in earth, the notion of a castle or fortified town as an inert, defensive mass was on the wane.

If we are to believe the chroniclers, and an expert like Jean de Bueil, the combination of heavy and light artillery in siege-craft was also understood by the 1450s. The *Jouvencel*, in its chapter on sieges, gave the following advice: 'When your bombards have begun to fire, make sure that the *veuglaires* [small cannon] and light artillery fire as much as possible after each bombard shot, so that those within have no chance to make *boulevards* nor to repair the damage which the bombard will have done to them.'[74] Guillaume Leseur, writing of the siege of Dax in 1451, gives an instance of this practice, when the French culverins picked off the defenders who were trying to repair breaches in their walls made by the heavier guns.[75] Jean de Bueil considered the older system of circumvallation—by building separate *bastilles*, as the English had done at Orléans in 1428—to be both ineffective and outdated.[76] The direction of siege-works was to be left to the technicians, he went on—above all, to the masters of the artillery. They were competent to advise not only on the deployment and laying of the guns, but also on the placing of shields and hoardings to protect the besiegers and gunners, as well as the digging of trenches and hauling of the cannon. The cannoneers—a distinct class—were to advise on the number of bombards, gun-stones, and gunpowder necessary for laying siege. 'It's their trade', wrote Jean de Bueil, and referred the aspiring siege engineer, tantalizingly, to 'the book of the master of the artillery'.[77]

In the regrettable absence of evidence for the nature and organization of Charles VII's artillery at the end of the Hundred Years War, one is forced to argue from sources of a rather later date. An inventory of Louis XI's artillery, drawn up in August 1463, gives a total of nine bombards and thirty-two smaller guns in and around Paris.[78] It would have

---

73. Ibid. i. 61.   74. *Le Jouvencel*, ii. 41.
75. *Histoire de Gaston IV*, i. 119–20.   76. *Le Jouvencel*, ii. 44.
77. Ibid. ii. 45 and 52.   78. B.N., MS. fr. 20492, fos. 16–16ᵛ.

been surprising if Charles VII's siege-train had been much smaller than his son's. The Bureau brothers were reputed to have founded sixteen bombards for the siege of Harfleur alone in 1449.[79] Gaspard Bureau, knight, *maître de l'artillerie*, went on to serve Louis XI in the same capacity:[80] his skill was too valuable for a king to lose. Around him was his *bande* of thirty cannoneers, a keeper of the artillery, a master-carter, and a *maître artilleur*.[81] This permanent personnel may have served with him in the last campaigns of the Hundred Years War. It was to these men that Jean de Bueil could delegate the responsibility for laying siege. But the *maître de l'artillerie* was a nobleman, although his nobility may have been recently acquired. The conduct and direction of war was not to be left entirely in the hands of technicians and artisans. It was to the Périgordin noble family of Genouillac that the mastership of the artillery was soon to be given.[82] The French nobility thus displayed a marked capacity for adaptation to the changing techniques of war.

A similar acceptance of the gun is to be found in the art and literature of the fifteenth century. The English verse paraphrase of Vegetius, written between 1457 and 1460, referred disparagingly to the older forms of siege engines:

> but now it is unwiste,
> Al this aray, and bumbardys thei cary,
> And gunne and serpentyn that wil not vary,
> Fouler, covey, crappaude and colueryne
> And other soortis moo then .VIII. or IX ne.[83]

In both naval warfare and sieges, the author had no illusions as to the value of fire-arms. They could destroy a besieger's siege-works and dismast a ship.[84] Their appearance in illuminated manuscripts is a commonplace by the middle of the century. In the magnificent copy of Froissart's *Chronicles*, made for Anthoine, *grand bâtard of* Burgundy in

79. See G. du Fresne de Beaucourt, *Histoire de Charles VII* (6 vols., Paris, 1881–9), v. 25–26; and Chartier, *Chronique*, ii. 178. Conditions at the siege were made exceptionally difficult by the bitterly cold weather (December 1449).

80. P. Contamine. 'L'Artillerie royale française à la veille des guerres d'Italie', *A. Bret.* lxxi (1964), 258–60. For an account rendered in 1469 for his expenses in that office, see B.N., nouv. acqs. frs. 21156, no. 58.

81. Ibid., no. 58; B.N., Pièces Originales 3051, no. 67943 (November 1458).

82. See Fleury Vindry, *Dictionnaire de l'État Major français au XVIe siècle*, i. 401–2 and ii. 205.

83. *Knyghthode and Bataile*, ed. R. Dyboski and Z. M. Arend (E.E.T.S., 1935), lines 148–52.

84. Ibid., lines 2544–52 and 2854–60.

about 1468, the Burgundian artillery of the time is faithfully depicted:[85] Philippe van Artevelde is shown, somewhat anachronistically, attacking at Ghent in 1381 with two field-guns mounted on their wheeled carriages by means of trunnions,[86] while Bertrand du Guesclin besieges Bourbourg with a large bombard on a wheeled carriage similar to those shown in use by the Turks at Constantinople in a manuscript of 1455.[87] The artist of the Froissart manuscript even incorporates the gun into the borders of his pages. A centaur is shown playfully firing a handgun.[88] The 'devilish instrument' was being domesticated and tamed. Men were curiously endeared to the gun by the end of the Hundred Years War. Siege-guns achieved a certain individuality. There was no standardization of calibre, and each gun was given a name. It was not only Pope Pius II who could christen cannon with names such as *Enea*, *Silvia*, and *Vittoria*.[89] In 1463, Louis XI had two bombards called *Jason* and *Medea*.[90] Others were called *La plus du monde*,[91] *Paris*, *La Dauphine*, *La Réalle*, *Londres*, *Montereau*, and *Saint-Pol*. Some of his cannon bore the names of Charles VII's captains: *La Hire*, *Barbaʒan*, *Flavy*, and *Boniface*.[92] The English had guns called *Bedford*, *Robin Clement*, *Brisebarre*, and *Herr Johan* in the castle of Rouen in 1435.[93] Christine de Pisan could even include a gun called *Seneca* in her chapter on siege-craft in the *Fais d'armes*.[94] Each gun was an individual,

85. See A. Lindner, *Der Breslauer Froissart* (Berlin, 1912); and for illustrations of surviving pieces captured by the Swiss from the Burgundians between 1474 and 1477, see *Die Burgunderbeute und Werke Burgundischer Hofkunst* (Bernisches Historisches Museum, Bern, 1969), figs. 161–78a and pp. 167–82.

86. Lindner, *Breslauer Froissart*, plate 1.

87. Ibid., plate 24; B.N., MS. fr. 9087; and *Voyage d'Outremer* of Bertrandon de la Broquière, reproduced in S. Runciman, *The Fall of Constantinople, 1453* (Cambridge, 1965), plate 1.

88. Lindner, *Breslauer Froissart*, plate 5. Handguns are frequently shown in action in the battle scenes from Swiss chronicles of the later fifteenth century. See J. Zemp, *Die Schweiʒerischen Bilderchroniken* (Zürich, 1897), plates 11, 18, and 19 (c. 1480–5).

89. Hale, 'Gunpowder and the Renaissance', p. 131.

90. B.N., MS. fr. 20492, fo. 16.

91. Ibid., fo. 16. 'La Plus du Monde' was evidently the motto of Pierre de Brézé, *grand sénéchal* of Normandy under Charles VII. See *Oeuvres complètes du roi René*, ed. H. de Quatrebarbes (4 vols., Angers, 1843–6), iii. 127. The bombard could thus have been named after Brézé and perhaps, as were other guns in the inventory of 1463, brought to Paris from Normandy.

92. B.N., MS. fr. 20492, fo. 16. *La Hire* = Etienne de Vignolles, *dit* La Hire (c. 1390–1443); *Barbaʒan* = Arnaud-Guillaume, lord of Barbazan (d. 1431); *Flavy* = Guillaume de Flavy, captain of Compiègne (d. 1449); *Boniface* = Boniface de Valpergue (*fl.* 1438–46).

93. *Letters and Papers*, ed. Stevenson, ii. 566.

94. See G. W. Coopland, '*Le Jouvencel* (Re-visited)', *Symposium*, v (1951), 179, where the point is made that the writer(s) of *Le Jouvencel* did not include these names when annexing passages from Christine de Pisan.

demanding careful treatment from its operators. The projectiles which it fired had to be specially made for it. A siege-gun in the fifteenth century still possessed a personality of its own.

Just as Italian Renaissance artists were to attempt to domesticate and even beautify the gun, so fifteenth-century Englishmen and Frenchmen made it acceptable to a chivalrous society. By 1445, Anthoine, *grand bâtard* of Burgundy, had chosen a wooden barbican with gun-ports as his emblem:[95] and by 1465, Louis de Bruges, lord of La Gruthuyse, had selected a bombard, with the motto *Plus est en vous*.[96] The *imprese* of the Este and Montefeltro were thus paralleled and anticipated in northern Europe during the fifteenth century.[97] The harsh reality of war, and of the gun's bite and sting, remembered in the words *couleuvrine, serpentine*, and *faucon*, was being smothered under a cloak of illusion. The gun had come to stay, and its influence on the final campaigns of the Hundred Years War was not derisory. If it had 'no serious influence on the issues of battles before the late fifteenth century', this was because there were so few battles in which it could play a part. Had it not been for the French siege-guns, the outcome of the Norman and Gascon campaigns which effectively ended the Hundred Years War might arguably have been very different. The challenge which they offered to traditional methods of siege-craft and fortification led to the creation of new techniques of both attack and defence. In the realm of ideas, the gun was accepted without serious reservations, just as former innovations had been accepted. The existing gulf between chivalrous idealism and the reality of war was merely widened as a result of its appearance. The gun posed no threat to a society in which 'chivalrous' behaviour in warfare was, perhaps, the exception rather than the rule.

95. Lindner, *Breslauer Froissart*, plates 5, 6, 9, 10, 23, and 28.
96. See P. Durrieu, *La Miniature flamande au temps de la cour de Bourgogne* (Brussels and Paris, 1921), plates LII and LXII (manuscript copy of *Le Jouvencel* executed for Louis de Bruges, B.N., MS. fr. 191, fo. 1); and L. Van Praet, *Recherches sur Louis de Bruges, seigneur de la Gruthuyse* (Paris, 1831), *passim*.
97. See E. Wind, *Pagan Mysteries in the Renaissance* (London, 1967), figs. 71, 81, and 82 and pp. 108–12 for these emblems of bombshells and cannonballs.

6

Spies and Spying
in the Fourteenth Century

J. R. ALBAN and C. T. ALLMAND

The use of spies, claimed Philippe de Mézières, is always necessary, but especially so in time of war, both to observe the enemy and those of doubtful loyalty, and to keep commanders fully informed of their intentions.[1] Perhaps it was Mézières's experience in Cyprus, and his contacts with the Byzantine and Islamic worlds, which had led him to appreciate this aspect of war.[2] The Venetians had long understood the importance of spying, were it but for primarily commercial reasons. But the need to have information of an enemy's military intentions was seen as equally pressing. Writing in the second half of the thirteenth century, Fidenzio de Padua advised the west that Christians should follow the Islamic practice of keeping themselves well informed of what was happening 'non solum in partibus propinquis, sed etiam in partibus remotis'. The use of faithful spies, he argued, could lead to much good and the avoidance of trouble and anxiety, especially in time of war,[3] a doctrine which Gilbert de Lannoy, for one, tried to put into practice in the course of his travels through the countries bordering on the eastern Mediterranean in 1422.[4]

1. Philippe de Mézières, *Le Songe du Vieil Pèlerin*, ed. G. W. Coopland (2 vols./ Cambridge, 1969), ii. 84–85 and 404–6; Dora M. Bell, *Étude sur le Songe du Viei, Pèlerin de Philippe de Mézières (1327–1405)* (Geneva, 1955), p. 175.

2. For Mézières's career, see N. Jorga, *Philippe de Mézières et la croisade au XIVe siècle*, Fasc.110, Bibliothèque de l'École des Hautes Études (Paris, 1896; repr. London, 1973), *passim*.

3. Fidentii de Padua, *Liber recuperationis Terre Sancte*, ed. G. Golubovich, *Biblioteca Bio-Bibliografica della Terra Santa et dell' Oriento Francescano* (Florence, 1913), ii. 33 ('De Exploratoribus'), cited in part by A. S. Atiya, *The Crusade in the Later Middle Ages* (London, 1938; repr. New York, 1965), p. 40.

4. 'A Survey of Egypt and Syria Undertaken in the Year 1422 by Sir Gilbert de Lannoy, Knight', ed. and trans. J. Webb, *Archaeologia*, xxi (1827), 281–444. 'Item, a sceu le dit messire Guillebert par information qu'il y a grant foison darballestres de romanie et asses de petis canons: et non mie nul gros dedens la ville [d'Alexandrie] et y'a grant nombre daballestries' (p. 317).

In the west, the wars of the late Middle Ages witnessed a developing attitude towards spies whose services were coming to be increasingly used on all sides. It is significant that the chroniclers Walter of Guisborough and Bartholomew Cotton should have recorded, with vividness, the treasonable activities and espionage of Thomas Turberville in 1295.[5] Later in the fourteenth century, as has been well pointed out, other chroniclers—Froissart and Geoffrey le Baker are instanced—recounted their versions of events in such a way as to show that they clearly understood that many military decisions had been based upon information obtained by persons who were, quite evidently, spies.[6] Their Scottish contemporary, John Barbour, archdeacon of Aberdeen, likewise made a number of detailed references to episodes in the military career of Robert Bruce in which spies, one of whom he named, were involved. Clearly Barbour saw nothing unusual in both sides using spies and other forms of 'slycht' and 'sutelte' in the guerrilla warfare which was fought in Scotland and the Border country in the early fourteenth century.[7]

Some medieval spies are known to us, in spite of a variety of disguises which it is not always easy to penetrate. If a *nuntius*, a *vespilio*, a *coureur*, or a *chevaucheur* may have been a spy, an *espie* or an *explorator* was almost certainly one. Governments were extremely reticent about referring to secret agents in their employ as spies. The necessarily clandestine nature of fourteenth-century espionage has to this day prevented historians from gaining a complete insight into it. A vagueness in terminology is apparent in many documentary sources which may be concerned with spies and spying. For example, English accounting documents of the period frequently contain references to payments made to messengers and other persons sent 'in negociis regis secretis', 'pour certaines busoignes qe nous touchent', or 'en noz secrees busoignes'. In many cases the absence of less ambiguous evidence makes it

5. *The Chronicle of Walter of Guisborough*, ed. H. Rothwell (C.S., 1957), pp. 252–4; *Bartholomaei de Cotton, monachi Norwicensis, Historia Anglicana*, ed. H. R. Luard (R.S., 1859), p. 306, cited by J. G. Edwards in 'The Treason of Thomas Turberville, 1295', *Studies in Medieval History presented to Frederick Maurice Powicke*, ed. R. W. Hunt, W. A. Pantin, and R. W. Southern (Oxford, 1948), pp. 296–309.

6. H. J. Hewitt, *The Organization of War under Edward III, 1338–62* (Manchester, 1966), p. 4.

7. John Barbour, *The Bruce; or the Book of the most excellent and noble prince, Robert de Broyss, King of Scots*, ed. W. W. Skeat (2 vols., S.T.S., 1894), Bk. vii, lines 522–63: B. W. Kliman, 'The Idea of Chivalry in John Barbour's *Bruce*', *Mediaeval Studies*, xxxv (1973), 489–96.

difficult to ascertain what precisely was meant by such terms. Indeed, a wide variety of inferences may be drawn from them. Sometimes they may mean nothing more than diplomatic intercourse with the heads or representatives of other states. The ambassadors who travelled from the English court to treat with Bernabo Visconti of Milan in 1379 were sent 'in secretis negociis regis'.[8] Often, however, such secret business was perfectly innocent. In 1371, Esmon Rose made three journeys to Flanders and Picardy on 'secrees busoignes dont nous lui chargasmes', although the object of his travels was, in fact, to purchase destriers for Edward III.[9] Evidently the term 'secret' often meant nothing more than 'private', although it is equally clear that in many cases it meant something more than run-of-the-mill letter-bearing.[10]

To the mind of the fourteenth century the distinction between the spy and the messenger was a fine one. This is made clear by the fact that in both England and France there was a tendency to include payments to persons whom we would regard as spies among the expenditure on messengers. The Wardrobe Book of 44 Edward III records, within a list of messengers' expenses, a payment of 110 marks to Frank de Hale, captain of Calais, for expenses 'sur divers messages et autres espies . . . as diverses parties pour espier et savoir la volente et les faitz des enemys de France'.[11] From this it appears that the term 'messenger' could be employed as a synonym for 'spy'. Similarly, in 1339, 'nuncii' were sent by Edward III to discover information about certain galleys in Norman ports,[12] while in 1425 and 1426 Burgundian 'messengiers' and 'chevauchiers' were sent to England and Holland to discover news of the English army.[13]

None the less, while spies might be coyly described as 'messengers', it is clear that ordinary messengers were always expected to be on the alert for information when travelling abroad, especially in the realm of a potential enemy. English messengers dispatched to the French court at Paris in 1323–4 sent Edward II a very detailed account of the movements of the French king and of the state of current affairs in France.[14]

8. P.R.O., E.364/13, mm. 5ᵛ, 6 (Exchequer: L.T.R., Rolls of Foreign Accounts).

9. P.R.O., E.404/10/66 (Exchequer of Receipt: Writs and Warrants for Issue).

10. M. C. Hill, *The King's Messengers, 1199–1377* (London, 1961), p. 98.

11. P.R.O., E.404/10/65; *Issue Roll of Thomas de Brantingham, bishop of Exeter, 44 Edward III, 1370*, ed. F. Devon (London, 1835), p. 493.

12. P.R.O., E.36/203, fo. 112ᵛ (Exchequer: T.R., Wardrobe and Household Accounts).

13. Arch. Dép., Nord, B.1933, fos. 62ᵛ, 77.

14. *Calendar of Chancery Warrants, A.D. 1244–1326* (London, 1927), pp. 548–9.

In addition, messengers travelling abroad on specific business could inform the king of any discoveries made incidentally; in 1385 Thomas atte Mille was paid 40s. for bringing to the king 'nouvelles ... de noz messages esteantz es parties de dela pour la trete de la pees'.[15] Occasionally, too, messengers were instructed 'par commandement de la buche' and were likewise expected to report orally to the king and council.[16] Messengers bearing important news or good tidings in addition to the letters which they carried were often rewarded for these additional services.[17]

Some, however, felt that not all information, however obtained, might legitimately be used in war. Besides Froissart's apparent assumption that the activities of spies were compatible with the practice of chivalric war must be placed Mézières's timely reminder that war must be pursued 'tousjours a la doubtance de Dieu, vaillamant, sans faire ou consentir ... aucune chose qui soit encontre loyaute et honnourable guerre'.[18] Among those who must always reflect an exemplary sense of honour were the messengers extraordinary, the heralds. In the fifteenth century both Anjou King of Arms and Sicily Herald lamented that heralds were not what they had once been: Anjou King maintained that pursuivants abused their diplomatic immunity to spy out military plans for their masters, while Sicily Herald reminded his fellows of their obligation to 'tenir secret tout ce qu'ilz verront tant de l'ung comme de l'aultre, soit de nombre de gens, d'ordonnance de batailles ... car, sans ce, foy ne seroit a adjouter à eulx, et seroient reputes et tenus pour espies'. But the information which the herald might pick up in the course of performing his duties could present him with a problem of loyalty. If he knew of an ambush, he might tell his master not to take a particular road but to choose another; he could not, however, give reasons for this advice which would be offered only in the fulfilment of every man's duty to save life.[19] But the matter went further still. A herald who betrayed the secrets or plans of his master's enemies must be punished by his master for having broken his trust, after which the

15. P.R.O., E.404/14/90.

16. For example, P.R.O., E.101/311/13 (Exchequer: K.R., Accounts, Various).

17. In 1369, for instance, Clayskin de la Haye was rewarded with 20 marks 'de nostre doun' for bringing news to Edward III concerning 'la nativite dun filz de la duchesse de Bayverer' (P.R.O., E.404/10/64).

18. Songe du Vieil Pèlerin, ii. 85 and 406.

19. A. Wagner, Heralds of England (London, 1967), pp. 43 and 45; F. Roland, Parties inédites de l'oeuvre de Sicile, héraut d'Alphonse V roi d'Aragon, Société des Bibliophiles de Mons, publication 22 (Mons, 1867), p. 47; and P. Adam-Even, 'Les Fonctions militaires des hérauts d'armes', Archives héraldiques suisses, lxxi (1957), 8–10.

enemies must be informed of what had been done, and assured that no advantage would be taken of the information which had been obtained in this manner:

Car sil fut advenir que lun desdis officiers eust, par aucune adventure, descouvert ou rapporte lestat et la discrecion dune partie a lautre ou des adversaires de son maistre ou seigneur, icellui seigneur eust tantost, et sans delay, assemble son conseil, et icellui officier eust este pugny tant et si largement que tous aultres y eussent prins exemple. Et eust tantost envoye devers sesdis adversaires ung autre officier darmes, en eulx faisant savoir la trayson, desloyaute et maudis rapport que icellui officier avoit fait deulx, en eulx signifiant que icellui ne eussent jamais eu foy ne eu credence, attendu que il avoit dit et declare la discrecion et estat deulx, ce que faire ne devoit.[20]

The opinion of another herald, Jean Herard, that there were too many pursuivants active in his day and that 'telz gens, a proprement parler, ne doibvent estre appellés heraulx ne poursievans, mais espyes',[21] is an interesting comment upon the situation at the end of the Middle Ages, emphasizing, as it does, that the activities of spies, however necessary they might be, constituted an aspect of war which was, in some measure, ignoble and certainly not proper for one who belonged to the international fraternity of heralds, and who swore to maintain its code of conduct.

Because of the diplomatic courtesies extended to them, ambassadors came to be regarded as being potentially among the best spies. But their very immunities caused many to be deeply suspicious of all that they did and of all to whom they talked. When emphasizing that the itineraries of foreign ambassadors should be closely controlled and their every movements carefully watched, Philippe de Commynes was only urging upon host countries the long-recognized need to preserve their secrets.[22] In both England and France ambassadors and royal messengers were

20. College of Arms, London, MS. M. 19, fo. 82ᵛ. This manuscript, which is here cited by kind permission of Sir Anthony Wagner, Garter Principal King of Arms, was printed in a slightly different version by Roland, *Parties inédites de l'oeuvre de Sicile*, p. 83.

21. Criticism is also aimed at the new captains who appoint heralds of their own, men of little or no virtue who betray their office by seeking out the enemy's secrets simply in order to please their masters. The indictment is levelled against both the heralds ('menteurs et désleaux rapporteurs') and their lords who do not understand that a herald's role in war must be an entirely honourable and disinterested one (Roland, *Parties inédites de l'oeuvre de Sicile*, pp. 84–85). In July 1377 William de Redineshull was granted 100s. by Richard II in part payment of his expenses incurred in travelling from Newcastle upon Tyne to London 'ad ducendum quondam heraldum de Francia, captum super marchiam Scotie ... coram consilio' (P.R.O., E.403/463, m.2. Exchequer of Receipt: Issue Rolls).

22. P. Dufournet, *La Destruction des mythes dans les mémoires de Philippe de Commynes* (Geneva, 1966), pp. 668–9.

escorted, partly as a mark of honour (especially in the case of large and notable embassies), partly to ensure their safety, but principally to make certain that they saw nothing, nor talked to any person who might give them evidence which could be of value to them.[23] In the early summer of 1415, the monastic chronicler Thomas Walsingham recalled, Henry V had gathered his army near Southampton in readiness for the invasion of Normandy which was soon to follow. The French, probably alerted to the English king's intentions but not knowing where he would land, sent a final embassy to Henry, who rejected its proposals and ordered it back to London. By now, however, the ambassadors had had a glimpse of the extensive preparations which the English had made for the expedition and, hoping to bring the news to their own countrymen so that effective measures for defence might be taken, they tried to make their escape without being noticed (*latenter*). Their plan, however, was frustrated and the ambassadors found themselves arrested and held in custody.[24] That such drastic action should have proved necessary is scarcely surprising. Only a few weeks before this incident Henry had written to the French king announcing his intention of reducing the period for which the ambassadors' safe conducts would be valid, since he regarded the time granted to them for the completion of their mission as being excessively long.[25] It is not unreasonable to deduce that Henry was himself suspicious in advance of the enemy's motive in wanting to send an embassy to him, and that events justified him in the detention of its members, a step which effectively prevented them from alerting the defences of the country which the English were about to invade.

The ready assumption that ambassadors, unlike heralds, might properly make use of, and report back, information gleaned during the period of their embassies is unlikely to surprise us. If, by the second half of the fifteenth century, Commynes regarded ambassadors as legalized spies, this was an opinion shared by many, if not most, of his contemporaries, especially Italians.[26] Most embassies, indeed, were equipped with a number of subordinate officials who could be sent back to their king or prince at a moment's notice, should the need for contact between him

23. Hill, *The King's Messengers*, pp. 96–97.

24. *The St. Albans Chronicle, 1406–1420*, ed. V. H. Galbraith (Oxford, 1937), pp. 85–86.

25. N. H. Nicolas, *History of the Battle of Agincourt* (2nd edn., London, 1832), Appendix I, p. 3. Mézières, too, strongly advised that persons coming under safe conduct should be very closely watched (*Songe du Vieil Pèlerin*, i. 512).

26. On this matter, see D. E. Queller, *The Office of Ambassador in the Middle Ages* (Princeton, 1967), p. 98.

and the ambassadors arise. The activities of ambassadors touched upon espionage in other ways, too. Medieval rulers usually kept agents permanently in the realms of their enemies, and such persons might carry out their work undetected for a considerable number of years. It appears that ambassadors, when on embassy, often made contact with undercover agents from the same court, and no doubt received information from them which was either to be conveyed to their masters or which might be relevant to the negotiations which the ambassadors were conducting. In 1413 Breton ambassadors, sent to the court of Henry V for truce negotiations, made contact with two agents, Langueffort and Le Meignen, who had been at work in England since at least 1406 in the pay of Duke John V, and whose task it was to find out what went on at Westminster.[27] Commynes's advice to rulers to watch carefully those who visited foreign ambassadors was indeed very fitting.[28]

Yet, although messengers and ambassadors were expected to uncover information, their involvement in matters of intelligence was only incidental to their other, main duties. Recorded evidence affords glimpses of agents whose sole function was concerned with espionage, although such references are relatively few. None the less, it is certain that English royal spies formed a class distinct from the royal messengers and others who were only occasionally involved in spying. It is, however, all too easy to overlook these professional spies since, in addition to the difficulties already adduced, many entries in the accounting documents of the period merely name the recipient and the sum paid, but make no mention of the services for which the payment was made. For instance, the Issue Roll of Michaelmas Term 1378, records a payment made on 25 October to a French esquire, Nicolas Briser, who was retained by Richard II for an annual fee of 50 marks.[29] Since many foreign knights and esquires were thus retained by the crown for military purposes during this period, the payment made to Briser could justifiably be

27. G. A. Knowlson, *Jean V, duc de Bretagne, et l'Angleterre (1399–1442)* (Rennes and Cambridge, 1964), p. 82. It is interesting to note that Langueffort's wife received payments from the duke, for unspecified reasons, while her husband was at work in England, and it is tempting to assume that these payments were made in respect of her husband's service (ibid., p. 46). It is known, too, that John V maintained agents in Paris to keep him informed of events there. We are indebted to Dr. Knowlson for drawing our attention to these matters.

28. Philippe de Commynes, *Mémoires*, ed. J. Calmette and G. Durville (3 vols., Paris, 1925), i. 219.

29. P.R.O., E.403/471, m. 5. He was again referred to by name only on 25 May 1379 (E.403/472, m. 6), and on 9 June 1379 (ibid., m. 6). On 8 September 1379 he was simply described as 'valletus de Harfleu' (ibid., m. 13).

construed as having been made for such a purpose. However, some indication of the true nature of Briser's employment was given in April 1379, when he received 71*s*. 1*d*. for 'jurato domino regi coram consilio suo ad faciendum comodum ipsius domini regis meliori modo poterit ad nocumentum inimicorum suorum in expedicionem guerrarum regis',[30] only a few months after he had been described as an 'explorator regis',[31] the nature of his position thus being clearly revealed. In other cases lack of further evidence means that many other spies probably remain undetected to this day.

Despite the reticence of the English authorities to describe their agents more exactly, a small number of individuals may positively be identified as spies. The names of the agents sent to Normandy in 1339, and those dispatched by Frank de Hale from Calais in 1370, are not recorded. From the 1370s onwards, however, named spies begin to appear more frequently in English records. In the years 1377–8, Nicolas Hakenet (or Hakynet), a French esquire, described as 'explorator regis', received several payments for intelligence work carried out in the English king's service. On 21 September 1377, he was paid 10 marks for a journey 'ad partes transmarinas ad explorandum de flota navium Francie et de ordinacione inimicorum regis in eisdem partibus',[32] while on 23 November he received expenses 'de dono regis' for 'morando in Londonia, ibidem expectando voluntatis ipsius domini regis et consilii sui';[33] later, on 12 December, he was paid 5 marks and another five on 29 January 1378, for going at the council's behest 'versus partes Francie, ad explorandum de ordinacione inimicorum pro guerra in partibus predictis'.[34] A further 40*s*. were paid to him on 25 September 1378, 'pro tempore quo stetavit Londonie, attendens voluntatem consilii regis'.[35]

An interesting point to note is that the payment of September 1377, was made by the hand of another known agent, the above-mentioned Nicolas Briser. Both are known to have been active in France in 1377–8, and may possibly have formed part of a spy-ring organized in enemy territory on behalf of the English crown. It is known that such a well-organized network of agents was established in Flanders by the English council in the 1380s, and was functioning in 1386–7,[36] although other

30. P.R.O., E.403/472, m. 1.
31. P.R.O., E.403/471, m. 8. He was also thus described on 14 July 1379 (ibid., m. 13).
32. P.R.O., E.403/463, m. 6.   33. P.R.O., E.403/467, m. 8.
34. Ibid., mm. 10, 14.   35. P.R.O., E.403/468, m. 12.
36. For a full account of this network, see J. J. N. Palmer, *England, France and Christendom, 1377–99* (London, 1972), pp. 123–4 and Appendix I.

groups of agents, and individual agents, were at work at the same time elsewhere. In October 1385, for instance, Arnald Turrour was sent 'apud Mergate in partibus de Pycardye, ad morendum et explorandum in dictis partibus de ordinacione inimicorum de Francia',[37] while in the following October Frederick Fullyng and Richard Henley were dispatched from Calais with news 'de exercitu adversarii regis de Francia'.[38]

It seems, too, that Edward III, by maintaining agents within the English companies in France, followed a dictum which was later to be expressed by Philippe de Mézières.[39] In February 1370, Roger Hilton and John de Neuby, 'esquiers de la grande compaignie', brought the king and council news from Normandy 'de certeines secrees busoignes dont ils furent charges depart nous', for which they received £100 in the king's gift.[40]

A striking feature of the agents employed by the English crown in the 1370s and 1380s was that many of them were aliens. All those working for the English in Ghent in 1386–7, with the exception of Brother Adam Bamford, appear to have been of Flemish stock. The appointment of French and Flemings as agents by the English had definite advantages: they spoke the enemy's language as natives and would thus arouse less suspicion than strangers with the enemy authorities.[41] Persons speaking Netherlandish dialects, for instance, could work without undue danger in Flanders, and it is known that Middelburg, in Zeeland, was an important centre for espionage from which the English, during the 1380s, dispatched agents speaking these dialects.[42]

Aliens working as agents might even hold positions of importance or responsibility in their native area, and would thus be more valuable to their masters. It was in return for his freedom that Thomas Turberville, captured in Gascony in April 1295, agreed to act as a French spy at the

---

37. P.R.O., E.403/510, m. 12.   38. P.R.O., E.403/515, m. 1.

39. 'Le chevetaine [of the army, town or castle] . . . doit tousjours ymaginer que le roy son seigneur (a) continuelment ses secretes espies en l'ost pour enquester et espier secretement le gouvernement du chevetaine et comment l'ost se porte' (*Songe du Vieil Pèlerin*, i. 519). Spies were also employed internally within the administration to check upon the functions of royal officers. In 1335, for instance, agents were named to investigate secretly the dealings of certain collectors of tenths and fifteenths who had 'borne themselves ill', and to report their findings to the council (*C.P.R., 1334–8*, p. 202).

40. P.R.O., E.404/10/65.

41. See Froissart's reference to spies 'moult bien parlant francoys, alemant et angloys' (Froissart, *Oeuvres. Chroniques*, ed. K. de Lettenhove (29 vols., Brussels, 1870–7), v. 545).

42. In September 1386, for instance, the mayor of the staple at Middelburg was ordered to certify the council 'de ordinacione Francigenarum' (P.R.O., E.403/512, m. 21).

court of Edward I, to which he returned, having 'escaped', in August 1295, leaving his children in France as hostages. A short while later he was writing to the *prévôt* of Paris that the Isle of Wight was undefended, and that if the Scots were to rise in rebellion against the English, the Welsh might do likewise. But Turberville was already uneasy about his position near the king: 'acone genz', he wrote to his French correspondent, 'unt suspecion vers moy, pur ceo ke jeo ay dyt ke suy eschape hors de la prison', a story which was evidently leading men to doubt his loyalty to the king. Betrayed and then arrested, Turberville was tried and executed.[43] Almost a century later, Sir Ralph Travers was unjustly accused of similar treasonable correspondence with the French: importance must be attached to the statement, made at his trial, that to have a spy who could pass on vital information personally obtained from Richard II's council would be of greater use to Charles VI than the possession of Calais and other castles round about.[44] That all spies did not have direct access to the king's council chamber, however, goes without saying.[45]

If it is difficult to estimate, from financial sources, both the numbers of spies employed by the English and the successes which they may have had, the reaction of the French populace and authorities to the threat of espionage may be a fair indication of the extent to which foreign agents were at work in France in time of war. The inhabitants of the border regions, the Calais March, the south-west, and the areas around other English-held territories were particularly aware of the threat. Local reaction was often one of violence. In September 1359, three inhabitants of Chitry were pardoned by the Dauphin Charles for having killed in error two valets whom they had mistaken for spies sent from the English garrison at Chablis.[46] At the same time, other pardons were granted to certain men of Monampteuil for the similar murder of Lamentier le Clay whom they had taken in error for an English spy from Vailly.[47]

---

43. See above, p. 74, n. 5.

44. ' . . . pluis profiteroit & plerroit al dit Adversaire & a son conseil d'avoir une telle persone come vous estes, de leur covyne & assent, en le conseil de notre seigneur le Roi d'Engleterre, pur lour conforter et acerter de privitees, purpos et affaires en notre Conseil, que d'avoir la ville de Caleys ou autre forteresce du Roi notre seigneur a lour volentee' (*Rot. Parl.* iii. 92).

45. One English agent, however, who escaped the vigilance of the Burgundian authorities in 1387 was no less a person than the clerk of the city of Ghent (Palmer, *England, France and Christendom*, p. 231).

46. Arch. Nat., JJ. 90, fo. 138ᵛ, no. 269.

47. Ibid., fo. 142, no. 275. At the time of the murder, the three men were engaged in the fortification of the church at Monampteuil, at the command of the bishop of Laon. It

These two examples were by no means isolated ones. On a less violent level were the numerous denunciations of persons suspected by their fellows of being enemy agents. Any dealings with the enemy, however innocent, might cause immediate suspicion. In 1369, Adam Hane, a monk at Le Tréport, was imprisoned for having dealings with the Navarrese, even though he had been merely involved in negotiations for the release of French prisoners held by them.[48]

Nor were the authorities slow to act. In June 1359, the abbess of Saint-Nicholas at Bar-sur-Aube was indicted by Jean de Chalons, the French king's lieutenant in Sens, Troyes, and Chaumont, on suspicion of treason and correspondence with the enemy.[49] Arrests of such suspects were frequent. Frenchmen who lived abroad, particularly in the realm of an enemy, were regarded as security risks on their return, and stood in danger of arrest. Such was the fate of the unfortunate Evrart Hostelier who, returning to France in 1369 after having lived eighteen years in England, was arrested by the French authorities as an enemy agent.[50] Other stringent security measures were taken. An *ordonnance* of 1370, for instance, decreed that prisoners of war held in the castle of Saint-Omer should be kept in rooms without windows lest they were to 'bien veoir et savoir le convenant, estat et forteresce de la dite ville. . . au tresgraunt domage, meschief et inconvenient de nous et de la dite ville',[51] while suspected spies captured in 1345 were provided with a heavily armed escort which accompanied them from Neuilly to Caen, where they were taken for interrogation.[52]

The extent of French reaction against espionage certainly implies considerable activity, and perhaps a certain success, by the English in this field, and although the role played by spies is, to a large extent, indeterminate, certain aspects of their functions are clear. Not only was there the obvious task of finding out the enemy's secrets, his plans, his military preparations and organization, and other information of interest, but such uncovered secrets had to be conveyed back to the appropriate authorities. The usefulness of agents, however, was not restricted to

---

may fairly be said that they thus had at least some justification for their suspicions that their victim had come to spy on the progress of the construction of the new defences.

48. Ibid., fo. 195, no. 386.   49. Ibid., fo. 108ᵛ, no. 197.

50. Ibid., fo. 27, no. 57.

51. Saint-Omer, Archives Municipales, CCXXVI. 3.

52. L. Delisle, *Actes normands de la Chambre des Comptes sous Philippe de Valois* (Paris, 1881), p. 185.

these roles. They were also employed in an offensive role, as *agents-provocateurs*, whose tasks included the spreading of false rumours to undermine the morale of the enemy and to mislead his military leaders. Of prime importance, too, were liaisons with dissident elements in regions under French rule: it is plain, for example, that in the summer of 1385 English agents were in constant contact with the anti-French and anti-Burgundian factions in the towns of Ghent and Damme.[53]

In all these activities, an important asset to English espionage was the possession of bases in France. These afforded footholds within enemy territory from which not only military expeditions could be launched but from which agents could also easily be dispatched. Calais was one such centre for spies. When Hennequin du Bos, captured on Jean de Vienne's expedition to Scotland in 1385, had decided 'd'estre Englès & de tenir la partie des Englès' and agreed to serve them as a spy, it was to Calais that the English sent him. There, according to the confession which he made some years later to the French authorities, he met other spies about to travel to different parts of France, to Rethel and Champagne, to the Lendit and other fairs, even as far as Poitou. All were to return in a variety of disguises, one dressed as a monk, another as a hospitaler, a third as a goldsmith. In all cases, Calais was to be their base.[54] This, and further evidence, suggests that the most was made of Calais, a great economic and military centre where French and English influences rubbed shoulders, a centre in which and from which spies and informers of all parties could hope to function with some success. From a petition filed by the captain in 1417, we learn of his need to spend £100 a year 'pour son espiaille en Fraunce et ayllours pour le bien et save garde de la ville du Calays, come autres capitans illoeques ount heuz devaunt ceste temps'.[55] If Calais was 'an admirable window for observing what the French were up to',[56] the reverse was almost equally true.

Bases such as Calais served, too, as centres for the accumulation of information which could then either be conveyed to England or acted

53. P.R.O., E.403/508, mm. 17, 18, 20, and 22.

54. *Registre Criminel du Châtelet de Paris du 6 septembre 1389 au 18 mai 1392*, ed. H. Duplès-Agier, Société des Bibliophiles Français (2 vols., Paris, 1861–4), i. 379–93. Professor Coopland drew attention to this evidence in *Le Songe du Vieil Pèlerin*, ii. 84, and in 'Crime and Punishment in Paris', *Medieval and Middle Eastern Studies in Honor of Aziz Suryal Atiya*, ed. S. A. Hanna (Leiden, 1972), pp. 79–80.

55. *P.P.C.* ii. 210.

56. C. G. Cruickshank, *Army Royal, Henry VIII's Invasion of France, 1513* (Oxford, 1969), p. 18. This study contains several references to spies in Calais. See too, *P.P.C.* ii. 343–4.

upon by the commander of the local garrison, as he saw fit.[57] Intelligence brought back there was treated as having the greatest priority, and was acted upon immediately. Thus William de Weston, arraigned before Parliament in 1377 for surrendering the fortress of Audruicq, sought to justify himself by claiming that he had been informed by a spy of the approach of a great enemy force armed with 'tres graundes et tres grevouses ordinances'. When the force did appear, indeed armed with a large number of guns, Weston, acting upon the information which he had received, surrendered the fortress.[58] In 1385, Calais likewise served as a clearing-point for information sent by different agents from Ghent concerning events which were then taking place in that town and in Damme.[59]

If information from agents in the field was to be of real value, it had to be conveyed to the king and council as rapidly as possible. To achieve this, good channels of communication were vital. English agents working abroad had the difficulty of having to bring their information across the sea if required to report directly to the king and council. One of the most regular crossings, frequently used by royal messengers, was between Wissant, some miles to the west of Calais, and Dover.[60] It was popular because it was the shortest distance across the Channel, both ports were in English hands from the 1340s, and, furthermore, fees for crossings had been regularized by statute early in the reign of Edward III.[61]

Within England itself, posting systems aided the swift passage of messages from the coast or the borders to the central authorities. One, ensuring rapid contact between the king and the captain of Calais, was in existence in 1372 between Dover and London. In June of that year arrangements were made for the provision of hackneys at a reasonable cost in Canterbury for the use of royal messengers travelling between

57. L. Puiseux, 'Étude sur une grande ville de bois construite en Normandie pour une expédition en Angleterre en 1386', *Mémoires de la Société des Antiquaires de Norman-die*, xxv (1863), 5.

58. *Rot. Parl.* iii. 39.   59. P.R.O., E.403/508, m. 18.

60. M. C. Hill, 'Jack Faukes, King's Messenger, and his Journey to Avignon in 1343', *E.H.R.* lvii (1942), 24.

61. *Statutes of the Realm*, i. 263 (Stat. 4 Edward III, cap. 8). Where speed was essential, boats could be hired for the crossing, although this was more expensive. Fees for a man and horse between Dover and Wissant generally cost about 1 mark (Hill, 'Jack Faukes', pp. 24–25). Charges for private hire could be even greater. In December 1369, £20 was paid 'pur le louer dune nief et deux barges pour conduire Rauf Barry et Johan Paulesholt et autres . . . alantz en nostre message vers Chirburgh en Normandie' (P.R.O., E.404/9/63).

London and Calais.[62] By May 1373 refinements in the system were evident: royal writs ordered the bailiffs of Dover and Southwark, too, to provide hackneys, and the orders to Canterbury and Rochester were repeated.[63] Evidence suggests that other roads in England may also have been posted to facilitate the passage of messages. In 1360, for instance, the council, then over a hundred miles away at Reading, was informed of the French descent on Winchelsea on the very day on which it took place.[64] That the conveyance of information was possible was a factor of the greatest importance in time of war.

Responsibility for matters of espionage lay ultimately with the king and council, who appointed agents and sent them on missions. Very often, as in the case of Nicolas Briser who travelled to Gloucester in 1378 to impart his information to the king, these agents reported back their findings in person. But it was not only agents who did this. Messengers and envoys were likewise expected to report in person to the king or his council on the completion of their missions. The link between the council and matters of espionage is further illustrated by the fact that while in the field the marshal and the constable, together with their subordinates (captains of garrisons in France or on the Scottish border, and commanders of armies) had responsibility for sending out their own agents,[65] such military commanders frequently passed on their information to the central authorities.

A great deal is known about the payment of messengers in the royal service in England, but the position regarding the remuneration of spies employed by the crown is much less clear. Royal messengers received daily wages at a fixed rate, according to their rank, together with annual

---

62. *C.C.R., 1369–74*, p. 399; *Foedera* (Rec.Comm.ed), III. ii. 947.

63. *C.C.R., 1369–74*, p. 505.

64. The French attacked Winchelsea on the morning of Sunday, 15 March 1360 (*Chronicon Anglie, ab anno domini 1328 usque ad annum 1388*, ed. E. M. Thompson (R.S., 1874), pp. 40–41; *Chronicon Henrici Knighton*, ed. J. R. Lumby (2 vols., R.S., 1889–95), ii. 109; *Thomae Walsingham Historia Anglicana*, ed. H. T. Riley (2 vols., R.S., 1863–4), i. 287). On the same day, the council issued writs mentioning the attack, and ordered the arrest of every ship and large barge for use against the French (*Foedera*, III. i. 476). Post roads connecting London with the Welsh and Scottish borders were possibly in existence during the reign of Edward I (Hill, *The King's Messengers*, pp. 108–9).

65. As in the case of William de Weston cited above (p. 85). The powers of the Marshal and Constable are well attested: 'Item, le Connestable a la cure d'envoyer messager & espies pour le fait de l'ost par tout où il voit qu'il appartient à faire, les coureurs & autres chevaucheurs, quand il voit que mestier en est' (P. Anselme, *Histoire généalogique et chronologique de la maison royale de France* (9 vols., Paris, 1726–33), vi. 234). 'Spyes specially ordeyned' must obey the Constable and Marshal (*The Essential Portions of Nicholas Upton's De Studio Militari, before 1446, translated by John Blount, Fellow of All Souls (c. 1500)*, ed. F. P. Barnard (Oxford, 1931), p. 36).

gifts of clothing and shoes. When on active service they received, in addition, expenses for travelling.[66] It is uncertain whether the same conditions applied to agents involved in the shadier business of spying, since evidence to determine this is slight. The Frenchman Nicolas Briser, was certainly paid an annual retaining fee of 50 marks and, in addition, was reimbursed the miscellaneous expenses he had incurred whilst travelling on the king's service.[67] The majority of payments made to secret agents, however, were usually extraordinary payments made in the king's gift ('de dono regis'), partly as wages, partly in recompense of the expenses incurred by the agent.[68] It is thus almost impossible to estimate the wages which a typical agent might receive. Payments made to them may possibly have depended upon results, as was sometimes the case for messengers who were frequently rewarded by the recipient of the letters which they bore.[69]

Mézières's Pilgrim was to advocate that at least one-third of military expenditure should be on espionage. It is difficult to estimate whether this was, in fact, the case in practice, but documentary evidence certainly does suggest that a substantial amount was spent on spies and spying. In 1370, for example, the sum paid to English spies working from Calais alone was in excess of £70, a trifling sum compared to the over-all war expenditure of that year, but significant when compared to the total expenditure on all royal messengers, which amounted to £183.[70] It is necessary to bear in mind that the sum of £70 did not include payments to agents working elsewhere, and that a large proportion of the moneys paid to ordinary messengers were for journeys of a special or secret nature.

So far we have dealt chiefly with spies working for the English crown. Such agents served as a valuable and necessary source of information, and were of great benefit to their masters. But there was a further side to the whole matter. Spies employed by the enemy caused many headaches for the central government and for military commanders. Record sources testify to the extensive use of secret agents by the French and other enemies against the English, both abroad and within the realm of

66. For payments made to royal messengers, see Hill, *The King's Messengers*, pp. 22 ff. and 46–51.
67. P.R.O., E.403/471, mm. 5 and 8; E.403/472, mm. 1, 6, 7, 10, and 13.
68. For example, P.R.O., E.403/463, m. 6; E.403/467, mm. 8, 10, and 14.
69. English kings habitually presented foreign messengers with moneys or valuables 'de dono regis' (for example, P.R.O., E.404/6/36/58, 60).
70. Hill, *The King's Messengers*, p. 98.

England itself. Time and again, the presence of enemy spies made itself felt in England, a fact reflected in royal writs which stressed the dangers to the realm presented by these persons, in statutes aimed at curtailing their activities, in reports of frequent arrests and detentions of suspects and, most significantly, in the complaints of the Commons in Parliament. It is, perhaps, all too easy to dismiss such references as manifestations of a fear which gripped crown and people subjected to the stresses of prolonged war, an interpretation which might certainly be applicable to the period after 1369, when the English reversals in the war were accompanied by an increased awareness and preoccupation with the needs of home defence. It is known that enemy agents were frequently sent to the English possessions in France, especially Calais, to uncover information,[71] and that French castles and towns situated near English possessions were also important bases for espionage. Saint-Omer, for instance, often acted as a dispatch centre for agents infiltrating into the English-held Calais March. Even in times of formal peace, the use of spies continued: in 1368, Pieret de Bourges was paid one écu 'pour aller secretement a Calais et ou pais de Ghisnes . . . pour enquerre et savoir sil avoit aucunes gens darmes a Calais et lestat et convenue des Engles'.[72] Agents were also sent to spy upon English armies in the field. Thus troops sent to aid the Gantois at Damme in 1385 came under the surveillance of agents sent by Duke Philip of Burgundy to discover the 'temps que les Anglois arriverent ou port de Hugheuliets'.[73] By far the most serious threat to English security, however, were agents actively at work within the realm itself—those sent to Scotland by the French in 1354 to persuade the Scots to stir up trouble in the north of England;[74] those dispatched to London by Louis de Mâle in 1382 to uncover information of importance to him;[75] or the Burgundians sent there in 1425 to secure details of the military preparations then under way.[76]

71. For Calais, Arch. Dép., Nord, B.15796, m. 6ᵛ; for Bordeaux, Chronique de Mathieu d'Escouchy, ed. G. du Fresne de Beaucourt (3 vols., S.H.F., 1863–4), iii. 387; for Gascony, B.N., MS. fr. 32511, fos. 142ᵛ, 143; the last two are cited by M. G. A. Vale, 'The Last Years of English Gascony, 1451–1453', T. R. Hist. S., 5th ser., xix (1969), 121–2.

72. Arch. Dép., Nord, B.15793, fo. 6 (Accounts of the bailliage of Saint-Omer).

73. Arch. Dép., Nord, B.1842/50006.

74. Chronique normande du XIVe siècle, ed. A. and E. Molinier (S.H.F., 1882), pp. 108–9.

75. Arch. Dép., Nord, B.1337/14596, printed by Palmer, England, France and Christendom, Appendix II.

76. Arch. Dép., Nord, B.1933, fos. 62ᵛ, 77.

It is certain, then, that the numerous measures taken against spies did have some positive foundation, and, from the extent of the measures employed, there can be little doubt that the menace presented by enemy agents was taken very seriously. With alarming regularity, English royal writs bore the startling information that enemy aliens were 'spying on the secrets of the realm and sending home intelligence',[77] or that 'divers aliens, enemies of the realm, have entered and daily enter the realm to spy out its secrets and reveal them to the French'.[78] The records of Parliament testify, perhaps better than any other single source, the extent to which Englishmen held enemy aliens in fear and suspicion, so that very few meetings of Parliament after the 1330s failed to refer to them or to the dangers with which they threatened the realm. Much of this was, admittedly, the result of a prejudice purely racial in its concept, although indubitably fostered by prolonged war. In 1347, for example, the Commons complained against the pope's appointment of aliens to English benefices and monastic houses,[79] and the Parliament of 1379 heard a similar petition that none of the best benefices should be granted to alien clergy.[80] But although much was based upon prejudice, the greater part of the Commons' complaints against aliens were the result of considerations concerning national security. In 1338, it was requested that all prelates should certify to Parliament the names and whereabouts of alien clergy in their dioceses;[81] some six years later, the Commons petitioned that the crown take in hand the goods and lands of aliens living within the realm, and that the profits from these be 'tournez a defens de la terre et de Seinte Eglise',[82] while in 1377 grievances levelled at aliens stated simply that they entered the kingdom as spies.[83]

English public opinion thus regarded the situation as one of extreme gravity, and the central government was not slow to take action against the threat of espionage. It is clear that the different ways by which enemy agents could operate were well recognized by the government, and that steps were taken to counter enemy operations in each of them. Briefly, the measures were directed towards four main ends: first, the prevention of the leakage of secret information to external enemies by

77. *Calendar of Documents relating to Scotland*, ed. J. Bain (4 vols., Edinburgh, 1881–8), iii. 294, no. 1614.

78 *C.P.R.*, *1377–81*, p. 475. Numerous other examples for the fourteenth century, taken from the Patent and Close Rolls, could be cited.

79. *Rot. Parl.* ii. 171.   80. Ibid. iii. 46.   81. Ibid. ii. 106.
82. Ibid. ii. 154.   83. Ibid. iii. 22.

hindering spies entering the realm or, failing this, by preventing them from leaving with their information; secondly, the control of alien clergy who constituted a threat, not always imagined, within the kingdom; thirdly, the prevention of the undermining of the country's economy by measures taken against the importation of inferior (usually Scots) coinage and the export of bullion (in specie or plate) or arms or victuals; and fourthly, the prevention of entry into the realm of undesirable, outside influences, such as anti-government propaganda, 'prejudicial bulls' and, above all, rumours (whether true or false) which might have a detrimental effect upon the morale of the population.

In putting such measures into effect, the ports played an important role. It was there that the first steps were taken to curtail the activities of enemy agents, and strict security was therefore essential. When a foreign expedition was in the offing, the crown frequently resorted to a complete ban on all persons or civil shipping wishing to leave the country. When Edward III's fleet set sail for Normandy in 1346, orders were sent to the mayor and sheriffs of London, and to officials in the Cinque Ports, particularly Dover, Winchelsea, and Sandwich that no-one, of whatever condition, should be allowed to leave the realm until eight days after the departure of the king's fleet, since 'intelleximus quod quamplures exploratores in civitate predicta London et alibi infra regnum nostrum Anglie conversantes secreta nostra ad partes externas ad inimicos nostros . . . mittunt'.[84] On other occasions, as in 1348, the ports were closed to all pilgrims.[85] At other times persons were permitted to leave the realm, but only from specified ports, usually Dover or, exceptionally, Orwell, or by some other controlled exit point.[86] Exceptions to the general ordinance were, however, often made, as when the bailiffs and wardens of the ports were instructed to permit 'known merchants' to leave.[87] Licences, too, were frequently granted by the crown for more specific reasons. These were varied. In 1368 the prior of Arundel was

84. P.R.O., C.76/23, m. 23ᵛ (Chancery, Treaty Rolls). Shortly afterwards the sheriffs of London were informed that French spies had infiltrated the kingdom to discover the king's secrets (*C.C.R.*, *1346–9*, p. 149).

85. P.R.O., C.76/26, m. 16ᵛ. In 1416 one Craquet was instructed to cross to England, disguised as a pilgrim travelling to Canterbury, to see to the interests of the abbey of Fécamp and to gather information and money (D. J. A. Matthew, *The Norman Monasteries and their English Possessions* (Oxford, 1962), pp. 130–1 and 166–7).

86. *C.C.R.*, *1381–5*, p. 1.

87. For example, P.R.O., E.364/3, m. 1. The prohibition against emigration of February 1383, however, stressed that even known merchants were to be prevented from leaving the ports (*C.C.R.*, *1381–5*, p. 281).

permitted to go to Rome 'pour aucunes busoignes tuchantz sa priorte',[88] while in 1381 the keepers of the port of Dover were instructed to allow John Myners and his retinue to leave the realm 'aller a Calais pour soi defendre illoeqes en gage de bataille'.[89] In order to receive licence to leave the realm, persons were sometimes requested to provide mainpernors to vouch for their integrity before a licence could be granted.[90] Yet, despite the legal methods which were available to those wishing to leave on legitimate business, many nevertheless tried to do so without proper authority.[91]

Alien clergy were singularly discriminated against by the government's security measures, in many cases with good reason. It was repeatedly reported that friars and other alien clergy entered and left England daily, so that 'the secrets of the realm are laid bare by such aliens to the king's enemies, to the peril of the realm'.[92] Widespread anti-clerical feeling no doubt had some bearing on the attitude towards alien clergy, but clerics, and more especially members of the mendicant orders, who had relative freedom of movement, were in a very good position to act as agents. More than one case could be cited to justify current suspicions. In 1369, the alien prior of Hayling, in Hampshire, was confined at his own cost in Southwark priory for having received letters from France;[93] while in 1384 Hugh Calveley, then keeper of the Channel Islands, was ordered to arrest without delay a French spy, Laurence Pussyn of Normandy, who had 'craftily intruded' into the church of St. Peter Port by means of a papal provision, and had since been spying on the secrets of the English in Guernsey.[94]

Such cases explain to a large extent the preoccupation with alien clergy in the Parliaments of Edward III and Richard II, and also the numerous measures levelled against them by the authorities. Heads of monasteries received orders to refuse alien clergy the right of admittance to their houses. The prior of Holy Trinity, London, was thus instructed in 1340;[95] the Dominican convent in Oxford received similar orders in 1373, the king having been informed that alien spies were active in Oxford under the pretext of studying there;[96] while in 1382, the

88. P.R.O., C.81/1712/5 (Chancery Warrants). 89. P.R.O., C.81/1656/6.
90. P.R.O., C.81/1715/19. 91. P.R.O., E.364/12, mm. 1, 4, 5ᵛ.
92. C.C.R., 1381–5, p. 64.
93. C.C.R., 1369–74, p. 63. This case was cited in the Parliament of 1379 as proof that alien clergy were in contact with the enemy (Rot. Parl. iii. 64).
94. C.P.R., 1381–5, p. 35. 95. C.C.R., 1339–41, p. 458.
96. C.C.R., 1369–74, p. 517.

warden and convent of the Friars Minor in London were told that no alien brethren 'coming from what realm or lordship soever' should remain in the house for longer than two days, and that those already there should be removed without delay.[97]

Apart from individual clerics, whole houses of alien clergy suffered from the government's security measures. 'Alien priories' presented a special security risk in coastal regions; periods of open war witnessed not merely numerous confiscations of their lands but more especially the removal of alien clergy from coastal areas, the principle having been established in 1295 that the coastal regions were to be free of alien (or, more specifically, French) clergy in time of war.[98] The practice was repeated in 1326, when all secular beneficed clergy who were 'subjects and adherents of the King of France, living near the sea or navigable rivers' were taken from the coastal region and accommodated inland for the duration of the troubles.[99] Such principles were to remain in force throughout the fourteenth century. For example, in July 1337 all alien priories in the Isle of Wight were taken into the king's hands, and their monks moved away from the sea,[100] while in the following year the monks of St. Michael's Mount and the denizen priory of Lewes shared the same fate.[101] In the Parliaments of 1346, 1369, 1372, and 1373 petitions against the alien clergy were put forward by the Commons,[102] and in the first Parliament of Richard II's reign measures were taken to expel all enemy aliens from England.[103] Although these measures meant by no means complete expulsions—conventual priors, known loyalists, and married secular clergy who could find sureties for themselves were exempted—they did represent a positive attitude by the government to the dangers presented by the alien clergy. Those who were permitted to remain were subject to the most stringent controls. The provision of 1377 amplified an order of 1369 whereby alien priors, to whom had been committed the custody of their own houses, were bound to find mainpernors to swear that each prior would remain continually in his house,

---

97. *C.C.R.*, *1381–5*, p. 64.   98. Matthew, *Norman Monasteries*, pp. 82–84.

99. *C.C.R.*, *1325–7*, p. 636. Only secular clergy were involved since, presumably, any action taken by alien regular clergy in an English religious houses could be controlled by its head.

100. P.R.O., C.61/49, m.19 (Chancery, Gascon Rolls). On the same day all alien clergy 'de potestate et dominio regis Francie' suffered a similar fate (ibid., m. 23).

101. *Foedera*, II. ii. 1061.

102. In 1373 the Commons entered a petition that all alien clergy living within twenty leagues of the sea-coast should be removed, since they were 'espiant les secretz et ordynancez de temps en temps a vostre Parliament et Conseil' (*Rot. Parl.* ii. 320).

103. Ibid. 162–3.

and that neither he, nor his monks nor servants, would 'pass out of the realm, or reveal the state, affairs or secrets of the realm to any foreign person, or transmit to foreign parts by letter or word of mouth . . . any thing prejudicial'.[104] Aliens who remained were not, in addition, to be involved in the keeping of the sea-coast. In 1379 the alien prior of Pembroke was given control of his priory with the proviso that he be exempt from the *garde de la mer*.[105] Nevertheless, despite the measures taken against them, alien clergy were to remain a security hazard until their more complete expulsion in the reign of Henry V.[106]

Controls at the ports were implemented for a number of reasons, not all of them directly connected with espionage. They played, for instance, an essential role in the sphere of royal finance, as in the case of searching for customs evaders. None the less, even such seemingly economic measures could have a bearing upon national security. It was often reported that enemy aliens were attempting to smuggle out arms, bullion, and victuals from the realm. While otherwise 'loyal' Englishmen were not averse to making their profit at the expense of the crown and possibly to the detriment of the kingdom, it is likely that such activities were undertaken by enemy agents as a positive part of their duties of espionage. This theory is supported by the fact that persons arrested on suspicion of spying were also frequently accused of economic offences. Mézières was one who noted the connection between merchants and spies; 'les espies', he wrote, 'par lesquelles on puet mieulx savoir lestat de ses ennemis ce sont les marchans Lombars et estranges'.[107] Money spent in procuring their services, and those of their factors, would be money well spent since, as men engaged in non-military activities, they could travel more freely than most, and suffered less from limitations imposed upon their movements. But it is clear that it was all too widely accepted that merchants might be spies in disguise. In April 1376 the Commons sought the expulsion of 'Lombard broukers' and others described as 'privees Espies' through whom aliens were alleged to be uncovering the secrets of the kingdom.[108] Hughlin Gerard, a merchant of Bologna Grassa who was pardoned in July 1388, had, since his entry into England in 1377, committed a number of crimes against the realm and the statutes. These were mainly of an economic

---

104. *Calendar of Fine Rolls, 1369–77*, pp. 13–17.
105. *Calendar of Fine Rolls, 1377–83*, pp. 155–6.
106. For a fuller account, see Matthew, *Norman Monasteries*, pp. 120 and 126–7.
107. *Songe du Vieil Pèlerin*, ii. 85 and 405.
108. *Rot. Parl.* ii. 332, 338, and 347.

nature, and included the illegal exportation of bullion, carrying on ex-changes without licence, exporting non-customed wools, and importing luxury commodities such as silk and pearls into England. In addition to these offences, he had 'betrayed the secrets and counsel of the realm to his master, a Frenchman, at Paris'.[109] It was merchants, too, who were responsible for warning the English of a proposed French attack on west Wales in 1377.[110] It is thus possible that the statutes concerning restrictions on such mercantile activities as the importation and expor-tation of goods may have been enforced, to a certain extent, with a view to countering espionage.[111]

Scrutiny at the ports was undertaken by several classes of officials. The mayors and bailiffs of coastal towns, or the sheriff of the county, were often commissioned by the crown to seize prohibited imports and exports, to prevent persons and shipping from leaving the realm, and to apprehend enemy agents.[112] Sometimes the king's serjeants-at-arms were commissioned in this way.[113] Regularly employed, too, were the searchers for bullion in the ports and, less frequently, the collectors of customs and subsidies. As the fourteenth century progressed, tem-porary mergers in the duties of these officials took place. In 1372, for example, Nicholas Potyn was appointed to search the ships of suspected persons for non-customed wools, bullion, and 'prejudicial bulls', and his findings were to be certified to the Chancery.[114] In Northampton, in 1385, a single commission was issued to the mayor and bailiffs em-powering them to search for spies, bullion, and counterfeiters, while in Holland, Lincolnshire, in the same year, commissioners were appointed to search for spies and 'prejudicial bulls'.[115]

Restrictions imposed at the ports were not simply intended to pre-vent persons or goods from entering or leaving the country. There was always the danger presented by subversive material such as 'prejudicial bulls' which might attack the king's prerogative; bearers of such material were immediately arrested on detection. But more serious was

109. *C.P.R., 1385–9*, p. 501.

110. *Anglo-Norman Letters and Petitions from All Souls MS. 182*, ed. M. D. Legge, Anglo-Norman Texts, iii (Oxford, 1941), pp. 162–6.

111. *Statutes of the Realm*, i. 132 (Stat. 27 Edward I); ibid. i. 273–4 (9 Edward III, Stat. 2, cc. 1, 9, and 10); ibid. ii. 17 (Stat. 5 Richard II, c. 2).

112. *C.P.R., 1385–9*, pp. 83 and 172; P.R.O., E.364/3, m. 1.

113. *C.P.R., 1377–81*, p. 475.

114. P.R.O., E.364/11, m. 1. Compare the appointment of searchers in Dartmouth in 1378 (E.364/12, m. 4).

115. *C.P.R., 1385–9*, p. 83.

the fear that rumours, fostered by enemy agents or by native English-men, and regarded by the crown, at least since the enactment of the Statute of Westminster in 1275 against 'devisors of tales' and those who caused discord between the king and his subjects, as a very serious evil, might creep into the realm.[116] Rumours could be a severe blow to the morale of the populace, particularly in regions such as the south-east of England and the Scottish border, both of which suffered heavily from enemy raids. Rumours, too, concerning the course of the war abroad were unwelcome if unfavourable to the crown in any way. Throughout the fourteenth century royal writs to local officials frequently contained orders that this clause of the Statute be applied,[117] and those found propagating false news were swiftly dealt with by the authorities.[118] The case of Hugh de la Pole shows this clearly. In June 1383 de la Pole was arrested in London and sentenced to the pillory for having invented stories concerning the taking of Ypres by Henry Despenser, bishop of Norwich. What sealed his fate was the fact that he had mentioned how dissent had broken out among the ranks of the English army at the siege. An example had to be made in this case; otherwise 'the whole kingdom might be easily disturbed and disquieted thereby'.[119] The authorities were only being consistent when they charged the anti-Lancastrian con-spirators in Essex in 1404 of having falsely proclaimed that Richard II was alive and that he intended to invade England from the north 'cum maxima multitudine populi Francigenorum, Scotorum et Walli-corum'.[120] Punishments for spreading rumours were heavy. Hugh de la Pole, as already noted, suffered the pillory for his crime, while in May 1383 Thomas Depham of Norfolk had also been arrested for declaring news from Flanders, concerning Bishop Despenser's 'crusade', to have been false. For his offence he was committed to prison.[121]

Apart from the measures already described, other means were also adopted to counter the threat of espionage in England. Royal and local officials were, as part of their general peace-keeping duties, expected to be on the alert for anyone engaged in nefarious activities of any sort.

116. *Statutes of the Realm*, i. 35 (Stat. 3 Edward I, c. 34).
117. B.L., Cotton MS. Julius C iv, fo. 8.
118. *Select Cases in the Court of King's Bench*, ed. G. O. Sayles (Selden Soc., 1939), iii, p. cxi.
119. *Memorials of London and London Life in the XIIIth, XIVth and XVth Centuries, 1276–1419*, ed. H. T. Riley (London, 1868), pp. 479–80.
120. *Select Cases in the Court of King's Bench*, ed. G. O. Sayles (Selden Soc., 1971), vii. 153, no. 26.
121. *Calendar of Plea and Memoranda Rolls of London*, iii. 36.

But such local officials frequently received writs containing explicit instructions to apprehend enemy agents. In March 1354 the mayor and bailiffs of Carlisle received a commission to arrest and imprison all Scots and others spying on the defects of the city walls, and also any others whom they suspected of being spies.[122] On other occasions, too, officers were appointed whose sole purpose was the apprehension of enemy agents. In 1387, for instance, Thomas de Milton was appointed with four associates to seek out and arrest all Irish rebels who had entered England as spies.[123] Sometimes commissions could authorize the arrest of named suspects; a commission of August 1359 appointed Nigel de Haukynton and others to arrest John de Cornwaille and William de Derby, 'adherents of the king's enemies of France', who were believed at that time to be spying in London and elsewhere.[124]

But it was not merely the authorities who were instrumental in the capture of enemy spies. The English people were themselves highly aware of the threat presented by enemy agents to national security. The large number of arrests and denunciations made by ordinary subjects testifies to this. In 1380 a number of suspected spies were arrested 'by the men of London'.[125] Such public awareness doubtless received a boost from the increasing growth of national (or, more accurately, anti-French and anti-Scottish) feeling. But there was more to it than that. Popular involvement was actively encouraged by king and council, and throughout the Hundred Years War was strongly evoked by those statutes known as the hosting laws which constituted one method of keeping a measure of control upon aliens 'come les Engloises sount tretez de par dela'.[126] The Statute of Winchester of 1285 had already ensured that watches be held in towns, had imposed curfews, and had provided that stringent checks be made on the movements of strangers. Moreover, by statute of 9 Edward III, innkeepers were obliged to search their guests and make report.[127] From time to time, too, the crown decreed that the peace statutes against strangers should be re-enforced, as in March 1341, when it was ordered that all strangers were to be arrested and, if suspected, to be delivered to the sheriff for custody in his gaol.[128] In cases of resistance, the hue and cry was to be enforced. In 1354 the inhabitants of Carlisle were ordered to assist the authorities in

122. *Calendar of Documents relating to Scotland,* iii. 287, no. 1573.
123. *C.P.R., 1385–9,* p. 265.   124. *C.P.R., 1358–61,* p. 284.
125. *C.C.R., 1377–81,* p. 416.   126. *Rot. Parl.* iv. 13.
127. *Statutes of the Realm,* i. 273–4 (9 Edward III, Stat. 2, c. 11).
128. *C.P.R., 1340–3,* p. 206.

the search for enemy spies.[129] The underlying principle, therefore, continued to be the general obligation to keep the peace, as embodied in the Statute of Winchester and other legislation.

The extent of activity against enemy spies in England may be measured by the large number of arrests on record. Many of these, however, were false arrests, based upon unfounded suspicion. It was not always easy for English port officials to distinguish between Flemish and other Netherlandish dialects, or between Castilian and Portuguese. Hence the not infrequent arrests of ships belonging to a friendly country in error for those of an enemy, or of natives of friendly countries who were taken in error for spies. The staplers of Middelburg wrote to Nicholas Brembre, mayor of London in 1381–2, pleading for the release of one Henrick Wilde who 'longment est detenuz en prison a Londres, a cause qil estoit pris en companie de Flamyngs, et que homme qui dist qil estoit Flamyng, dount, seignour, vous plese assaver qil est neez de Zeland, et qil est cousyn le burghemestre de Midelburghe'.[130] More unfortunate was the case of Stephen Philip, who entered England in 1375 to visit a Norman monk at Long Bennington.[131] Arrested by the sheriffs of London and imprisoned on suspicion of espionage, it was ordered by the king that he should be released on bail, provided that he was not guilty. Apparently, however, his release was never secured, since an endorsement on the document states that he was unable to find bail.[132] Nevertheless, in many cases there was good cause for suspicion. The enemy agents discovered in London in 1346 were certainly up to no good; they were said to have 'hung out on a lance the shield of arms of some great Scots lord, so that the king's enemies might know their retreat'.[133]

129. *Calendar of Documents relating to Scotland*, iii. 287, no. 1573.

130. P.R.O., S.C.1/43/82, p. 83 (Special Collections, Ancient Correspondence). An item in the Chancery Miscellanea concerning persons detained by the sheriff of London in 5 Richard II refers to 'Henricus Wylde de Middelburgh in Seland, detentus et captus . . . pro suspicione exploratoracionis' (C.47/28/6/22).

131. *C.C.R., 1374–7*, p. 139.

132. *Calendar of Inquisitions, Miscellaneous, 1348–77*, p. 982.

133. *Calendar of Documents relating to Scotland*, iii. 268, no. 1472. The same fear of strangers is reflected in a letter from Charles VII to the mayor and *jurat* of Bordeaux, dated November 1459, some years after the expulsion of the English from Gascony: 'Item, et pour ce qu'on dit qu'on tollere aux Angloiz qui viennent en ceste ville, sans guide et garde, et de nuyt, sans lumiere, et aussi d'aler par le pais de Medouc et d'Entre-deux-Mars, achater les vins d'ostel en hostel, et communiquer et converser avecques ceulx de ladicte ville et du pais en secret, et oyr la conduicte des gens de guerre, qui est chose trop dangereuse, et en quoy est necessaire mettre autre remede, car aucunes foiz es flotz sont venuz si grand nombre d'Anglois, et encores pourroient venir, qui n'y mettra ordre, dommaige irreparable sen pourra ensuir' (*A.H.G.* ix. 404).

Persons arrested on suspicion of spying in England were usually sent to the king or council, or sometimes to both, for interrogation. In 1378, and again in 1382, all spies and persons carrying bulls were also to be brought before the king and council;[134] in October 1373 enemy alien friars were sent before the council for questioning;[135] while in 1377 the council interrogated French spies captured on the Scottish border.[136] Less frequently, arrested suspects were questioned in Chancery, as was the case in March 1380 when serjeants-at-arms, appointed to arrest alien spies, were ordered to conduct them either before the Chancery, or before the king and council.[137] Where it was more convenient, captured suspects were brought for initial questioning before other high-ranking or trusted officials, such as the captain of Calais or the wardens of the Scottish Marches. If it was decided that their case was important enough they might be sent before the council. If, however, it were only a small issue of local importance, the matter might go no further; in 1389, John, Lord Cobham, and Sir William Heroun were deemed to be of sufficient standing to investigate the case of Hugh Pot of Gelderland, 'pris comme espie', who was sent before them 'pour estre examine de certainez piecez... pris dil dit Hugh'.[138]

Spies and suspects awaiting interrogation were held in prison until they could be dealt with. The most usual place of detention in London was Newgate prison. Bearers of 'prejudicial bulls' arrested in London in 1342 were cast into Newgate, prior to their interrogation by the council.[139] In the 1380s the prison was bursting at the seams with spies and suspects detained there.[140] Outside London, royal castles were frequently used to accommodate captured enemy agents. Windsor Castle housed more than one French spy in 1379, while the castles of York, Gloucester, Corfe, and others were also often employed for the same purpose.[141]

Although evidence shows that spies were held in prison pending

134. C.P.R., 1377–81, pp. 163 and 219; C.P.R., 1381–5, pp. 200, 350, and 424.
135. C.C.R., 1369–74, p. 517.
136. P.R.O., E.403/463, m. 3. See above, p. 77, n. 21, for the French herald interrogated on suspicion of spying in those parts.
137. C.P.R., 1377–81, p. 475.
138. P.R.O., C.47/2/49/16.
139. C.C.R., 1341–3, p. 660.
140. C.C.R., 1377–81, p. 416; R. B. Pugh, Imprisonment in Medieval England (Cambridge, 1970), pp. 106–7.
141. For Windsor, P.R.O., E.404/10/70/20 and C.C.R., 1377–81, pp. 174 and 319; for York (1338), C.P.R., 1338–40, p. 77; for Gloucester (1378), C.C.R., 1377–81, p. 164; and for Corfe (1384), C.C.R., 1381–5, p. 364.

questioning by the authorities, less is known concerning the punishments inflicted upon those convicted of spying. It has been noted that spreaders of false rumours were liable to gaol or the pillory. Pilgrims and others leaving the realm clandestinely in 1381 ran the risk of one year's imprisonment if detected.[142] Beyond this, there is little evidence concerning the fate of proven spies. The fact that Thomas Turberville paid the extreme penalty has been taken to show that by the end of the thirteenth century spying could incur the penalty for treason.[143] A century and a half later Nicholas Upton was in no doubts that 'men of warre schall lese there heddys [as] Spyyse that schew the secretes off the hooste to ther enmyys'.[144] But there is none the less evidence to suggest that the English crown's policy towards spies was less severe than a lawyer like Upton might regard as fitting. When Nicholas de Wantham, the parson of Banbury, was accused in 1285 of associating with Guy and Emeric de Montfort and with Llewellyn of Wales, the king's enemies, and of passing on to them by letter information which he had gathered at the English court, he was said to have acted 'contra fidelitatem suam et contra foedus suum et ligeitatem quam debuit Domino Regi', an accusation which branded him as a 'proditor'. Wantham does not appear to have been captured, so that outlawry and deprivation of his cure were the only effective penalties which could be applied against him.[145] In December 1380 a large number of suspects who had been 'found wandering in . . . [London] . . . at the time when the galleys were at sea, running hither and thither about the city like spies', were released, on royal instructions, from Newgate for Christmas.[146] Even convicted spies stood a fair chance of receiving a pardon. In 1378 Roger Foucate, a spy for the French cardinals, was arrested and imprisoned, and then interrogated sporadically by the council throughout 1379 and 1380, only to be released in August 1380.[147] Robert Rillyngton of Scarborough was convicted by the justices of Oyer and Terminer for Yorkshire in 1382 on charges of having 'dealt with the king's enemies, bought of them ships and goods captured from the king's subjects, conveyed victuals

142. *C.P.R.*, *1381–5*, p. 1.
143. J. G. Bellamy, *The Law of Treason in England in the Later Middle Ages* (Cambridge, 1970), p. 16.
144. *De Studio Militari*, ed. Barnard, p. 5.
145. *Oxford City Documents*, *1268–1665*, ed. J. E. Thorold Rogers, Oxford Historical Soc. (Oxford, 1891), pp. 183–4 and 204–5.
146. *C.C.R.*, *1377–81*, p. 416.
147. *C.P.R.*, *1377–81*, pp. 163 and 219; *C.C.R.*, *1377–81*, pp. 164, 174, 319, and 398.

and moneys to their ships, and led them secretly by night to inspect the town and castle of Scarborough'. In November of that year he was fortunate enough to receive a pardon for these offences on payment of a fine of 100 marks at the Hanaper, and a second pardon, too, for other offences, the chief of which was that 'at the bidding of the king's enemies he went to sea and traitorously assisted them against the king'.[148]

This leniency was quite out of keeping with the strict precautions taken against spies to ensure the security of the realm. Occasionally, however, agents were committed to gaol. In 1384 a malefactor who had stirred up trouble 'to the peril of the realm' was arrested on the king's orders by Nicholas Brembre, mayor of London, and was imprisoned in Corfe Castle at the king's pleasure.[149] Such a sentence is what would be expected in view of the fact that enemy espionage was regarded, by both crown and people, as a serious threat to the security of England. It also accorded with the sentences meted out to spies by the French authorities. Thus Hennequin du Bos paid for his treason and espionage with his life in 1390, while the Parisian informer, significantly 'ung varlet boucher qui estoit devenu poursuivant, qui portoit aux ennemis anciens tous les secretz que on faisoit a Paris' was duly executed in the French capital during Holy Week, 1437.[150] On the other hand it must also be noted that the French could choose to be merciful, as in the case of Jean Thiebout and his wife, who were pardoned in 1359 for having been forced to work for the English under threat of death.[151]

Espionage played an important role in fourteenth-century warfare. If its extent has been largely under-estimated by recent historians, its importance was better recognized by contemporary writers such as Mézières, Christine de Pisan, and Commynes. The value of espionage

148. *C.P.R., 1381–5*, pp. 190–1. It is strange that this man should have been treated so lightly, since he was so plainly a traitor. The crime of Thomas Turberville, who had suffered the extreme penalty for aiding the king's enemies, was alluded to frequently throughout the fourteenth century. A schedule of 1337–8 naming traitors as one of the chief dangers facing the realm, cited Turberville as the supreme example. It had recommended the sternest penalties for any such transgressors in the future (P.R.O., C.47/28/5/34, 35, 36).

149. *C.C.R., 1381–5*, p. 364.

150. *Journal d'un Bourgeois de Paris, 1405–1449*, ed. A. Tuetey (Paris, 1881), pp. 330–1; *A Parisian Journal, 1405–1449*, trans. J. Shirley (Oxford, 1968), p. 315. For the herald's opinion regarding pursuivants, see above, p. 77.

151. Arch. Nat., JJ. 90, fo. 118, no. 218.

was certainly well appreciated by contemporary monarchs, who often based military decisions upon intelligence received. English writs issuing instructions for coastal defence frequently gave reasons why the orders which they contained should be carried out. In 1343, for instance, defensive measures were implemented because 'pro certo iam noviter intelleximus quod galee guerrine in non modico minimo cum magna multitudine armatorum ... venientes versus Angliam'.[152] Such predictions were almost certainly based upon information sent to the king by his agents. In many cases, the intelligence was accurate. The English saw for themselves, with their capture at Caen, in 1346, of the French invasion plan of 1338, that the news sent home by their agents in that year of plans to descend upon England with an 'immensa multitudine galearum et navium' had been perfectly accurate.[153] On other occasions, intelligence was inevitably defective. Nevertheless, it is certain that all governments set great store by information sent to them by their agents, and that all rulers and military leaders employed numerous secret agents to spy upon the secrets of their enemies during the prolonged warfare of the fourteenth century.

152. P.R.O., C.76/23, m. 20.
153. *Foedera*, II. ii. 1055 (for the writs of warning); for the captured document outlining the French invasion plan, see *Rot. Parl.* ii. 158–9, and *The Black Book of the Admiralty*, ed. T. Twiss, (4 vols., R.S., 1871–6), i. 426–9. For details of the French naval and military preparations for the invasion of England in that year, see B.N., MS. fr. 25996/126–7, 129, 139–41, 152–3, 160, 165–7, 173–4, and 183; nouv. acqs. frs. 3654, p. 2, nos. 8 and 10–11; ibid. 3653, p. 21, no. 79; Arch. Nat., Marine, B⁶ 136 – Galères 1337.

7

The War Literature of the Late Middle Ages: The Treatises of Robert de Balsac and Béraud Stuart, Lord of Aubigny

P. CONTAMINE

Among the didactic and technical literature written at the end of the Middle Ages, those works concerned with the art of war or the many problems which touch upon war assume an importance which reflects their differing origins.

To limit ourselves to works in the French language, let us consider those which, written in ancient Rome, came to be the object of translations. For example the *Epitome rei militaris*, or *De Re Militari*, written by Vegetius in the fourth century A.D., was continually referred to throughout the Middle Ages and was rendered into French by Jean de Meun (author of the second part of the *Roman de la Rose*), at the instigation of Jean de Brienne, count of Eu, under the title *Virgesse les establissemens de chevalerie* or *Li livres de Vegece de l'art de chevalerie* (1284).[1] Basing himself very closely upon this translation, Jean Priorat adapted it into octosyllabic verses, to which the title *Li abrejance de l'ordre de chevalerie* was given. This poem, dedicated to Jean de Chalon-Arlay, was probably written between 1284 and 1290.[2] During the course of the fourteenth century two further translations of Vegetius emerged: one by Jean de Vignai in about 1330, another half a century later in

---

1. *L'Art de Chevalerie, traduction du 'De Re Militari' de Végèce, par Jean de Meun*, ed. U. Robert (S.A.T.F., 1897). English translation of the same work: *Knyghthode and Bataile. A XVth-century verse paraphrase of Flavius Renatus' Treatise 'De Re Militari'*, ed. R. Dyboski and Z. M. Arend (E.E.T.S., 1935).

2. *Li Abrejance de l'Ordre de Chevalerie, mise en vers de la traduction de Végèce par Jean de Meun, par Jean Priorat de Besançon*, ed. U. Robert (S.A.T.F., 1897). For another translation of Vegetius, also dating from the thirteenth century, see M. L. Thorpe, 'Mastre Richard, a Thirteenth-Century Translator of the "De Re Militari" of Vegetius', *Scriptorium*, vi (1952), 39–50, and 'Mastre Richard at the Skirmish of Kenilworth?', ibid., vii (1953), 120–1. See too, M. D. Legge, 'The Lord Edward's Vegetius', ibid., pp. 262–5.

1380.[3] The *Stratagemata* of Frontinus, written in the first century A.D., were less well-known. If the Latin text was to be found in a number of individual libraries—in that of the Louvre in 1373 and among the books owned by Jean de Berri in 1402, for instance—it was only in 1439, at the very earliest, that Jean de Rovroy, doctor of the Faculty of Theology in Paris, translated the work into French at the request of Charles VII. The date of this translation is not unimportant, for it was made at a time which was both witnessing the advance of humanistic studies in a much devastated country and, in a different sphere, was facing up to the important issue of the reform of the royal army. If the first three books of the *Stratagemata* are little more than a tedious collection of military ruses drawn from Greek and Roman history, the fourth book, which was then thought to have been the work of Frontinus, is concerned with the matter of military discipline. In addition to that of Jean de Rovroy, two other translations exist which, although done in the fifteenth century, were both subsequent to Rovroy's work.[4]

The humanistic tradition was to be abandoned by Geoffroy de Charny. This important Burgundian lord was the author of a treatise in which were set out the various classes of men-at-arms, followed by a definition of the *raison d'être*, role, vocation, and ideals of the order of chivalry, these being completed by a triple series of questions (*demandes*), 'pour la jouste', 'pour le tournoy', and 'pour la guerre' which Charny addressed, soon after the creation of the Order of the Star by John II in 1351, to the 'haut et puissant prince des chevaliers Nostre Dame de la Noble maison'.[5] These two treatises, imbued with the same spirit and seeking the same ends, together act as important

3. P. Meyer, 'Les Anciens traducteurs français de Végèce et en particulier Jean de Vignai', *Romania*, xxv (1896), 401–23; C. Knowles, 'A Fourteenth-Century Imitator of Jean de Meung: Jean de Vignai's Translation of the "De Re Militari" of Vegetius', *Studies in Philology*, liii (1956), 452–8; J. Camus, 'Notice d'une traduction française de Végèce faite en 1380', *Romania*, xxv (1896), 393–400.

4. R. Bossuat, 'Jean de Rovroy, traducteur des *Stratagèmes* de Frontin', *Bibliothèque d'Humanisme et Renaissance*, xxii (1960), 273–86 and 469–89.

5. The first of these works was published by Kervyn de Lettenhove, under the title *Le Livre de Chevalerie*, in his edition of the *Chroniques de Jean Froissart* (29 vols., Brussels, 1870–7), i, pt. 2, 463–533. Of the second, as yet unpublished, two manuscripts survive: B.N., MS. nouv. acqs. frs. 4736 and Bibliothèque Royale, Brussels, MS. 1124–6. On Charny, who was keeper of the *Oriflamme* and died at the battle of Poitiers, see A. Piaget, 'Le Livre messire Geoffroi de Charny', *Romania*, xxvi (1897), 394–411; P. Contamine, *Guerre, état et société à la fin du Moyen Âge. Études sur les armées des rois de France, 1337–1494* (Paris and The Hague, 1972), pp. 184–92; Contamine, 'L'Oriflamme de Saint-Denis aux XIVe et XVe siècles. Étude de symbolique religieuse et royale', *Annales de l'Est*, 5e sér. xxv (1973), 179–244.

witnesses not only to the practicalities of war but, above all, to the mentality of the men who waged it.

Of a rather more legal and historical nature was the learned and justly famous work of Honoré Bouvet, *The Tree of Battles*, dedicated to Charles VI, one of whose chief sources, as Professor Coopland has clearly shown, was the *De Bello, de Represaliis et de Duello* of the Bolognese jurist, John of Legnano.[6] This was followed, in 1408–9, by the work of Christine de Pisan, *Le Livre des faits d'armes et de chevalerie*, a work written for an occasion which relied shamelessly upon Vegetius and Bouvet, but to which the author added certain contemporary details, many of a technical nature, which had in all probability been supplied to her by the captains and technical experts of the day.[7]

Later in the century came *Le Jouvencel*, or *Le Jouvencel introduit aux armes*, a work which its modern editor, C. Favre, described as a real text-book of moral and military education based upon historical allusions and illustrations. Composed between 1462 and 1466–7, when its chief author was more or less in official disgrace, and intended both to teach and to entertain, this famous work was written by Jean de Bueil and three collaborators, Jean Tibergeau, lord of la Motte, Nicole Riolay, and Martin Morin. It should be read with the brief commentary of explanation, or *Exposition du livre du Jouvencel*, which Guillaume Tringant wrote between 1477 and 1483 to help lay bare the pseudonyms which the work contained.[8]

At about the same time Pierre Choisnet, physician and astrologer to Louis XI, composed the *Rosier des Guerres* for the edification of the dauphin, the future Charles VIII. It was a work whose merits, however, can be summed up as consisting of a few acute historical observations, some well-turned phrases, and a few words of wisdom based upon sound sense—but very little else.[9]

6. *L'Arbre des Batailles d'Honoré Bonet*, ed. E. Nys (Brussels and Leipzig, 1883); *The Tree of Battles of Honoré Bonet*, ed. and trans. G. W. Coopland (Liverpool, 1949); and John of Legnano, *Tractatus de Bello, de Represaliis et de Duello*, ed. T. E. Holland and trans. J. L. Brierly (Oxford, 1917).

7. A list of the manuscripts and early editions of this work is to be found in *The Book of Fayttes of Armes and of Chyualrye*, ed. A. T. P. Byles (E.E.T.S., 1932). See too, C. C. Willard, 'Christine de Pizan's Art of Medieval Warfare', *Studies . . . L. F. Solano* (Chapel Hill, 1970).

8. Jean de Bueil, *Le Jouvencel*, ed. L. Lecestre and C. Favre (2 vols., S.H.F., 1887–9). The opinion of C. Favre which is cited is in i, p. ccixc. See also, G. W. Coopland, '*Le Jouvencel* (Re-visited)', *Symposium*, v (1951), 137–86.

9. *Le Rosier des Guerres*, ed. M. Diamant-Berger (Paris, 1925). *Le Guidon des Guerres* (Paris, 1514), attributed to the Chevalier de la Tour-Landry, is only *Le Rosier des Guerres* without its last chapters.

These may be supplemented by two further treatises of a more technical nature: one on the *Art de l'artillerie et canonnerye,*[10] the other on the *Art d'archerie.*[11] Together these add up to a mixed collection of works of very varying natures, but whose practical influence may not have been negligible.

The aim of the present essay is to complete this panorama by drawing attention to a group of three short treatises, dating from the late fifteenth and early sixteenth centuries; all are closely related to one another, and have hitherto been almost completely ignored by students of the period.[12]

The earliest of the three treatises is found in a book printed at Lyons in September 1502 by Guillaume Balsarin, printer to the king, and entitled *La nef des princes et des batailles de noblesse, avec aultres enseignemens utilȝ et profitables a toutes manieres de gens pour congnoistre a bien vivre et mourir, dediqués et envoyés a divers prelas et seigneurs ainsi qu'on pourra trouver cy aprés, composés par noble et puissant seigneur Robert de Balsat, conseiller et chanbrelan du roy nostre sire et son senechal au pays d'Agenés. Item plus le regime d'ung jeune prince et les proverbes des princes et aultres petis livres trés utilȝ et profitables, lesquelȝ ont esté composés par maistre Simphorien Champier, docteur en theologie et medecine, jadis natif de Lionnoys.*

This collection includes not only several short works by Symphorien Champier but also two brief treatises by Robert de Balsac. The first is a short essay of satire, not lacking in verve: *Le droit chemin de l'ospital et les gens qui le trouvent par leurs oeuvres et maniere de vivre et qui pour vraye succession et heritage doivent estre possesseurs et heritiers dudit hospital et jouyr des privileges, droitȝ et prerogatives, ou aultrement leur seront fait grant tort et injustice.*[13] As for the second, its character and author are best described in its concluding lines:

10. B.N., MSS. frs. 2015 and 1244; MS. lat. 4653, fos. 125–70. See Napoleon III and I. Favé, *Études sur le passé et l'avenir de l'artillerie* (6 vols., Paris, 1846–71), iii. 138–62.

11. *L'Art d'archerie; publié avec notes d'après un manuscrit du XVᵉ siècle*, ed. H. Galice (Paris, 1901).

12. The treatise of Béraud Stuart was noticed by C. Favre in his introduction to *Le Jouvencel* (i, pp. cci-ccii). J. R. Hale refers briefly to *La Nef des Princes et des Batailles* of Robert de Balsac as 'the outstanding example of a work dealing with war in a soberly realistic spirit' (*New Cambridge Modern History*, ed. G. R. Potter (Cambridge, 1957), i. 276).

13. *La Nef des Princes*, fos. 62–65. This text was re-edited, under the title *Le Chemin de l'ospital et ceulx qui en sont possesseurs*, by P. Tamizey de Larroque, *Revue des langues romanes*, 3ᵉ sér. xvi (1886), 294–300.

Cy finist l'ordre et train que ung prince ou chief de guerre doit tenir tant pour con-quester ung pays et passer ou traverser celluy des ennemys, aussy pour assieger une place, que pour soy deffendre et garder aux siens quant on l'assault ou se doubte d'estre assailly, aussy pour faire la guerre guerreante, fait et composé par noble et puissant seigneur Robbert de Balsac, seigneur d'Autregues [sic] et de Saint Amand es Montaignes, conseiller et chanbellan du roy nostre sire et son seneschal es pays de Gascongne et Agenés.[14]

In the edition of 1502, in which the treatise occupies folios 54ᵛ–62, a wood engraving, found on the right-hand side at the foot of folio 54ᵛ, depicts the figure of the author, framed between columns surmounted by foliated scrolls, standing bareheaded, beardless but with flowing locks, hands joined, dressed in a full coat, the folds of which fall to the ground. On the left, also at the foot of the folio, is the author's crest, although not accurately depicted.[15] Three further illustrations are found in this treatise: on folio 55, surrounded by a framework of tree trunks, stands a fully equipped man-at-arms, sallet on his head and halberd in his hand; on folio 58ᵛ, a fortification is attacked by two pieces of artil-lery on wheels and by two soldiers; while on folio 59ᵛ, four horsemen, in pairs, ride against one another; one of them, by the crown which he wears and the imperial eagle inscribed on his breastplate, is doubtless intended to symbolize the emperor, probably Maximilian of Habsburg.

The treatise exists, too, in a manuscript copy to be found in the Biblioteca Nacional, Madrid. If, when compared to the printed version, it offers only slight variations of details, the omission of the passage cited above has hitherto hindered the identification of the author. The Madrid manuscript was studied by R. Anthony and J. Meurgey who did their best to date it by way of the miniature on the first folio depicting the figure of a nobleman seated upon a white horse, galloping from the left through the ranks of his men.[16] Upon the rider's tunic is painted a coat of arms which can have belonged only to a ruler of the kingdom of Navarre who was at the same time count of Foix and vicomte of Béarn: according to these authors, the only person who held all three honours at once was François Phébus, king of Navarre from February 1479 until January 1483. However, doubts about the accuracy of such a dating are raised by a close inspection of the foot soldiers who

14. La Nef des Princes, fo. 62.
15. The coat of arms on Balsac's memorial plate is reproduced in Contamine, Guerre, état et société, plate 13.
16. R. Anthony and J. Meurgey, 'Note sur un manuscrit aux armes de François Phébus, comte de Foix, vicomte de Béarn, roi de Navarre (1467–1483)', M.A. xliv (1934), 176–88.

surround the horseman, for these are dressed in a style which was typical of some twenty years later. Furthermore, the Madrid manuscript, like the edition of 1502, contains certain precise references to historical events which provide a *terminus a quo* for dating purposes. The latest of these refers to the recapture of the town of Arras by the soldiers of Maximilian on Sunday, 4 November 1492:

Item, qu'ilz facent souvent remuer les clefz de leurs portes a serreuriers loing de la et qu'ilz gardent bien que les clefz ne soient en mains de gens qui ne soient bien seurs, car entre aucuns ilz les pourroient imprimer en cire et faire pareilles clefz, et que la nuyt il ait ung fort guet a la porte qui ne puisse venir gens pour l'ouvrir comme ilz firent a Arras.[17]

The treatise must, therefore, have been completed between 4 November 1492 and 12 September 1502, the day it came off the presses of Guillaume Balsarin. In these circumstances it cannot have been François Phébus who was depicted in the miniature, but his sister Catherine de Foix, queen of Navarre from January 1483 until February 1517, the artist having decided to show her dressed for war, in the manner of Joan of Arc.

Robert de Balsac, the author of the treatise, is not unknown to history: he was the subject of a fairly complete and generally accurate article written at the end of the last century.[18] It may be useful, however, to rehearse with greater precision what may have been his military role in the light of some documents unknown to his earlier biographer.

The house of Balsac took its name from a place in the *commune* of Saint-Gérond, near Brioude (Haute-Loire). Robert's father, Jean, who was lord of Entragues, had married Agnès, daughter of Robert de Chabannes, and, in so doing, had become the brother-in-law of two important persons, Jacques and Antoine de Chabannes. Such a marriage was bound to further the fortune of Jean's children. The eldest, Ruffec, seneschal of Beaucaire and Nîmes from June 1465 until his death in October 1473,[19] was also captain-general of 4,000 *francs-archers* from 1466 until 1473, while also being given command of twenty-five,[20] and

---

17. Biblioteca Nacional, Madrid, MS. Vitr. 24–28 (Hh 88), fo. 30 (see too fo. 32); B.L., Cotton MS., Vesp. A. xvii. The event was recalled by Jean Molinet, *Chroniques*, ed. G. Doutrepont and O. Jodogne (3 vols., Brussels ,1935–7), ii. 337–43.

18. P. Tamizey de Larroque, 'Notice sur Robert de Balsac, sénéchal d'Agenais et de Gascogne', *Revue des langues romanes*, 3ᵉ sér. xvi (1886), 276–93; *Dictionnaire de biographie française*, iv, cols. 1531–3.

19. G. Dupont-Ferrier, *Gallia Regia ou état des officiers royaux des bailliages et des sénéchaussées de 1328 à 1515* (7 vols., Paris, 1942–66), i. 272–3, no. 2988.

20. Contamine, *Guerre, état et société*, p. 595; B.N., MS. fr. 21479, no. 149.

then of one hundred lances in the royal army.[21] One of his brothers, Antoine, became bishop of Valence.[22] As for Robert, he was born probably about 1435.[23] By 1453 he was already serving as a man-at-arms in the king's army,[24] and in 1464 he was to be found seeking his fortune in Italy. Three documents help us to trace this stage of his career. In the first, a letter sent on 27 May 1464 by Louis XI to Francesco Sforza, duke of Milan, the king, having set out how his 'bien amé serviteur, Robert de Balsac, escuier' had a 'grant desir et affection d'aler veoir le monde et de s'y emploier en fait de guerre', recommended him as a man 'de bonne maison et noble et bien expert au fait de la guerre', and begged Sforza to retain him in his service.[25] A second letter to Sforza, sent only a few days later by his ambassador, Alberico Malleta, added greater precision to the request: this 'bon homme d'armes', a gentleman from the Auvergne, the nephew of Antoine de Chabannes, count of Dammartin, was also favoured by Jacques d'Armagnac, count of La Marche and duke of Nemours; the king would much like to have him near him, in his pay (a statement which appears to imply that Balsac was still, at that time, a man-at-arms in the royal army), but the young man was desirous of leaving France to enter the service of the duke of Burgundy or that of the duke of Milan; it had been Louis XI himself who had made the second suggestion.[26]

On 12 June, in a further dispatch, Malleta provided his master with information of a different type: Balsac was far from being in favour with the king and his family link with Dammartin, at that moment a political prisoner, was barring him from all hope of promotion. The duke of Milan would be well advised not to associate himself with one whose service could be of embarrassment to him.[27]

This first experience beyond the Alps, the duration of which is

21. B.N., MS. fr. 20498, fos. 106–9.

22. Antoine de Balsac was bishop of Valence and Die from May 1474 until November 1491 (C. Eubel, *Hierarchia catholica*, ii. 262).

23. Previous writers have given his year of birth, but without proof, as being about 1440. But, referred to as a man-at-arms in 1453, he must have been at least eighteen years old in that year; it therefore seems more sensible to suggest that he was probably born a few years before 1440.

24. Arch. Nat., AB XIX, 690–3 (Dictionnaire généalogique de Dom Bévy, *sub* Balsac).

25. *Lettres de Louis XI*, ed. J. Vaesen and E. Charavay (11 vols., S.H.F., 1883–1909), ii. 183.

26. *Dépêches des ambassadeurs milanais en France sous Louis XI et François Sforza*, ed. B. de Mandrot and C. Samaran (4 vols., S.H.F., 1916–23), ii. 173–5, no. xiv.

27. Ibid., pp. 183–4, no. xvii.

unknown to us, should be borne in mind. One thing is certain: the return to favour of Antoine de Chabannes, after the War of the Public Weal (1465), could only be to the advantage of his nephew, who then obtained the patronage of the king's brother, Charles de France. In 1468, as duke of Normandy, Charles gave Balsac command of four men-at-arms and eighteen archers,[28] a modest enough responsibility but one which was increased in the following year when Charles, having become duke of Guyenne, promoted him to the rank of councillor and chamberlain, and gave him the position of seneschal of the Agenais and Gascony.[29] By 1471, Balsac had thirteen men-at-arms and twenty-six archers under his command.[30] Taking part in a number of campaigns against the count of Armagnac,[31] he continued to act as seneschal of the Agenais,[32] and maintained the command of his soldiers, now increased to twenty-five complete lances,[33] after the death of Charles of Guyenne on 24 May 1472. Between 1474 and 1478 he and his men served in garrisons in Burgundy,[34] and by 1478 he had command of one hundred lances,[35] the company, however, being discharged on 1 October of that year and the money thus saved earmarked for the payment of the Swiss.[36] Although he maintained his seneschalcy and his pension, he held no active command until the accession of Charles VIII.[37] Indeed, the reaction which followed upon the death of Louis XI worked against Balsac's interests for, at the meeting of the Estates held at Tours in 1484, he was very strongly taken to task for the death of the count of Armagnac.[38]

28. B.N., Pièces Originales 178 (Balsac), no. 6.

29. Tamizey de Larroque, 'Notice sur Robert de Balsac', 281.

30. B.N., MS. fr. 25779, no. 28; C. Stein, *Charles de France, frère de Louis XI* (Paris, 1921), pp. 789–804, *pièce justificative* 139.

31. On these campaigns, in which his uncle Antoine de Chabannes also participated, see C. Samaran, *La Maison d'Armagnac au XVᵉ siècle et les dernières luttes de la féodalité dans le midi de la France* (Paris, 1908).

32. Dupont-Ferrier, *Gallia Regia*, i. 7–9, no. 36.

33. Morice, *Preuves*, iii. 265–6; B.N., MS. fr. 20498, fos. 106–9.

34. In garrison at Vézelay on 17 April 1474 (B.N., MS. nouv. acqs. frs. 8608, fo. 50); on 5 June 1475 (BN., MS. fr. 21499, no. 261); on 26 August 1475 (B.N., MS. nouv. acqs. frs. 8609, fo. 82); on 7 January 1476 (B.N., MS. fr. 21500, no. 315); and on 8 April 1476 (B.N., MS. fr. 21498, no. 255). He kept his force of twenty-five lances in 1476 (B.N., MS. fr. 2906, fos. 49–50) and in 1477 (Morice, *Preuves*, iii. 324–5); he was present in Burgundy in 1478 (Arch. Dép., Côte-d'Or, B 1781, fos. 48–49).

35. Morice, *Preuves*, iii. 350–1.   36. B.N., MS. fr 2906, fo. 17.

37. An annual pension of 800 *livres tournois* in 1482 (Tamizey de Larroque, 'Notice sur Robert de Balsac', p. 286).

38. Jean Masselin, *Journal des États généraux de France tenus à Tours en 1484 sous le règne de Charles VIII*, ed. A. Bernier (Paris, 1835), pp. 278 and 296.

A new phase of Balsac's career began in 1486. He first served the king in Burgundy with thirty lances; then, in 1488, he saw service in the war in Brittany at the side of Louis de la Trémoille, one of whose closest lieutenants he became.[39] A witness of the capture of Marcillé, present at the surrender of Châteaubriant (2 April 1488), active at the siege of Fougères (24 April), Balsac took part in the fighting at Saint-Aubin-du-Cormier a few months later, being ordered to 'chevaucher sur les ailes pour se rendre a l'avant garde'.[40] During the winter of 1489-90, his thirty lances formed the garrison at Pontorson;[41] in 1491 these were reduced to twenty-five, mustered at Dinan on 12 March, at Guingamp on 10 June, at Acigné on 9 September, and at Châteaugiron on 14 November.[42] In 1492 he commanded fifty lances, inspected at Villeneuve-d'Agenais on 28 August.[43]

It is possible that Robert de Balsac took part in the invasion of Italy in 1494. He may be identified, in the different accounts of that enterprise, as the 'Entragues' referred to by Philippe de Commynes in his *Memoirs*, 'homme mal conditionné, serviteur du duc d'Orleans', yet able enough to receive from Charles VIII, at the request of Louis de Luxembourg, count of Ligny, the command of the citadel of Pisa, where he provided the garrison in the company of foot soldiers from Berri.[44] Later he also obtained Sarzana, Pietrasanta, Motrone, and Librefate. Acting against the king's orders, he sold the citadel of Pisa to the Pisans, Sarzana to the Genoese, Pietrasanta and Motrone to the Luccans, and Librefate to the Venetians, all for his own profit. Such action resulted in the king

39. *Lettres de Charles VIII, roi de France*, ed. P. Pélicier (5 vols., S.H.F., 1898–1905), i. 312–13, 316–17, 319 and *passim*.

40. Ibid. iii. 384.

41. A. Raison du Cleuziou, 'Gilles Rivault, maître d'hôtel du roi Charles VIII. Documents inédits pour servir à l'histoire des événements du règne de Charles VIII de 1484 à 1492: instructions du roi, état des garnisons', *Bulletins et mémoires de la Société d'émulation des Côtes-du-Nord*, liv (1922), 129–30.

42. B.N., MS. fr. 8269, fos. 329–33.   43. B.N., MS. fr. 25782, no. 113.

44. Philippe de Commynes, *Mémoires*, ed. J. Calmette and G. Durville (3 vols., Paris, 1924–5), iii. 148. All sources, French as well as Italian, refer to the lord of Entragues, and never to Robert de Balsac. It is certain, however, that Balsac, although he had inherited the lordship of Entragues from his father, normally had himself addressed as Robert de Balsac (his signature is witness to this). The problem goes deeper: Commynes (iii. 66) refers to the lord of Balsac who pillaged the house of Piero de Medici on the occasion of Charles VIII's entry into Florence; why does he use these two different ways of describing the same man on different pages of the same book? Furthermore, Robert de Balsac was councillor and *chamberlain* to the king (see *Lettres de Charles VIII*, iv. 39); but the lord of Entragues is described as the king's councillor and *maître d'hôtel* (ibid. iv. 315 and v. 262). Finally, how can one explain the fact that he was able to preserve his seneschalcy and command? It is not without hesitation and some scepticism that I here accept the traditional identification.

receiving strong protests from the Florentines, and publicly denouncing his treachery and even threatening him with death.[45] It is all the more surprising, therefore, to note that, in spite of the royal anger, he was able to preserve, throughout this period, not only the seneschalcy of the Agenais but also his pension and his command in the army.[46] Under Louis XII, no great change was to occur. By 1499 his pension was worth 2,000 *livres tournois*;[47] in 1501 he was in charge of fifty lances,[48] a command which he maintained until his death on 9 August 1503.

Robert de Balsac's career was never to achieve the greatest heights; he never obtained the command of an army, nor did he receive the reward of the insignia of the Order of St. Michael; indeed, he was still an esquire at the time of his death. None the less, he had been a councillor and chamberlain to three kings, a seneschal for almost thirty-five years, and a captain in the royal army for over twenty years; he had also been able to take advantage, on more than one occasion, of the support of powerful patrons. Such are the factors which plead in Balsac's favour in our estimate of him as a soldier, a man of the world, and a courtier.

As shown above, Balsac wrote his treatise between 1492 and 1502. Is it possible to be more precise about the date? Although the work makes no specific reference to any event of the Italian wars, the feeling remains that the author had in mind an expedition similar to that of 1494–5. Thus he wrote of the prince whom he was addressing as one obliged to forsake his country for a considerable period in order to achieve the conquest which he was planning:

Item, doit [le prince] aviser et faire que, ce pendant qu'il yra a ceste conqueste, qu'il laisse son pays en bonne surté ou n'y aller point, affin que, si aucun de ses voysins le venoient assaillir ou si aucun de son païs luy vouloit faire quelque seducion ou

45. Marino Sanudo, *La Spedizione de Carlo VIII in Italia*, ed. R. Fulin (Venice, 1883), pp. 105 and 647; A. Desjardins, *Négociations diplomatiques de la France avec la Toscane* (6 vols., Paris, 1859–86), i. 633, 641, 649–51, 661, 668 ,and 691–3.

46. Dupont-Ferrier, *Gallia Regia*, i. 7–9, no. 36; B.N., MS. fr. 26105, no. 1200 and Pièces Originales 178 (Balsac), nos. 23 and 27. In this last manuscript, Louis XII refers to the 'grans, vertueux et recommandables services' rendered by Robert de Balsac to Charles VIII, especially in the Breton war. Such flattering language would seem incomprehensible if Balsac were the traitor of Pisa. Tamizey de Larroque, who cited the passage, liked to think that it was an ironical reference; but, one must ask, was irony customary in the royal chancery? Furthermore, in his treatise Balsac recommends to the king that he should leave places conquered from the enemy in the hands of men in whom he had trust; would he have been cynical enough to have made such a remark if he had betrayed, for money and contrary to orders from his king, those places which had been left in his care?

47. Tamizey de Larroque, 'Notice sur Robert de Balsac', p. 289.

48. B.N., MS. fr. 2927, fos. 34–37.

rebellion, qu'il laisse le plus feable homme qu'il ayt pour luy et plus seur et grant personnage pour la garde de son pays et les principalles places laisse a gens de bien et qui luy soient bien seurs.[49]

The same impression is given by the passage in which Balsac recommended that the prince should review his troops before entering enemy territory (so as to unburden himself of those of no value to him, thus reducing the baggage-train and the need for provisions) and that steps be taken to set up adequate lines of communication for the provision of supplies.[50] In another significant piece of advice, Balsac counselled that the king's army should take adequate measures to protect itself:

en chascune bataille aye ung petit nombre de colevriniers et bons arbalestiers avec eulx au derriere de la bataille pour garder l'ennuy que font ces gens legiers a cheval comme janeteres et estradiotz en chevauchant, et avec cela ilz se aprocheront point de si pres.[51]

If the existence and tactics of *genétaires*, or lightly armed horsemen, had long been familiar to the French, it was, by contrast, only the Italian wars which gave them their first experience of the Albanian (*e*)*stradiots*, or light cavalry. Indeed, when using the word, Commynes felt it necessary to explain it to his readers:

Stradiotz sont gens comme genetaires, vestuz a pied et a cheval comme les Turcs, sauf la teste ou ilz ne portent ceste toile qu'ilz appellent toliban; et sont dures gens et couchent dehors tout l'an et leurs chevaulx.[52]

To this it may be added that the treatise recommended the prince to 'faire mettre en painture', or draw up plans of the country which he hoped to conquer.[53] We know that Charles VIII acted in this fashion in his conquest of Italy, using in particular a map which Jacques Signot, his agent in Ferrara, had provided.[54] It is thus probable that Balsac wrote his work after 1495, perhaps for Louis XII, and just before the Italian expedition of 1499.

Apart from one passage referring to Caesar's conquest of Gaul,[55] the work contains no classical or literary allusions. Must one think, therefore, that it is based on the author's personal experience?

---

49. *La Nef des Princes*, fo. 55.   50. Ibid.   51. Ibid., fo. 58.
52. Commynes, *Mémoires*, iii. 163–4, for the presence of *stradiots*, in particular at the battle of Fornovo (1495).
53. *La Nef des Princes*, fo. 55 ᵛ.
54. C. Maumené, 'Une Ambassade du pape Alexandre VI au roi Charles VIII. Le cardinal François Piccolomini', *Revue des Deux-Mondes*, 5ᵉ pér. lii (August 1909), 695.

Only three captains are mentioned: Talbot (who will be referred to again later), Rodrigue de Villandrando, and Charles the Bold, duke of Burgundy. Villandrando is held up as an example of an adventurer who has achieved the heights of fame and success:

Item, que ledit prince entretiengne le plus qu'il pourra de ses voysins pour s'en ayder a son affaire et, s'il n'est point contraint, de ne prandre guerre que a l'ung aprés l'autre, car malles gens sont trop, et faire comme disoit Rodigues et faisoit en France et pour bien faire ses besoignes il falloit chevaucher les uns et mener les autres en main, et, par ce moyen, regna longuement et fist ses besoignes et s'en retourna en Espaigne a grant honneur et riche homme, accompaigné de deux cens hommes d'armes.[56]

As for Charles the Bold, he is cited as the example of one not to be imitated. A prince should not risk 'l'aventure de bataille' immediately after one defeat, for eighteen times out of twenty he will lose this second battle, too, and thus bring complete ruin upon himself under the pretext of defending his reputation:

Car tel cuide venger sa honte qui la croist et tel se cuide venger qui se excille, car il n'est pas bon vouloir rompre l'anguille au genoil ne precipiter les choses ne les faire contre raison, et n'est pas vaillance, mais opiniatrie, obstinacion et follie, car, comme chascun scet, le trés redoubté duc Charles de Bourgoigne se perdit par ce moyen la.[57]

The earliest episode referred to is the defeat suffered, in July 1391 before Alessandria in Italy, by John III, count of Armagnac, who met his death on this occasion.[58] Froissart had already described the events in considerable detail,[59] but it is not impossible that Balsac learned about the episode from other persons, especially when his links with the Armagnac family are recalled. One may note, too, that he uses a sobriquet for John III, 'la bosse d'Armegnac' of which Froissart makes no mention.[60] Otherwise, all the events cited are taken from the fifteenth century: the capture of Chartres in 1432;[61] the taking of the bridge at

See the map by Jacques Signot in H.-F. Delaborde, *L'Expédition de Charles VIII en Italie; histoire diplomatique et militaire* (Paris, 1888), p. 393.

55. *La Nef des Princes*, fo. 57ᵛ.   56. Ibid.

57. Ibid., fo. 58. See too, the allusion to the siege of Neuss in 1474–5 (fo. 59ᵛ).

58. Ibid., fo. 59.

59. Froissart, *Chroniques*, xiv. 305. See P. Durrieu, *Les Gascons en Italie; études historiques* (Auch, 1885), pp. 15–104.

60. This name is all the more remarkable since the Saint-Denis chronicler emphasized his fine presence: 'Ainsi périt, victime d'une embûche, ce fier chevalier, issu d'une antique et noble race, si remarquable par sa haute taille et sa force physique, si célèbre par ses nombreux exploits' (cited by Durrieu, *Les Gascons en Italie*, p. 91).

61. *La Nef des Princes*, fo. 62. See Thomas Basin, *Histoire de Charles VII*, ed. and trans. C. Samaran (2 vols., Paris, 1933–44), i. 148–50.

Meulan in 1435;[62] and the premature attempt to capture Rouen on 16 October 1449.[63] A passage which recalls the capture of Lectoure is rather difficult to identify. Although the text is ambiguous, it must be taken to be a description of the reconquest of that town by John V of Armagnac on the night of 18–19 October 1472, at a time when the place was controlled by the troops of Louis XI.[64]

In spite of having seen active service in the Breton wars, Balsac refers to them only once:

Item, ne doit on marcher de dans pays s'il n'est contraint de ce faire, si n'est que l'en voie qu'on s'en puisse retourner a son ayse et honneur, ou y demourer en seurté et pouvoir avoir secours, car ce n'est pas la maistrise de aller bien avant en pays, mais de y demorer en seurté ou s'en povoir venir a son honneur, car quarante compaignons prindrent la grosse tour de Rouan d'amblee qui ne peurent avoir secours et furent tous perdus au tempz de Tallebot, aussi a Vanes en Bretaigne qui furent prins et destrousséz.[65]

Certainly Vannes, taken by the French on 5 June 1487, was occupied by a garrison commanded by Gilbert de Grassay, lord of Champéroux. Besieged from 25 February 1488 by the duke of Orléans and the marshal de Rieux, and too isolated to receive relief within the required time, Vannes was obliged to surrender on 3 March following.[66]

It was, perhaps, from his brother, a knight hospitaller, that Balsac obtained the interesting detail concerning the siege of Rhodes (1480) that the Turks, having made a breach in the wall, all but surprised the Christians when the Grand Master, Pierre d'Aubusson, was hearing Mass.[67]

Finally, still fresh in the memory of men, were the struggles between

62. *La Nef des Princes*, fo. 61ᵛ. See G. du Fresne de Beaucourt, *Histoire de Charles VII* (6 vols., Paris, 1881–91), iii. 4.

63. *La Nef des Princes*, fo. 57ᵛ. See Basin, *Histoire de Charles VII*, ii. 114–18; and *Narratives of the Expulsion of the English from Normandy, MCCCCXLIX–MCCCCL*, ed. J. Stevenson (R.S., 1863), pp. 125–7 and 293–6.

64. Samaran, *La Maison d'Armagnac*, pp. 184–5.

65. *La Nef des Princes*, fo. 57ᵛ.

66. A. Le Moyne de la Borderie and B. Pocquet, *Histoire de Bretagne* (6 vols., Rennes and Paris, 1896–1914), iv. 544.

67. *La Nef des Princes*, fo. 60. Robert's brother, who was called Louis or Raymond, was commander of Chezel in the Forez (P. Anselme, *Histoire généalogique et chronologique de la maison royale de France* (9 vols., Paris, 1726–33), ii. 437. This episode in the siege of Rhodes is not mentioned in the *Obsidionis Rhodiae urbis descriptio* of Guillaume Caoursin, first printed in 1496. However, a letter written by a Burgundian knight, who was present at the siege, alludes to an attack by the Turks, while the Christians were hearing Mass ('Le Voyage de Pierre Barbatre à Jérusalem en 1480', ed. P. Tucoo-Chala and N. Pinzuti, *Annuaire-bulletin de la Société de l'histoire de France*, 1972–3 (Paris, 1974), p. 160).

the French and the Burgundians, at the end of Louis XI's reign and at the beginning of that of Charles VIII, over the possession of Hesdin, Béthune, Thérouanne, Arras, and other places which are mentioned on a number of occasions. Whether Balsac took an active part in these events we cannot say, for the sources have nothing to tell on the matter.

This rapid survey suggests that Balsac was not trying to recall his own campaigns, nor was he trying to underline his own military skill. The treatise is not a nostalgic and prejudiced account of past events as seen by a former soldier, as is *Le Jouvencel*, but rather a collection of practical recommendations, all functional in character, expressed in simple and unadorned language which is usually lacking in literary qualities,[68] and relying on examples which would have been sufficiently known to make anything more than a passing reference to them unnecessary.

Let it be noted, too, that like his predecessors, Balsac divided his work according to the different types of war. In only one sense was he original, in his description of the *guerre guerreante*, which consisted of *chevauchées*, ambushes, surprise attacks, and sallies, in short those forms of military activity out of which was woven the daily existence of the soldier of the time.

As often happened in the Middle Ages, a time when writers were not afraid to borrow the ideas of others and when the notion of literary ownership was almost unknown, Balsac's text was, within a very short time adapted, corrected, and completed by an anonymous author whose work, in manuscript, has survived to this day.[69]

From all outward appearances it would be impossible to tell whether this work predated or postdated Balsac's treatise. An analysis of the text itself, however, reveals that the author took up and enlarged upon developments described by Balsac, adding remarks and examples of his own. These examples, which number some fifteen in all, cover the period from the battle of Poitiers (1356) to the operations outside Brest

---

68. It should not be forgotten that the mother-tongue of Robert de Balsac was, theoretically at least, the *occitan*, or speech of the south. I emphasize, however, that *Le Droit Chemin de l'ospital* is composed by a man with a complete command of the *langue d'oil*, or speech of the north, a command characteristic of men such as Honoré Bouvet and Antoine de la Sale, who also stemmed from those parts of France in which the *occitan* was spoken. A holograph letter of Robert de Balsac (B.N., Pièces Originales 178 (Balsac), no. 27), is further evidence that he wrote the *langue d'oil* perfectly easily.

69. B.N., MS. fr. 1245, small bastard hand on paper, late fifteenth or early sixteenth century, 32 folios, the last 8 being blank.

(1492), passing by way of Agincourt (1415), the capture of Gerberoy (1449), and the siege of Beauvais (1472). They constitute, in effect, a collection of references parallel to that drawn up by Robert de Balsac, and bear witness to the fact that the two treatises relied upon the same historical and military background.

Of the developments which were clearly the work of the second, anonymous author, it will be sufficient to cite one passage. Discussing the battles of Poitiers and Agincourt, the author showed how, at the end of the fifteenth century, it was possible to explain these French defeats of the past:

Plus, qu'il [le prince] se garde bien de passer un mauvais passaige s'il n'est contrainct de ce faire, qui ne puisse bien estre, luy et toute sa compaignie, de dela ledit passage et y avoir mis son ordre avant la venue de ses ennemys, et si, estant en son ordre et ayant ses gens, qui les puisse tout esplecter ne trouver ses ennemys en champ plain et qu'ilz soient puissans a cheval et qu'il ait ung boys ou un fort au derriere d'eulz apréz, qu'ilz les assaillent, car ilz en auront meilleur marché que ailleurs, et se mec- tront plustost en desordre pour gaigner le fort que s'ilz avoient le fort bien loing d'eulx, car il fault tousjours laisser ung passaige ouvert a ses ennemys par ou ilz se puissent retirer ou fouyr, car qui les enferme de tous coustéz ilz jouent au desespere et se vendent bien cher comme a la bataille de Gincourt et de Poictiers que les Angloys estoient encloux et ne povoient fouyr, ne aussi ne fault point desesperer les ennemys ne dire que on ne les prendra point a mercy, car a Poytiers fut faicte ceste responce, dont en print mal et le prince de Galles le dist et prescha aux Engloys qu'il n'eussent nul esperance d'appoinctement car ilz n'en trouveroient point ne en riens fors que en Dieu et a leurs braz et deffence.[70]

Some years later another writer, Béraud Stuart, lord of Aubigny, used a copy of Balsac's treatise which he, too, remodelled and enriched with his own personal reflections. It is enough to recall here that this man, grandson of John Stuart who, in about 1420, had come to place his services at the disposal of the king of France, was born about 1447. Referred to by Commynes as 'bon chevalier et saige et honnourable',[71] Stuart had served as a man-at-arms in the Scottish company in 1469, being given command over a hundred lances in 1483. Sent by Charles VIII to renew the alliance between France and Scotland in 1484, he was present at the battle of Bosworth in the following year with a French contingent, lending his support to the future Henry VII; it was perhaps at about this time, too, that he went to fight the Moors in Spain. Ap- pointed captain of the Scottish guard in 1493, he was present at the first, and again at the second conquest of the kingdom of Naples, when his

70. B.N., MS, fr. 1245, fo. 5.   71. Commynes, *Mémories*, iii. 136.

role was a decisive one. He died in 1508 while on another mission to Scotland. These brief facts concerning Stuart's career as a war leader, administrator, and diplomat suggest that he was a man of wider experience, if not of greater importance, than Robert de Balsac had been.[72]

The prologue to Stuart's work, of which a number of sixteenth-century manuscripts are extant,[73] outlines the circumstances in which the work was compiled:

S'ensuyt ung livret et traicté pour entendre quel ordre et train ung prince ou chef de guerre doibt tenir pour conquester ung pays ou passer ou traverser le pays des ennemys, composé par messire Berault Stuart, chevalier de l'ordre du roy nostre sire, son conseiller et chambellain ordinaire et seigneur d'Aulbigny, en allant par luy en ambassade pour le roy au royaulme d'Escoce ou il mourut, pour confirmer les anciennes allyances dudit seigneur, appellé avec luy a rediger et escripre ledict livret et traicté maistre Estienne le Jeune, natif dudict Aulbigny, son secretaire et chappellain ordinaire.[74]

Stuart was therefore at least sixty years old when he dictated his treatise to his secretary, the same age at which both Balsac and Bueil had taken up the pen. It was often fairly late in life that members of the nobility, by contrast with professional writers, committed their ideas to paper in the earnest hope that their wisdom, born of long experience, would not be wasted. The text states the author's aims:

C'est peu de chose de sçavoir l'art et avoir la vertu de force, laquelle doibvent avoir principalement tous ducz, capitaines et conducteurs de exercices et gens de guerre s'ilz n'ont l'experience de ce, laquelle est mere et maistresse de toutes choses: a ceste cause me suis mis a addicioner et faire escrire, au plus prés de la verité, de la forme, maniere et experience de la conduicte et exercice de la discipline militaire, pour la conduicte et enseignement de tous nobles, vertueux et chevalereux hommes, ainsy que moimesmes j'ay veu practiquer et experimenter en plusieurs royaumes, terres, pays et seigneuries.[75]

One must think, therefore, that Stuart had taken a copy of Balsac's treatise with him, and that, perhaps during the long hours spent sailing to Scotland, had decided to embellish, if not to recast it by making some

72. E. Cust, *Some Account of the Stuarts of Aubigny, in France, 1422–1672* (London, 1891); *Dictionnaire de biographie française*, iv, cols. 179–80. His commands in the army are mentioned in the following documents: Arch. Nat., JJ 216, no. 129 and B.N., MS. lat. 5414A, fos. 143-4 (1483); Bibliothèque de l'Institut de France, Paris, MS. Godefroy 317, fo. 6 and Arch. Nat., JJ 219, no. 129 (1488); B.N., MS. fr. 8269, fos. 332-3 (1490); and MS. fr. 2928, fos. 10–11.

73. For example, B.N., MSS. frs. 2070 and 20003; B.L., Add. MS. 20813; Hamilton Collection, Berlin, MS. 470; MS. in the Marquis of Bute's possession (Historical Manuscripts Commission, *Third Report* (London, 1872), p. 208).

74. B.N., MS. fr. 20003, fo. 2.   75. Ibid., fo. 3.

additions of his own. He certainly intended his contribution to be a personal one, the deposit of the fruits of his own experience, practical knowledge, and years of service which, here and there, happily complemented the work of his predecessor. Whether he had completed the treatise when death overtook him one cannot say for certain: one thing, however, is clear, that his secretary tidied up the text and brought it back to France with him.

The following passage, which contains references to the battle of Gioia, in Calabria, which Stuart fought and lost against the Spaniards, will give some idea of the recastings which he undertook:

Car la chose au monde qui faict plus tost gaigner les batailles, c'est que de tenir bon ordre et estre bien serré et en trouppe s'il est possible. Nonobstant ce, les Françoys n'ont point ceste façon de faire, par quoy plusieurs foys ilz ont esté deffaictz, tant du temps des Angloys que comme ledict seigneur d'Aulbigny fut deffaict a Joye pour ce qu'il alla assaillyr les ennemis en mauvais ordre par ce qu'il ne les prisoit point ne estimoit, et les trouva tous en trouppe; la grande audace des Françoys et la grande craincte des Espaignolz firent avoir victoire auxdicts Espaignolz et la fut prins ledict seigneur d'Aubigny.[76]

None the less Stuart did not limit himself to citing events, usually in Italy, in which he had participated with greater or lesser success;[77] he also referred to earlier campaigns and to famous captains of earlier generations: the 'bon seigneur de Torcy' when mentioning the battle of Guinegatte (1479);[78] the lord of Aubijoux and the marquis of Rothelin when discussing the conquest of Burgundy (1477);[79] 'Monsieur de Bueil, qui estoit bon capitaine';[80] La Hire and Poton de Xaintrailles;[81] even 'messire Jehan Quiziel, capitaine angloys' who 'disoit qu'il falloit mectre tousjours deux barres a sa porte quant il y auroit tresves ou traictié de paix'.[82] It is significant, too, to note the respect with which, even in the early sixteenth century, French soldiers often treated the

76. B.N., MS. fr. 20003, fo. 5. See too fos. 15 and 23. Another personal touch: 'Non obstant plusieurs capitaines dyent depuis que ceulx de dehors sont deboutés une foys qu'ilz perdent le cueur, je ne suis pas d'avis que ceulx qui ont esté reboutéz retournent a l'assaut mais d'autres tous frais' (fo. 13ᵛ).

77. Allusion to the battle of Garigliano (1503) on fo. 11: 'Comme feist le roy Loys douziesme de ce nom, aprés que ses gens furent deffaictz a Garillain par leur faulte, les feist sejourner et mectre aux garnisons jusques a ce qu'ilz eussent prins leurs esperitz, car il doubtoit que, s'il les envoyoit en la guerre ou en bataille, eulx estant tout appisiz, qu'il ne s'en trouvast pas bien.'

78. Ibid., fo. 5.   79. Ibid., fo. 6ᵛ.   80. Ibid., fo. 17.

81. Ibid., fo. 6.

82. Ibid., fo. 9. This probably refers to Thomas Kyriel, who was defeated at Formigny in April 1450.

memory of the English of an earlier age. Their composure, their discipline, their efficiency were all admired:

Les Angloys ont une bonne façon de faire car, du premier jour qu'ilz vont a la bataille et qui est maistre de la compaigyne a le tout en sa subjection, et est une trés bonne ordonnance et façon de faire pour le bien du peuple. Car, s'ilz avoyent fortes places et feissent la guerre guerreante comme on faict en France et ailleurs, leur pays seroit destruict.[83]

As for the allusions to Hannibal[84] and Scipio Africanus,[85] can it be said that these reveal a knowledge of classical culture in some way richer than that displayed by Robert de Balsac, or are they the handiwork of the chaplain, Étienne le Jeune? It may further be added that Béraud Stuart slightly altered the order of paragraphs put forward by his model, and that he then added two short chapters: 'S'ensuyvent les provisions qu'il fault pour bien garnir une place'[86] and 'S'ensuyt le guect qu'il fault pour bien garder une ville'.[87]

Apart from the corrections, additions, and omissions by which they distinguish themselves, our three authors adhere to the same conception of war and its attendant problems. They take for granted a certain *corpus*, or *thesaurus* of the art of war whose main features, for the sake of completeness, are worth drawing out.

Glossing over, as rapidly as possible, the theological and moral justifications for war,[88] the three treatises emphasize the underlying importance of the need for manpower and money, provisions and artillery. They propose a whole range of types of leader, some fit to lead a company, others an army; some skilled in war in which armies confront each other in ranks and columns, others more accustomed to a war of sieges and raids; some expert at theorizing about war, others better at fighting it on the ground. Nor should the specialists be forgotten: the artillerers, the engineers, the spies, those expert in diplomacy. The prince must employ men skilled in all these activities.

The rules concerning battles are deceptively brief, and are chiefly concerned with such matters as the composition of the advance and rear

---

83. Ibid., fos. 16^v–17.   84. Ibid., fo. 8^v.   85. Ibid., fo. 17^v.
86. Ibid., fo. 26.
87. This chapter, not found in B.N., MS. fr. 20003, is in MS. fr. 2070, fos. 24^v–25 and in B.L., Add. MS. 20813, fos. 24^v–25.
88. 'Premierement et avant tout ovre doit adviser s'il a bonne et juste querelle pour mettre Dieu et la raison pour luy', says Robert de Balsac (*La Nef des Princes*, fo. 55). The Anonymous writer adds: 'Car autrement ce seroit tirannie et faire contre Dieu de prendre les biens d'autruy' (B.N., MS. fr. 1245, fo. 1).

guards, the need for commanders to protect their artillery, to maintain close formation, and the importance of allowing the whole army to seek booty. The authors' advice with regard to attacks upon fortified places is a good deal clearer: they emphasize the use of several 'sieges', batteries of cannon, the blockade ('enclour la place du siege'); they write about the approaches to the fortifications and the use of waves of attacking forces. The greatest danger for the assailant, we are reminded, is to be surprised by a relieving force.

The chapter on defensive war gives the opportunity of emphasizing the role of ambassadors, whose task it is to keep a watchful eye on neighbouring states. If one of them makes preparations for an attack, the first task will be to put the frontier lands into a state of preparation. Then, as the threat becomes more clearly defined, the prince will gather the largest army available to him to meet the enemy as he enters the country. But if the risk of a battle is regarded as too great, the prince will instead put into action a comprehensive plan of defence: strongholds which cannot be held will be destroyed, while others will be reinforced so that men, animals, and provisions can find safety within their walls; the enemy will be harassed, too, so as to impede the work of his spies and foragers. The aim of such activity is to oblige the enemy to remain near the frontier, and to prevent him from penetrating into the country. The relative peace thus achieved will allow the prince to assemble his available forces away from the front line, and they will be used, in due course, to rescue the places which have been threatened.

The fourth chapter, given over to the defence of a particular fortified place rather than to that of a country as a whole, opens with some advice on the matter of fortification. Ditches will be reinforced, and those shaped like a V are to be preferred to those like a U.[89] The side of the ditch which protects the wall should be raised ('haulser la douhe qui couvre la muraille de la place')[90] in order that the besiegers' batteries shall strike the escarpment rather than the very wall itself. There are also to be 'moineaux', or chambers built into the escarpment, from which it shall be possible to fire into the ditches themselves. There are references, too, to *boulevards*, not, in these circumstances, platforms on which to place artillery, but false breaches running along the foot of the ramparts. Houses should not be allowed to touch the interior face of the walls: the space left free will provide an opportunity to dig a ditch on

89. 'Fortifier leurs fossez et les faire estroictz dans le bas' (*La Nef des Princes*, fo. 60).
90. Ibid.

which a rampart can be built. On this rampart, an artillery battery will be set up so that, if the attackers force a breach, they will come up against this unexpected obstacle when they make the assault.

With regard to the control and distribution of provisions, the needs of artillerers and bowmen, the presence in the army of pioneers, apothecaries, and surgeons, little is said that is not commonplace. It should be emphasized, however, that close attention was paid to signals, to the fear of betrayal, to mutinies, and to the importance clearly attached to morale. Last, but certainly not least, is the emphasis placed upon the *guerre guerreante*, with its use of surprises and stratagems.

However ordinary may be their qualities and schematic their content, the fact remains that these treatises have a three-fold interest to the historian. First, they are all drawn up in the tradition of the art of war of the Middle Ages, based upon the wisdom of experience, while also touching upon modern thinking which suggests a wider political appreciation found among some of the contemporaries of Commynes and Machiavelli. Secondly, these treatises serve to remind us of what could be the theoretical *vade mecum* which French captains at the very end of the Middle Ages were thought to need, demonstrating that only a very limited instruction derived from the book was regarded as sufficient since, as the texts say, 'la guerre se faict a l'ueil'.[91] Finally, these works indicate to us what was, in their specialism, the historical culture of captains of the time of Charles VIII and Louis XII: a few great names gleaned from antiquity; the memory, still very fresh, of the wars waged against the English; but, above all, a good knowledge of the most recent events.

91. Biblioteca Nacional, Madrid, MS. Vitr. 24–28 (Hh.88), fo. 36. One is reminded of Napoleon saying that 'la guerre est un art simple et tout d'exécution'.

8

Of Breton *Alliances*
and Other Matters

P. S. LEWIS

It appears to be accepted that a form of political contract which can be termed non-feudal existed in later medieval France, and that its emergence can be traced back to the last quarter of the fourteenth century. In about 1389 Philippe de Mézières could put into the mouth of 'la Riche Precieuse, Verite la royne' a detailed commentary upon 'l'aliance publique et, il se doit dire, secrete de tes serviteurs roiaulx, grans princes royaulx et autres du royaume de Gaule' in her interminable discourse to Charles VI in his guise of 'jeune Moyse couronne'.[1] She was quite clear about the nature of the contract: indeed, she might have had an example of the letters giving the terms of such an *alliance* before her.[2] A great lord, she explained, would say to a royal officer well-in with the king:

Beaux amis, pour ta grant vaillance, pour ta vertu, ou pour aucune legiere acointance nouvellement trouvee, et principaument affin que tu me teignes en la grace et amour de mon seigneur le roy, et que je soie souvent garniz et enformez par toy des voulentez et commandemens de mon seigneur le roy, je te donne v^c, mil ou ii^m frans tant comme tu vivras; et se bien me serviras, plusgrant chose je te donray. Mais quoy je veuil que tu soies mon frere espicial et mon alie et te donne ma devise, et que tu me faces serement d'estre avecques moy en tout et par tout, contre tous ceulx du royaume, voire excepte mon seigneur le roy; et que mon bien et mon honneur tu garderas et me feras savoir tout ce qui me pourra touchier, ou bien ou mal, par les lectres secretes ou par loyal messaige, ou par un tel signet.

Nothing could be clearer than that; and nothing, in Mézières's view, could be worse than the effect of the system upon 'gouvernement moral'.

---

1. *Le Songe du Vieil Pelerin*, ed. G. W. Coopland (2 vols., Cambridge, 1969), ii. 350–5. The remaining quotations from Philippe de Mézières are taken from this section of the *Songe* (§264).
2. See the letters printed in P. S. Lewis, 'Decayed and Non-Feudalism in Later Medieval France', *B.I.H.R.* xxxvii (1964), 183–4 (document 8) and those cited there, p. 172, no. 7.

Comment, if comparatively private, was not lacking; some fifty-five years later Jean Juvenal des Ursins could again complain about the evils of clientage.[3] Nor, when Mézières wrote, was the system, in a general sense, new: it can be detected in the political society of the reign of Philipe VI,[4] though we know nothing of the way in which the relationships between lord and client were created. But Mézières's commentary upon the *alliance* is valuable not only for its views upon the organization of patronage and its effects: it shows also, as we shall see, that the distinction in his mind between feudal and non-feudal forms was arguably a clear one. But he saw, too, that there might in a sense be an overlap: royal officers who held land of the great lords could do them 'homage et serement' for that land, but should not be bound by 'autre aliance particuliere, car ilz scevent tout ce qu'ilz doyvent fere ou servir aux seigneuries ou aux seigneurs 'pour le dit homage'. Mézières repeated the point: royal servants could inherit land held of the princes, or the princes could give them land for life or hereditarily for past or future service; 'en cestui cas', he thought, 'il est bien raison qu'ilz en facent le serement et homage, tel qu'il appartient au seigneur du fief, et non pas autre aliance expresse qui n'appartient pas au fief et que un simple homme ne feroit qui ne seroit pas serviteur ou officier royal'.

How is one to disentangle this last statement? To keep a lord in royal 'grace et amour', to inform a lord of the king's 'voulentez et commandemens', were clearly beyond the capacity of someone not a royal officer. But other elements in the contract which Mézières sketched out were equally clearly not beyond the capacity of the simple man: wearing the lord's livery badge—a practice admittedly all too obscure at present, as far as later medieval France, as opposed to later medieval England, is concerned; swearing to be with the lord against all men except the king; pursuing the lord's 'bien et ... honneur' and informing him of things concerning him. All these were familiar enough, indeed, from the obligations that one might expect to find in some of the oaths linked with homage in the phrase 'homage et serement'[5] in a relationship that was 'feudal'. But if a royal officer was in fact in a feudal relationship

3. P. S. Lewis, *Later Medieval France: The Polity* (London, 1968), p. 129.

4. R. Cazelles, *La Société politique et la crise de la royauté sous Philippe de Valois* (Paris, 1958), pp. 267–9.

5. See, for instance, the terms of the oath sworn by the sire de Curton when he did homage to Gaston III Fébus, comte de Foix, in February 1382 (P. Tucoo-Chala, *Gaston Fébus et la vicomté de Béarn, 1343–1391* (Bordeaux, 1960), pp. 361–2 (pièce xix)). This text is typical of a number to be found in the registers of the notary-general of Béarn, Arch. Dép. Pyrénées-Atlantiques, E 302 and 304.

with his would-be patron, would not the patron already derive from the 'serement et homage, tel qu'il appartient au seigneur du fief', the advantages made perhaps only more explicit by the specific duties imposed upon his vassal, now his *allié* as well, in the contract of *alliance*? Or does Mézières really mean to say that the whole of the new contract of *alliance*, one made on top of the contract of vassalage, creates somehow a different relationship from the original homage and oath of fidelity done to the lord upon entry into the fief, despite the fact that some of the stipulations may have been the same in both fealty and contract of *alliance*? In short, did this new, non-feudal contract, despite the similarity of wording, create a new and particular relationship for the *allié* on top of the relationship of vassalage?

Given the nature of the contract of *alliance* which Mézières sketched out, it is difficult to avoid the belief that he thought a vassal could also be an *allié*, and that were he not discussing the particular case of the royal officer who entered into an *alliance* with a great lord, his view would be clearer. The similarity between the obligations of 'vassals' and '*alliés*' has been pointed out; and it has been argued that the distinction between the two seems to turn finally upon whether homage was done or not, a distinction perhaps lacking a difference, but one which, in doing so, provided a smooth crossing from the 'feudal' into the 'non-feudal' world.[6] Can one now argue that the crossing was even smoother: that one can find an even more transitional situation than that offered by the two contracts made in 1404 with Louis, duke of Orléans, in one of which Waleran de Luxembourg, comte de Ligny and Saint-Pol, took a money fee and became Louis's vassal, and in the other of which Édouard de Bar, marquis de Pont, took a pension for the same amount and became Louis's *allié*—each contracting otherwise to perform the same services?[7] Could an *alliance* indeed reinforce vassalage, the two relationships existing simultaneously between lord and man?

Here, perhaps, one should turn to the *Trésor des Chartes des ducs de Bretagne*. It seems clear that the *alliance* was known in Brittany as elsewhere. It can be found expressed in an unequivocal form, for instance, in contracts made with Duke John V by Georges de La Trémoïlle in February 1431 and February 1434,[8] by William Stuart, James Rovan,

---

6. Lewis, 'Decayed and Non-Feudalism', p. 160.   7. Ibid., p. 159.
8. Letters of 22 February 1431, Arch. Dép. Loire-Atlantique, E 181, no. 8 and of 1 February 1434, ibid., E 144 no. 9; reproduced below, Appendix, document 1. Documents from this archive are henceforward cited by series, file, and document indication alone.

and John Stuart in April of that year,[9] by perhaps a different William Stuart in September 1436,[10] and by Jean, seigneur de Bueil, in June 1439.[11] It is perhaps unnecessary to expand upon them; some have been printed, two in the Appendix to this article. Rather more equivocal, perhaps, are the documents in which men with Breton names became, apparently, the *alliés* of Duke John IV. In July 1371 Eon Le Moine, chevalier, made his relationship with John IV known in a letter patent remarkable only for its brevity;[12] in October of the same year Rolland de Kergorlé did the same in a slightly longer document.[13] John IV had 'retained' Eon Le Moine 'des siens et de sa retenue', and Rolland de Kergorlé 'un de ses escuiers et gentilx hommes'; there is no breath of vassalage. Nor is there in the contract made in March 1380 by Raoul de Kersaliou in which, recognizing that John IV 'm'a ordiené pour mes gages et pension la somme de doux centz livres par an affin de le servir', he promised to perform the usual duties, with the topical addition of 'pourchacer la delivrance de son duché de Bretaigne',[14] a service we shall encounter again.

But more often, however, in the surviving documents in the ducal archive at Nantes, there is some reference, explicit or implicit, to a 'feudal' relationship with a duke of Brittany. In August 1387, in the court of Vannes, Jean de Poulglou, chevalier, recognized that he was 'de sa nativité dou duché de Bretaigne et de sa droite nature comme vroy home estre tenu voloir le bien et honnour' of John IV 'et estre son subgiet et home feal'.[15] Some contractors, like Rolland, vicomte de Coatmen, described themselves as 'homme lige' of John IV;[16] some, like Jean de Kerenlouët, recognized that the duke was their 'prochain seigneur lige'.[17] In other documents—as, for instance, the contract of

9. Letters of 21 April 1434, E 144, no. 6.
10. Letters of 27 September 1436, E 144, no. 7; reproduced below, Appendix, document 2. The signature of 'G. Stuart' is different from that of 'Guillaume Stuart' on E 144, no. 6, which is unsealed.
11. Letters of 16 June 1439, E 147, no. 8; printed in Jean de Bueil, *Le Jouvencel*, ed. L. Lecestre and C. Favre (2 vols., Paris, 1887–9), ii. 319–20, and see i, p. lxxxj, n. 2. Further *lettres d'alliance* with dukes of Brittany are those of Archambaud de Périgord of 12 March 1393, E 181, no. 14; Jean de Rochechouart, seigneur d'Aspremont, of 13 September 1424, E 181, no. 15; Charles d'Anjou, comte de Mortain, of 13 September 1436, E 179, no. 8; and Jean de Blanchefort of 5 Feburary 1440, B.N., MS. 22332, fo. 222.
12. Letters of 30 July 1371, E 142, no. 16.
13. Letters of 14 October 1371, E 142, no. 20.
14. Letters of 8 March 1380, E 143, no. 3; reproduced below, Appendix, document 3.
15. Letters of 9 August 1387, E 143, no. 19.
16. Letters of 1371, E 142, no. 18.   17. Letters of 1371, E 142, no. 19.

Prigent Le Moine made in April 1380[18]—a 'feudal' element appears to be detectable in the phrases 'mon tres souverain seigneur monseigneur monsr. Jehan duc de Bretaigne', 'estre avecques mondit seignour le duc bon, vroy et loial servant et obboissant' (or, in other documents, 'subgit'),[19] and 'plus proche a lui que a nuls autres', a tag which appears to be associated closely with homage in Brittany.[20]

Equally remarkable, if less common, are those documents in which the phraseology of the 'non-feudal' world appears alongside that of the 'feudal'. In a number for the reign of John IV the concept of retainer appears. In February 1371 Even Chesnel, chevalier, confessed that it had pleased the duke 'me retenir avoucques luy de son conseil et des chevaliers de son ostel';[21] in May 1372 Jean du Juch, chevalier, too, was 'retenu' by Jean IV 'a un de ses chevaliers';[22] in 1379 Brient de Châteaubriant, chevalier, seigneur de Beaufort[23] and Raoullet, seigneur de Coëtquen;[24] in 1380 Jean Raguenel, chevalier, vicomte de Dinan,[25] and Prigent Le Moine;[26] in 1382 Alain Tivarlen;[27] and in 1398 Eustache de La Houssaie, chevalier,[28] each recognized that the duke 'me avoir retenu avecques lui'.[29] In the contracts of Prigent Le Moine and of Eustache de La Houssaie there is mention of a 'pension'. In two or three cases a man refers to himself as an *allié* of John IV: ' . . . confesse estre alié . . . et par ces presentes lettres me ralie' was the formula used by Rolland, vicomte de Coatmen, for instance, in his letters of March 1380.[30]

Probably a month earlier than Rolland de Coatmen, Silvestre de La

18. Letters of 3 April 1380, E 143, no. 6.
19. See, for instance, the letters of Brient de Châteaubriant, chevalier, seigneur de Beaufort, of 29 December 1379, E 142, no. 14.
20. See, for instance, the evidence given in an inquiry into the taking of homage in Brittany on 24 March 1392, E 142, no. 34, printed in Morice, *Preuves*, ii. 595–7; and see the letters of Eustache de La Houssaie of 20 January 1398, cited below, p. 128. But cf., also, the letters of Thibaud du Perrier of 22 February 1391, reproduced below, Appendix, document 5.
21. Letters of 22 February 1371, E 142, no. 13.
22. Letters of 4 May 1372, E 142, no. 27.
23. Letters of 29 December 1379, E 142, no. 14.
24. Letters of 29 December 1379, E 142, no. 15.
25. Letters of 8 January 1380, E 143, no. 7.
26. Letters of 3 April 1380, E 143, no. 6.
27. Letters of 11 October 1382, E 143, no. 9.
28. Letters of 20 January 1398, E 143, no. 32.
29. The term 'retenu . . . de noz genz et de nostre ostel' can be found again in the ducal letters of 10 September 1369 retaining Eustache de La Houssaie and granting him a *fief-rente*, E 154, no. 9. (I am grateful to Dr. M. C. E. Jones for this reference.)
30. Letters of 1 March 1380, E 143, no. 2.

Feuillée, chevalier, used almost an identical wording in his contract with John IV, like Raoul de Kersaliou, 'a la conqueste, pourchaz et recouvrement de sa duchié de Bretaingne'.[31] But in another, longer, document Silvestre de La Feuillée promised 'loyalment a mon tres redoubté seigneur lige monsr. Jehan duc de Bretaigne, conte de Mont-fort, que tout le cours de ma vie je li seray vray et loial soubgeit lige'.[32] This contract, made some twelve years earlier,[33] did not preclude the shorter contract, nor the inclusion in it of some of the more common general stipulations. But other examples of multiple contracting are not hard to find;[34] nor, indeed, are two examples of a contract with Duke John V by men who had contracted with John IV. On 22 November 1406 Rolland, vicomte de Coatmen,[35] and Raoul de Kersaliou sealed almost identical documents, in which the latter's obligation, apparently 'non-feudal' in 1380, was now, in its recognition of an anterior 'sere-ment de feaulté' seemingly containing the phrase 'prouche a lui que a nul autre', apparently 'feudal'.[36]

But such recognition of, as it were, two layers of contract, one con-taining an oath of fidelity and the other a seemingly separate obligation, helps, one may argue, to make the matter clearer. In February 1391 Thibaud du Perrier 'sire de Querpignac en l'evesché de Saintes' acknowledged '[je] cognois et confesse par la teneur de ces lettres que combien que j'ey fait fay et homage a mon souverain seigneur [John IV] ... comme son subgit et feal, que ce noiantmains je me suis alié

31. Letters of 8 February '⟨   ⟩9', E 142, no. 12; events would seem to indicate a date of 1379 o.s. rather than 1369 o.s. as given on the modern dossier of this document. Raoul de Kersaliou's contract is cited above, p. 125, and reproduced below, Appendix, document 3.

32. Letters of 5 March 1368, E 142, no. 7.

33. The date is admittedly barely decipherable; but the letters of Girard, sire de Retz, of 20 February 1368, E 142, no. 9, are an almost precise word for word parallel with E 142, no. 7.

34. By Jean, vicomte de Rohan: letters of 21 February 1372, E 142, no. 26, and of 13 April 1381, E 143, no. 5. (The reference to Olivier de Clisson in this document would appear to indicate a date of 1381 rather than 1380. Easter 1380 fell on 25 March, Easter 1381 on 14 April. Another document which falls between the two dates, the letters of Prigent Le Moine of 3 April, E 143, no. 6, I have, in the absence of other indication, assigned to 1380. But the reader should perhaps be warned.) By Geoffroy, sire de Quin-tin: letters of 11 August 1385, E 143, no. 12, and of 3 January 1389, E 143, no. 16; and by Jean Tournemine, seigneur de La Hunaudaie: letters of 26 January 1386, E 143, no. 13, and of 16 August 1389, E 143, no. 14. The reasons for the multiple letters are sometimes clear—Jean Tournemine, for instance, was going off on pilgrimage to Jerusalem—but the general contract was repeated.

35. Letters of 22 November 1406, E 144, no. 2.

36. Letters of 22 November 1406, E 144, no. 1; reproduced below, Appendix, document 4.

avecques lui a touzjours mes; et par ces presentes li ay promis et juré par la foy et serement de mon corps' to carry out the obligations stipulated, to John IV, to his duchess, Joan of Navarre, and to his heir, the comte de Montfort.[37] In April 1389 Alain du Perrier announced that

comme de raison touz et chascun les habitanz et demoranz ou duché de Bretaingne soient tenuz servir et oboir a mon souverain seigneur [John IV] . . . et plus pres a lui que a nul autre, ce noiantmains je par superhabundant fais savoir que je en esgart et consideracion aus grans biens, honneurs et profitz que mondit seigneur m'a fait, de ma liberale, pure et franche volanté et sens nul pourforcement, combien que paravant ces hores j'ey fait certaines promesses, aliances et confederacions avecques mondit seigneur, ce nonobstant en les confermant et ratiffiant je me alie presentement pour moy, mes heritiers et sucesseurs par la teneur de ces lettres [with John IV and the heirs of his body] . . . a touzjours mes, et li promais et jure par la foy et serement de mon corps et en leauté de chevalerie estre son bon, vroy et loial alié, subget, servant, aidant et oboissant

and also that of Joan of Navarre during her marriage to the duke and of the heirs of his body.[38]

Here the layers become triple: or, rather, the second layer divides itself into two. But the simple bifurcation finds adequate support in other documents. In 1386 the contract of Jean Tournemine, seigneur de La Hunaudaie, had also been made 'par superhabondant';[39] in 1398 Eustache de La Houssaie, having been, as we have seen, retained, swore 'en oultre le serment de fealté et hommaige lige que . . . [j'] ay fait', to John IV 'proche a lui que a nul autre senz nul en excepter'.[40] A number of contracts between 1388 and 1399 introduced the phrase 'combien que ge soye homme lige . . . ';[41] in 1397 Jean, vicomte de Dinan, and his associates, having recognized their 'feudal' relationship with the duke, continued 'toutesfoiz pour le grant desir que nous avons de plus aquerir et deservir sa bonne graice et seignourie . . . ';[42] and in the same way the contracts of Raoul de Kersaliou and Rolland, vicomte de Coatmen, with John V in 1406 continued 'que encores je promois et m'oblige . . . '.[43]

37. Letters of 22 February 1391, E 143, no. 23; reproduced below, Appendix, document 5.
38. Letters of 28 April 1389, E 143, no. 21.
39. Letters of 26 January 1386, E 143, no. 13.
40. Letters of 20 January 1398, E 143, no. 32.
41. Letters of Pierre de Tournemine, chevalier, of 8 April 1388, E 143, no. 15; of Guillaume, seigneur de Montauban, of 5 March 1389, E 143, no. 20; of Raoul, sire de Coëtquen, and others, of 11 November 1397, E 143, no. 31; of Bertrand, seigneur de Matignon, of 19 August 1399, E 143, no. 28.
42. Letters of 7 November 1397, E 143, no. 26.
43. Letters of 22 November 1406, E 144, nos. 1 and 2.

Finally, nearly three-quarters of a century later, in their contracts made in June and September 1475, Françoise de Dinan, comtesse de Laval, and Jean de Laval, sire de La Roche, used, amongst a great deal of grand verbiage, the old formula 'combien que par droit et raison naturelle ... nous soions tenuz et obligez ... et encores est nostre intencion de y perseverer ... mais ce neantmoins ... nous lui promectons d'abondant ...' in obliging themselves to Duke Francis II.[44]

If one compares this with, say, the document issued by Pierre de Lesnerac in May 1371, in which he confessed 'que ge suy devenu homme de foy' of John IV 'et que ge li ay fait fay et ligence a cause de doux centz livres de rante ... le temps de ma vie'[45]—a document recognizing the acceptance of a *fief-rente*—the anteriority of the homage and the oath of fealty to the oath of the contract recorded in the other documents which we have discussed is emphasized. In apparently only one document of this group is it necessary to imagine a fairly close connection between homage-and-fealty and another obligation. In September 1398 Jean Le Barbu, chevalier, announced that John IV had given him the lands, rents, and heritages of a number of defunct persons, and other rents and heritages in the bishopric of Léon, at present held by Tanguy de Kermaon, for which property held directly of the duke he had done him 'foy et homage'. 'Et par ce ait voulu', Jean Le Barbu continued, 'que je en jouisse tantost et incontinent amprés le decés dudit monsr. Tangui senz aucun debat ne impechement selon la teneur des lectres de mondit seigneur a moy sur ce baillees j'ay parmi ce promis et juré et par ces lectres promais et jure' a second obligation.'[46] But this situation must be regarded as exceptional. It seems safe to argue that normally the contract enshrined in our documents represents a secondary contract imposed upon an anterior 'feudal' contract: a secondary contract which would, were it not for that anterior contract, bear more purely the marks of a 'non-feudal' *alliance*: indeed, an *alliance* superimposed upon a contract of vassalage. And if this is so of the documents which give evidence of such bifurcation, it is arguably so of those that do not. In

---

44. Letters of 17 June and of 23 September 1475, E 147, nos. 11 and 13. It is not my intention to discuss here the documents recording the oaths taken by captains of Breton places on taking office; but one may point out that in a number of these, too, a 'bifurcation' takes place: the captaincy oath is taken 'en oultre' liegeancy. See, for instance, the oath of Jean de Juch of 6 November 1406, E 134, no. 15. Cf., also, the contract of Jean de Bueil cited above, p. 125, n. 11: the oath of *alliance* is taken on top of the *chambellan*'s oath.
45. Letters of 15 May 1371, E 142, no. 5.
46. Letters of 1 September 1398, E 143, no. 27.

this respect, all the documents of this kind from the *Trésor des Chartes de Bretagne* could be classed as Breton *alliances*; in this sense, as much 'non-feudal' documents as that rare life-indenture exchanged between John IV and Thomas 'Aldroiche', an Englishman, on 14 May 1363.[47]

As such the Breton documents compare well with those late medieval French letters of *alliance* that have so far been disinterred.[48] With one interesting exception, which will be discussed later, the documents range in time from that life-indenture of 1363 to the contract of Jean de Laval, sire de La Roche, in 1475.[49] The bulk of them derives from the reign of John IV;[50] a much smaller number coming from that of John V, two in 1406, one in 1422, the rest in the period 1434–9.[51] Two contracts[52] derive from the reign of Duke Peter II; two[53] from that of Francis II. The normal form[54] was a letter patent under a single name, though contracts made by small groups were not infrequent[55] and in 1437 contracts were made with the Breton nobility in mass groups.[56] Not infrequently,

---

47. E 142, no. 4; reproduced below, Appendix, document 6.

48. A few contracts have come to my attention to add to those cited in 'Decayed and Non-Feudalism'. Professor Philippe Contamine was good enough to bring to my notice the *lettres d'alliance* of Guillaume, seigneur de Marville, contracting with Renaud VI de Pons, of 9 October 1376, printed by J. Chavanon, 'Renaud VI de Pons', *Archives historiques de la Saintonge et de l'Aunis*, xxxi (1902), 91–92 (pièce xii); and Dr. M. G. A. Vale those of Guy de La Roche, seigneur de Montendre, contracting with Jean de Bretagne, comte de Penthièvre, disguised as comte de Périgord, of 30 October 1440, in Arch. Dép. Pyrénées-Atlantiques, E 643 (I have not been able to see this document). The contract of François, sire de Rieux, with Alain IX, vicomte de Rohan, of 19 February 1443, survives in Bibliothèque Municipale de Nantes, MS. 1693, no. 10. A contract between the seigneur de Mussidan and Charles d'Artois was referred to in litigation before the *Parlement* of Paris on 26 June 1385 (A.N., X¹ᴬ 1472, fos. 292–3: see P. Anselme, *Histoire généalogique et chronologique de la maison royale de France* (9 vols., Paris, 1726–33), i. 387).

49. Excluding those cited above, pp. 124–5, nn. 8–14 and n. 47 above, they are to be found in E 142–7. There are post-medieval copies of some of these contracts in B.N., MS. fr. 2709, fos. 182–222ᵛ; MS. fr. 22339, fos. 83,157; MS. fr. 22340, fo. 130; MS. fr. 22362, fos. 20, 27–50.

50. Numbers by years, including renewals: 1368, 2; 1371, 5; 1372, 8; 1379, 7; 1380, 5; 1381, 3; 1382, 2; 1385, 1; 1386, 1; 1387, 2; 1388, 1; 1389, 4; 1391, 1; 1392, 1; 1393, 2; 1395, 1; 1397, 2; 1398, 2; 1399, 1.

51. Numbers by years: 1434, 1; 1436, 2; 1437, 4 (as well as the oaths taken *en masse*; see below and n. 56).

52. Of 1453 and 1455, both, admittedly, barely within the category we are discussing.

53. Both of 1475.

54. Contracts were recognized before the court of Vannes by Jean de Poulglou, chevalier (letters of 9 August 1387, E 143, no. 19) and of Nantes by Jean Tournemine, seigneur de La Hunaudaie (letters of 16 August 1389, E 143, no. 14). An indenture of 1363 is cited above.

55. See, for example, the letters of Jean, vicomte de Dinan, and his associates, of 7 November 1397, E 143, no. 26.

56. The surviving documents are in E 144–7.

too, as we have seen, the preamble to the document includes a recognition of vassality, occasionally a recognition of alliance or retainer;[57]
occasionally there is a 'grand' preamble.[58] The commonest oaths were
upon the body and upon the Gospels, sometimes regarded as associated,
sometimes as not;[59] other oaths, when they appear, are primarily in
reinforcement of one or both of these.[60] Frequently a contractor's
property is obliged for non-fulfilment of the contract;[61] frequently, he
accepts the penalty of diffamation.[62] The obligations of the contract include a larger or smaller number of elements from the common litany:
the contractor promises to be a duke's good subject (or some synonym)
or good servant (or some synonym), or both, more or less long-
windedly, against all persons, normally without exception,[63] not infrequently *plus proche à lui*, occasionally to live and die with him.[64]
Sometimes, too, the promise to hold to a duke's party appears;[65] not
infrequently, the promise to help him preserve his rights,[66] particularly,
in the spirng of 1380, as we have seen, to help him recover his duchy.

57. I have omitted from those cited above the contract of 'Franscico de Lescasses'
of 9 October 1391 (E 143, no. 24), which seems to have a particularly military flavour.
58. See, for example, the letters of Jean, sire de Malestroit, of 20 April 1387, E 143,
no. 18.
59. They seem to be regarded as associated in, for instance, the contracts of Rolland
de Kersaliou of 28 May 1380 (E 143, no. 4) and of Prigent Le Moine of 3 April 1380
(E 143, no. 6), as separate in, for instance, the contract of Pierre de Tournemine of 8
April 1388 (E 143, no. 15) and, particularly clearly, in that of Guillaume, seigneur de
Montauban, of 5 March 1389 (E 143, no. 20).
60. A number of oaths, particularly in the 1370s, were sworn additionally upon God
(see, for instance, the letters of Even Chesnel of 22 February 1371, E 142, no. 13); some,
particularly in the 1380s and 1390s, upon some chivalric concept (see, for instance, the
letters of Alain du Perrier of 28 April 1389, cited above, p. 128). Thomas Pean, écuyer,
swore additionally upon the head of St. Guillaume de Saint-Brieuc (letters of 18 May
1393, E 143, no. 25) but he was outdone by Jean, vicomte de Rohan, who swore to
Francis II in 1484 on the *Corpus Christi*, the true Cross, the relics of St. Hervé, St.
Sebastien 'et autres plusieurs saintes Reliques' (letters of 4 September 1484, printed by
Morice, *Preuves*, iii. 439–40; I have not included this document, which came from Blain,
in the tally for Francis II's reign: it does not appear to survive in the *cartons Biçuel* in the
Bibliothèque Municipale de Nantes). An oath upon God alone was taken, for instance, by
Jean de Juch (letters of 4 May 1372, E 142, no. 27); upon the honour and estate of his person by René de Retz, sire de La Suze (letters of 24 August 1436, E 144, no. 5). No particular oath is mentioned in the contracts of Girard, sire de Retz, of 20 February (E 142,
no. 9) and of Silvestre de La Feuillée of 5 March 1368 (E 142, no. 7).
61. See below, Appendix, documents 4 and 5.
62. See below, Appendix, document 4.
63. For an example of such exceptions see below, Appendix, document 2.
64. See, for instance, the letters of Brient de Châteaubriant, seigneur de Beaufort, of
29 December 1379, E 142, no. 14.
65. See below, Appendix, documents 4 and 5.
66. See, for example, the letters of Brient de Châteaubriant of 29 December 1379,
E 142, no. 14.

Pursuing a duke's good and eschewing his damage appear fairly commonly;[67] less common, is the obligation to obey a duke's summons.[68] Informing one's lord of matters detrimental to him is a frequent stipulation;[69] other miscellaneous obligations also appear.[70] In a number of contracts the obligation is extended to a duke's heirs,[71] and in some, in 1383–99, to his duchess as well.[72] That the contract is for life is explicit in a large number of cases[73] and presumably implicit in the others. In some cases recourse against the contract is explicitly renounced.[74] The documents are normally sealed, sometimes by the seals of persons other than the contractors in the absence of their own,[75] sometimes by those seals in reinforcement of the contractors'.[76] Not infrequently the document is signed as well;[77] and other forms of attestation also appear.[78]

Evidence of the counter-obligation of a duke to his subject, servant, or *allié* in the Breton material, unlike that derived from Foix-Béarn,[79] is admittedly much rarer. In 1475 Françoise de Dinan stated in her contract with Francis II that

il a pleu a mondit seigneur de sa grace nous promectre et asseurer par ses lectres patentes que de ce il nous a baillees nous estre bon et leal seigneur et prince, garder, preserver et deffendre a son pouoir par touz moiens licites et raisonnables la personne, bien et estat de nous et de noz terres et seigneuries vers et contre toutes

67. See, for instance, the letters of Silvestre de La Feuillée of 5 March 1368, E 142, no. 7.

68. See below, Appendix, document 5.

69. See the letters of Silvestre de La Feuillée of 5 March 1368, E 142, no. 7.

70. See, for instance, those cited below, p. 133, and in the Appendix, document 5.

71. Ibid.   72. Ibid.   73. Ibid.

74. See the letters of Brient de Châteaubriant, seigneur de Beaufort, of 29 December 1379, E 142, no. 14.

75. See, for instance, the letters of Even Chesnel of 22 February 1371, E 142, no. 13.

76. See the letters of Thomas Pean of 18 May 1393, E 143, no. 25.

77. See, for instance, the letters of Françoise de Dinan, comtesse de Laval, of 17 June 1475, E 147, no. 11.

78. The letters of René de Retz of 24 August (E 144, no. 5) and of André de Laval of 25 August 1436 (E 144, no. 10) are signed only, with additional signatures. The letters of Bertrand de Dinan, seigneur de Châteaubriant, and Jacques de Dinan, seigneur de Montafilant, of 8 October 1437 (E 144, no. 13) are signed in the absence of their seals; Bertrand de Dinan not knowing how to write, Pierre de L'Hôpital signed for him. Occasionally there is the attestation of a tabellion: see, for instance, the letters of Jean Tournemine, seigneur de La Hunaudaie, of 26 January 1386, E 143, no. 13. That a proper seal was regarded as important may be seen from the letters of Jean, vicomte de Rohan, and his associates, of 11 April 1381 (E 143, no. 33) and of Bertrand and Jacques de Dinan, cited above. Documents in which a *constat* is given to interlineations or erasures (as in the letters of Alain de Malestroit of 22 May 1392 (E 143, no. 17) and of Hervé de Voluyre of 22 June 1395 (E 143, no. 30)) again emphasize the evidentiary aspect of these letters.

79. Lewis, 'Decayed and Non-Feudalism', p. 162.

personnes qui mal, grief, ennuy ou domaige nous vouldroient faire ou porter en quelque maniere que ce soit.[80]

The letters of Raoul, sire de Montfort and de Lohéac, and others, of 28 November 1393 included sworn counter-promises of the same kind by John IV and by Joan of Navarre, who sealed the document as well.[81] In a very few cases, as we have seen, a pension was given; but in the main the nature of the contractor's interest is passed over in silence.

One must, of course, take into account the possibility that some of these obligations were, in fact, imposed upon a contractor because of some dereliction of duty or as a pledge of good behaviour. Hervé de Voluyre, chevalier, seigneur du Pont, a liege man and subject of John IV for the fees and lands he held in the duchy of Brittany, had failed to appear for military service and had had his Breton property confiscated; his contract was made in June 1395 when the duke released them to him.[82] Jean de Poulglou and his father had committed 'plusours granz cas de quoy peussent estre pugniz ou reprins a plusours fins, lesquelx mondit seigneur de sa graice lour a debonairement passez' before he made his contract in August 1387—a contract which contained particularly severe penal terms and which seems something like acceptance of a suspended sentence.[83] The contract made by a repentant Jean, vicomte de Rohan, returning to the fold in the autumn of 1484, has again the nature of a submission rather than a free contract.[84] One might well imagine that promises such as those not to leave the duchy without the duke's permission,[85] or not to make 'confederacion, alliance ne ligue a personne quelxconques de son pais ne d'ailleurs senz son assentement de quelconques matiere que ce puist estre',[86] have an overtone of constraint for good behaviour. Again, the emphasis placed upon obligation of goods[87] does seem to underline the penal aspect of these documents;

80. Letters of 17 June 1475, E 147, no. 11.
81. E 143, no. 29. John V's letters of 2 November 1437 (see below, pp. 136–7) in fact again recorded a counter-promise (Morice, *Preuves*, ii. 1315).
82. Letters of 22 June 1395, E 143, no. 30.
83. Letters of 9 August 1387, E 143, no. 19.
84. Letters of Francis II of 4 September 1484 (Morice, *Preuves*, iii. 439–40.)
85. See, for instance, the letters of Silvestre de La Feuillée of 5 March 1368, E 142, no. 7.
86. See, for instance, the letters of Jean, sire de Malestroit, of 20 April 1387, E 143, no. 18.
87. Obligation of goods is otherwise rare in the contracts known to me. It can be found, however, in those of Guillaume de Marville with Renaud VI de Pons of 9 October 1376, cited above, p. 130, n. 48; of Archaumbaud de Grailly, comte de Foix, and his two sons, the future Jean I de Foix and Gaston, captal de Buch, with Louis, duke of Orléans, of 4 April 1401; of Humbert, seigneur de Villars, with Louis II, duke of Bourbon,

and in one case, that of Rolland, vicomte de Coatmen, in 1406, a contractor agreed specifically to pay 5,000 *livres* 's'il avenoit que nous feissons du contraire, que Dieu ne vueille', as well as to incur the other penalties specified.[88]

There is perhaps no more than an echo here of the kind of pledge taken on both sides of the Channel in the early thirteenth century;[89] but it does serve to remind us, too, that the sort of contract we have been discussing might be thought to have had a respectable ancestry. In May 1241, for instance, Olivier de Termes made a contract at Pontoise in which he recognized that he had sworn on the Gospels faithfully to serve Louis IX against all men who could live and die, never to leave his service, never to join in confederation with his enemies but to make war against them, and finally to protect his men and lands and to warn them of danger to them.[90] But without an investigation of the circumstances of the making of each of these earlier 'fidelities' one cannot be certain of the status of such documents. On 14 June 1270, for instance, Geoffroy de Lanvaux, chevalier, issued letters patent in which he announced, very simply, 'que nous avons juré sur les saints Evangiles servir le Comte de Bretagne byans & loyaument à nostre poer, & li bailler mes lettres saellées'.[91] There is no breath here of a 'feudal' terminology. La Borderie, who discussed the tribulations of the Lanvaux family, seems to have assumed that Geoffroy swore fidelity to Count Jean *le roux* in 1270 because his elderly father Alain had ceded his lordship to him;[92] but Geoffroy seems already to have been co-seigneur of Lanvaux with Alain since at least 1267.[93] What, then, is one to make of his letters?

There would thus seem to be some room for doubt. An apparent emphasis on penalty clauses, and the general absence of ducal counter-obligation in our documents—the Foix letters of *alliance*, as we have seen, generally recorded a counter-promise to the *allié* by the count—

---

of 18 August 1402; of Jeanne de Voisins, dame de Mirepoix and de Lagarde, as guardian of Philippe de Lévis-Mirepoix her son, with Jean I de Foix, of 5 September 1418; and of Nompar II de Caumont with Gaston IV de Foix of 21 May 1439 (Lewis, 'Decayed and Non-Feudalism', p. 166, n. 4).

88. Letters of 22 November 1406, E 144, no. 2.
89. J. C. Holt, *Magna Carta* (Cambridge, 1969), p. 85.
90. *Layettes du Trésor des Chartes*, ed. A. Teulet and others (5 vols., Paris, 1863–1909), ii. 449, no. 2914.
91. Morice, *Preuves*, i. 1021.
92. L. A. Le Moyne de La Borderie, *Histoire de Bretagne* (6 vols., Rennes and Paris, 1896–1914), iii. 345–6.
93. Morice, *Preuves*, i. 1007.

might seem to place the emphasis upon submission rather than recruitment. But the general obligation of a lord—'aid, help, succor and support', which Lord Hastings in England promised Henry Willoughby, esquire, in 1478[94]—was the same in the 'non-feudal' as in the 'feudal' contract; there was little need for a Breton duke, already in a 'feudal' relationship, albeit perhaps a precarious one, with the persons with whom he was contracting, specifically to state his own duty to them— though on occasion, as we have seen, he did so. The existence of documents much earlier than the later fourteenth century, of the same general purpose as the documents we have been primarily discussing, might seem to cast doubt upon the status we have given them. But perhaps the doubt should turn the other way: if these earlier acts of fidelity were made separately from an act of homage and fealty, then one must ask what their precise purpose within the system was.[95]

Perhaps, as in other matters, we should indeed concentrate upon purpose, rather than precedent. A Montfort duke of Brittany, perhaps more than most, had a need to acquire support. Like other lords, he might find it amongst the members of his household,[96] or the members of his Order. After the second treaty of Guérande in 1381 John IV, according to Guillaume de Saint-André

> ... fist assembler les prélaz,
> Abbez et clercs de touz estats,
> Barons, chevaliers, escuiers,
> Qui lors portoint nouveaulx coliers
> De moult bel port, de belle guise,
> Et estoint nouvelle devise
> De doux jolez bruniz et beaux,
> Couplez ensemble de doux fermaulx

94. Indenture of 28 February 1478 (W. H. Dunham, Jr., 'Lord Hastings' Indentured Retainers, 1461–1483', *Transactions of the Connecticut Academy of Arts and Sciences*, xxxix (1955), 129).

95. One may take, for instance, the letters of Hervé IV de Léon making his peace with Jean *le roux* in September 1260 (*Layettes*, iii. 550–1, no. 4637; for the circumstances, La Borderie, *Histoire de Bretagne*, iii. 343–4) as presumably recording the equivalent (but without mention here of homage) of the *hommage de paix* referred to very briefly by R. Boutruche, *Seigneurie et féodalité* (2 vols., Paris, 1959–70), ii. 160–1. (For another possible 'purpose' of such documents, see F. L. Ganshof, *Feudalism*, trans. P. Grierson (London, 1964), p. 80.) For the comparatively rare instances of a 'vassalitic' relationship apparently created 'by a simple oath of fealty, without any homage being required'; see Ganshof, *Feudalism*, pp. 79–80; Boutruche, *Seigneurie*, ii. 156–7; but see also R. Boutruche, *Une Société provinciale en lutte contre le régime féodal. L'Alleu en Bordelais et en Bazadais du xie au xviiie siècle* (Rodez, 1947), p. 56, no. 3.

96. See, for instance, the obligations of Jean de Vendôme, chevalier, vicomte de Chartres, on becoming John V's *chambellan* on 19 April 1441, E 181, no. 9.

> Et au dessouz estoit l'ermine
> En figure et en coleur fine;
> En deux cédules avoit escript:
> A MA VIE, comme j'ay dit;
> L'un molt est blanc et l'autre noir,
> Il est certain, tien le pour voir.[97]

The creation of what became a highly eclectic company[98] at such a significant time should not need comment. The *alliance* between equals —again a time-hallowed practice, of which examples can be found in the south-west as far back as about 1174[99]—was of course to be found in Brittany.[100] The *alliance* between unequals was likewise to be found there. If a duke wanted to be recognized as 'vray duc de Bretaigne',[101] or needed support in the 'conqueste, pourchaz et recouvrement' of his duchy of Brittany,[102] or support 'par especial' against Olivier de Clisson;[103] or if he needed assistance against Jean de Penthièvre, seigneur de L'Aigle,[104] his *funeste* mother, Marguerite de Clisson, and the whole *cohue* of the 'aliez et bienveillans de la maison de Bluys',[105] or even imagined the need for support against his own cooks or at least against those shadowy figures behind them in Anjou and elsewhere whom his spies had warned him had 'machiné la mort, prinse, mal, ennuy, ou domage de nostre personne, cell. de nos enffans et freres, ou division de nostre seignourie';[106] in circumstances such as these, what

97. *C'est Le Libvre du bon Jehan, duc de Bretaigne*, ed. E. Charrière, *Chronique de Bertrand du Guesclin par Cuvelier* (Documents inédits sur l'histoire de France) (2 vols., Paris, 1839), ii. 544–5, lines 3766–79.

98. See, for instance, G. A. Lobineau, *Histoire de Bretagne* (2 vols., Paris, 1707), ii, *Preuves*, 628–9; Morice, *Preuves*, ii. 1394–5.

99. See, for instance, the letters of Raymond V, comte de Toulouse, contracting with Bernard-Aton VI, vicomte de Narbonne, *c.* 1174, and Bernard-Aton's counter-letters, *Layettes*, i. 107–8, nos. 254–5.

100. See, for instance, the letters of Bertrand du Guesclin and Olivier de Clisson of 24 October 1380, Morice, *Preuves*, i. 1642–3.

101. See, for example, the letters of Rolland, vicomte de Coatmen, of 1371, E 142, no. 18.

102. See the letters of Silvestre de La Feuillée of 8 February 1380, E 142, no. 12.

103. Letters of Jean, vicomte de Rohan, of 13 April 1381, E 143, no. 5.

104. Letters of Jean de Bueil of 16 June 1439, cited above, p. 125, n. 11.

105. Ibid.; cf. the letters of Jean Harpenden, seigneur de Belleville and de Montagu, establishing a protection treaty with John V, of 10 August 1433 (E 181, no. 19) and of 6 August 1438 (E 144, no. 14); similar letters to the first were issued by Jean de Belleville, seigneur de Mirabeau, again on 10 August 1433 (E 181, no. 20). Cf. also the contracts of Jean de Rochechouart of 13 September 1424 (E 181, no. 15) and of Jean de Blanchefort of 5 February 1440 (B.N., MS. fr. 22332, fo. 222).

106. Bibliothèque Municipale de Nantes, MS. 1691, no. 19; printed in Morice, *Preuves*, ii. 1314. For the 'conspiration des cuisiniers' of 1437, see La Borderie, *Histoire de Bretagne*, iv. 247.

was a duke to do? He could appeal for assistance outside his duchy, as indeed John V did against Jean de Penthièvre and Margot de Clisson in retaining Jean de Bueil in 1439.[107] But in general it was to their own subjects that the dukes of Brittany turned, as John V in 1437 turned to Alain IX, vicomte de Rohan, and his associates 'ausquelx ayons fait declerer et exposer ce que en avons peu jucques a savoir et descurir' of the machination in Anjou, 'lesquelx acertanez desd. auterissemens et tres deplessans de lad. deslealle machinacion nous ayent promis et juré et baillé leurs sellez de nous servir en celle matere'.[108] The Breton dukes do not seem to have regarded—understandably, perhaps, in the circumstances—the 'feudal' nexus as strong enough, at least in those cases in which they seem to have felt a supplementary oath and a legal contract as necessary to reinforce it: hence our documents. The purpose of these contracts is clear enough. The form which they took, derived from the circumstances in which they were made, might appear 'feudal'. But arguably it is yet another illustration of that shadowy world in which 'feudal' and 'non-feudal' met. Contracts which established a *fief-rente* without a *rente* belonged, according to M. Sczaniecki, 'déjà à une nouvelle époque où l'on ne se soucie plus du droit et du vrai sens des institutions féodales'.[109] It is not, in our case, the use of a 'feudal' form for a purpose arguably 'non-feudal'; it is an attempt to use arguably a now essentially 'non-feudal' form to reinforce a decayed 'feudal' situation.

Perhaps we should forget about form as well as precedent. Did the Breton contracts ensure the fulfilment of their purpose? This, perhaps, is a question for the historian of the late medieval Breton nobility. In his letters of May 1380 Rolland de Kersaliou, chevalier, was prepared to promise 'que toutes autres lettres et promesses que j'ai fait paravant ces houres contraires de cestes, qu'ils soient anullees et mis hors de nulle value';[110] and in April 1381 Jean, vicomte de Rohan, too, made his promise 'non obstant autres sermanz quiconques que nous aions fait a

107. Letters of Jean de Bueil of 16 June 1439, cited above, p. 125, n. 11.

108. Bibliothèque Municipale de Nantes, MS. 1691, no. 19; printed in Morice, *Preuves*, ii. 1314. This document, one of the *Titres de Blain*, represents John V's counter-letters to those issued by Alain de Rohan, of 19 October 1437, E 144, no. 12. These letters, like those of Bertrand de Dinan, seigneur de Châteaubriant, and Jacques de Dinan, seigneur de Montafilant, of 8 October (E 144, no. 13), Jean de Beaumanoir, seigneur du Bois de La Motte, Jean de Beaumanoir and Guillaume de Beaumanoir of 26 October (E 144, no. 11) and Guy, comte de Laval, and Louis de Laval, sire de Châtillon, of 12 November (E 147, no. 12) took the form of the mass contracts of 1437.

109. M. Sczaniecki, *Essai sur les fiefs-rentes* (Paris, 1946), p. 164.

110. Letters of 28 May 1380, E 143, no. 4.

quiconques persomes'.[111] The views of Jean I de Rohan's great-grand-son, Jean II, vicomte de Rohan, on the question of loyalty in the second half of the following century might have been interesting. But if this question must remain open it is still possible to add an element towards the answer concerning that of the enforcement of such political con-tracts—in this case in English Gascony; an element which illustrates, too, the attitude of English law to the life-indenture. K. B. McFarlane at one stage seems almost to have doubted whether such a contract could be enforced in the courts.[112] Later he was able to cite such a case in which, towards the end of Henry IV's reign, Sir Ivo Fitzwarin and Ralph Brit alleged before justices on circuit in the West Country that the other was responsible for the breach of the terms of their life-indenture.[113] It would be out of place here to go fully into the ensuing litigation;[114] but rather earlier than this, Gilibert, called *Petit* de Pellegrue, chevalier, brought an action before the king against Guillaume-Amanieu de Madaillan, chevalier, sire de Lesparre and de Rauzan.[115] His case was that Florimond, sire de Lesparre, Guillaume-Amanieu's uncle and predeces-sor, had retained him for life at an annuity of 100 francs, and had con-firmed this in his will; but Guillaume-Amanieu had refused to pay him, and the arrears over three years amounted to 600 francs (Pellegrue was including the fringe benefits of the contract). Guillaume-Amanieu's case was that Pellegrue had lost his pension because of some delict com-mitted towards him and for other reasons. Henry IV, or his advisers, seem to have felt rather in a quandary: Pellegrue had been an old

---

111. Letters of 13 April 1381, E 143, no. 5.

112. 'A first impression is that we must not accept the apparent finality of the phrase "for life" in the indentures at its face value. In the early days of the system some of the contracts had a sanctions clause for breach of the engagement; but after the middle of the fourteenth century this clause disappears. What is more so far no evidence of any attempt to enforce a contract in the courts has been published' (K. B. McFarlane, ' "Bas-tard Feudalism" ', *B.I.H.R.* xx (1945), 173).

113. K. B. McFarlane, *The Nobility of Later Medieval England* (Oxford, 1973), pp. 105–6.

114. I hope to do so elsewhere. McFarlane appears to have relied on an incomplete copy of the initial action, B.L., Add. Roll 74138. (I am grateful to Mr. James Campbell for this information.) A full record of this action, on Monday, 24 February 1411 before the royal justices William Hankford and William Skrene at Dorchester, can be found on the relevant assize roll, P.R.O., Just. Itin. 1/1519, m. 30.

115. Letters of Henry IV, of 12 July 1401, recording the settlement between the par-ties, Gascon Roll 2 Henry IV, P.R.O., C.61/108, m. 3. The document was printed in *Lettres de rois, reines et autres personnages des cours de France et d'Angleterre*, ed. J. J. Champollion-Figeac (Documents inédits sur l'histoire de France) (2 vols., Paris, 1839–47), ii. 310–11; but the transcription contains enough minor faults to justify printing it again below, Appendix, document 7.

pensioner of John of Gaunt in Gascony—Henry IV was to retain him for life and confirm his annuity on 19 July 1401[116]—yet the sire de Lesparre, especially one who was to depart from England with seventy 'familiares' and twenty-two sailors in his own barge,[117] could not be overlooked. A tactful compromise was reached. Guillaume-Amanieu was to pay Pellegrue 500 francs at Michaelmas the following year; Pellegrue was then to abandon all claim on Guillaume-Amanieu de Madaillan and his heirs and surrender to him the indenture received from Florimond de Lesparre. Pellegrue may have been more concerned with his pension and his arrears than with the joys of serving a sire de Lesparre; but at least his contract was thought to be legally binding.

Appendix

1. *Letters of Georges de La Trémoille, 1 February 1434*

Sachent touz que je, George seigneur de La Tremoille, de Sully et de Craon, en faveur du mariage nagayres accordé par mon tres redoubté seigneur le duc de Bretaigne et mon tres chier et honnoré sr. et cousin le conte de Laval, de madamoyselle Yolant de Laval, aysnee fille dudit monsr. le conte de Laval et de Jehan de La Tremoille mon filz, considerant que mondit sr. le duc me veult ayder et secourir comme a son parent et serviteur en mes afferes, je, pour lesdictes causes et pour les grans honneurs, biens et pleisirs que je espere que mondit sr. le duc me face en temps advenir, ay promis et prometz par ces presentes en bonne foy a mondit tres redoubté seigneur le duc de Bretaigne de luy estre bon, vray et leal serviteur, porter et soustenir ses faitz, estat et honneur, et le servir, conseiller et conforter en ses afferes, le ayder et garder et deffandre sa personne, messrs. ses enffens, biens, villes, chasteaux, forteresses, terres et seignouries a tout mon pouoir toutes foiz que besoign en aura, contre touz ceulx qui invader, assaillir ou grever le vouldroient, en sa personne, messrs. ses enffens, villes, forteresses, terres et seignouries dessusdictes; et luy reveleray ce que je scauray que on vouldra faire ou pourchasser ou prejudice, ennuy et domage de luy et de ses choses dessusdictes; et ainsi l'ay promis en tiltre de bonne foy sanz fraude, barat ne malengin le tenir a mondit sr., messrs. ses enffens et messrs. d'Estampes et de Laval, desquelx mondit sr. le duc se tient fort de le leur fayre tenir paraillement. Et en tesmoign et a plus grant fermecté desdictes choses j'ay signé ces presentes de ma main et fait seeller de mon seel. Fait a Nantes le premier jour de fevrier l'an mil iiijᶜ trante et troys.

[*signed:*] George de La Tremoylle

[*Parchment, seal applied. Arch. Dép. Loire-Atlantique, E 144, no. 9.*]

116. Gascon Roll 2 Henry IV, P.R.O., C.61/108, m. 7.
117. Licence for the passage of Guillaume-Amanieu, seigneur de Lesparre and de Rauzan, to Aquitaine with this company, 12 June 1401, ibid., m. 15.

2. Letters of William Stuart, 27 September 1436

Je, Guillaume Stuart escuier, natiff du pais d'Escoce, cappitaine des gens d'armes et de trait dudit pais estanz en France, promet et m'oblige par la foy et serment de mon corps et sur mon honneur estre bon, vroy et loyal serviteur tant que vivroy a tres hault et puissant prince et mon tres redoubté seigneur monseigneur le duc de Bretaigne et a son aisné filz, et les servir a mon poair vers touz et contre touz qui peuent vivre et mourir, sanz riens en excepter sauff le roy d'Escoce mon souverain seigneur et la personne du roy de France seulement, et empescher celx qui vouldroint faire ou pourchacer ennuy ou domage a mondit seigneur de Bretaigne ou a sondit aisné filz, leurs pais, subgiz, terres ou seigneuries en aucune maniere, et s'aucune chose venoit a ma cognoessance qui fust prejudiciable a eulx ou a l'un d'eulx, leursd. pais, subgiz, terres ou seigneuries, le leur reveler ou faire savoir a mon lige poair, et generalment vouloir et procurer le bien et empescher le mal et domage de mondit seigneur de Bretaigne et de sondit aisné filz et de leursd. pais, subgiz, terres et seigneuries, et tout ce tenir, fournir et acomplir sanz jamais encontre venir ne y commettre ne obmettre, et tout sanz fraude, barat ne malengin. Et en tesm. de ce j'ay signé ces presentes de ma main et seellees du seau de mes armes, le xxvij^me jour de septembre l'an mil quatre cens trante seix.

[*signed:*] G. Stuart

[*Paper, seal applied. Arch. Dép. Loire-Atlantique, E 144, no. 7.*]

3. Letters of Raoul de Kersaliou, 8 March 1380

Sachent touz que je, Raoul de Kaersaliou, faz savoir que comme mon tres redobté et puissant signeur monsigneur monsr. Jehan duc de Bretaigne, conte de Montfort et de Richemont, m'a ordiené pour mes gages et pension la somme de doux centz livres par an affin de le servir, dont je li ay juré et promis, jure aux sainctes Euvangiles de Dieu touchees et promet par mon serement et en bone foy et foy d'armes et de gentilece, que je le serviray bien et loiaument a mon pouoir contre et vers toutes persomes de quelque estat qu'ils soient qui pueent mourir et vivre, a pourchacer la delivrance de son duché de Bretaigne et de toutes ses autres terres et heritaiges quelque part qu'ils soient; et en cas que je puisse sentir ou apparcevoir aucune mauvestié, domage ou traison envers mondit signeur je suy tenu a les li reveler affin de y pourvoir de remede. Et ce je promet et jure en la maniere dessusdicte tenir et acomplir bien et loyalment, sur poine d'estre repputé faux, parjure et desloyal en toutes courz et devant toutes persomes et juges qui soient ou puissent estre, ou cas que je feroie le contraire. Doné soubz le saell monsr. Jehan Kazvallen a ma priere et requeste le viij^e jour de marz l'an mill trois cenz sextante deiz et neuff.

[*Parchment, sealed on a tongue. Arch. Dép. Loire-Atlantique, E 143, no. 3.*]

4. Letters of Raoul de Kersaliou, 22 November 1406

Je, Raoul de Kaersaliou, cognois et suy confessant que comme feal de monseignour le duc ly dois et ay juré par le serement de feaulté a vouloir et procurer son prouffit et son domage eschiver, le servir, ly oboir, le guarantir et deffandre a mon lige pouoir vers touz et contre touz, prouche a lui que a nul autre, que encores je promois et m'oblige faire a mondit seigneur les choses desurdictes sanz nulle faintise, estre o lui et tenir son parti vers touz et contre touz qui peuent vivre et morir a mon lige pouoir, a paine d'estre reputé faux et parjure vers mondit seigneur et encourir les autres paines qui en tel cas appartient; et quant a ce je m'oblige avecques touz et chascun mes biens meblés et heritages presentz et avenir, et ce jure et promois par mon sere-ment ainssin le tenir sanz aler encontre. En tesmoign desquelles choses en ay baillé a mondit seignour ces presentes seellees de mon propre seell le xxij ᵐᵉ jour de novem-bre l'an mil quatrecenz et seix.

[*Parchment, sealed on a tongue. Arch. Dép. Loire-Atlantique, E 144, no. 1.*]

5. *Letters of Thibaud du Perrier, 22 February 1391*

Sachent touz qui ces lettres verront et orront que je, Thebaud Perier sire de Quer-pignac en l'evesché de Saintes, cognois et confesse par la teneur de ces lettres que combien que j'ey fait fay et homage a mon souverain seigneur monseigneur Jehan duc de Bretaingne, comte de Richemont, comme son subgit et feal, que ce noiant-mains je me suis alié avecques lui a touzjours mes; et par ces presentes li ay promis et juré par la foy et serement de mon corps de tenir son parti et de vivre et morir pour sa querelle et de madamme Jahanne de Navarre sa compaigne, de monseigneur le comte de Montfort son filz et de touz leurs enffanz qui essirent d'eulx ensamble vers touz et contre touz ceulx qui peuent vivre et morir, sens fraude ne malengin et sens nulli excepter, et plus pres a lui que a nul autre, et de li aider et venir a ses com-mandemens toutes foiz qu'il lui plera me mander et que il ait a faire de moy; et que¹¹⁸ le chastel de Plaineseve que je tiens a present sera au commandement de mondit seigneur et de ceulx qui tendront son parti; et que de tout mon pouoir, tant de corps, de biens, de forteresces que j'ey a present et pourré avoir et conquester ou temps futur par quelconque maniere que ce pourra estre, et touz ceulx que je pourré induyre et amener, serons et tendrons la partie de mondit seigneur ainsi que dit est. Et ces choses et chascune d'elles promais et jure par le serment de mon corps tenir fermes et estables de point en point sens jamés venir encontre par moy ne par autres, et quant ad ce je me oblige a mondit seigneur corps et biens presens et advenir par ces presentes seellees de mon seel. Donné a mon ostel de Cropignac le xxij ᵉ jour de fevrier l'an mil iij ᶜ iiij ˣˣ et dez.

[*Parchment, sealed on a tongue. Arch. Dép. Loire-Atlantique, E 143, no. 23.*]

6. *Indenture of Jean IV, duke of Brittany, and Thomas 'Aldroiche', 14 May 1363*

Ceste endenteure faite parentre tres noble seigneur monsr. Jehan duc de Bretaigne, conte de Montfort et viconte de Lymoges d'une part, et Thoumas Aldroiche d'autre part, tesmoigne que ledit Thoumas est demoré et demorra toute sa vie o ledit duc pour le servir bien et loiaument vers toutes manieres de gienz, fors contre le roy 'd'Engleterre' et sauff sa ligence vers luy, ⟨   ⟩renent dudit duc chascun an quatre

---

118. me *crossed out.*

cenz escuz et boche a court, lesqueulx quatre cenz escuz ledit duc li a assignez
un⟨   ⟩ner sur la renczon de la paroisse de Rex durant la guerre; et si ladicte
renczon monte plus par an que ladicte somme led⟨   ⟩s est tenu et obligé de
rendre le sourplus audit duc, et si mains vaut ladicte renczon ledit duc est tenu de le
⟨   ⟩lours ladicte somme, et en temps de paez ledit duc li assignera ou paiera
ladicte somme chascun an ou il porra estre bon⟨   ⟩e. Et tendra ledit Thoumas
par guerre deux archiers pour servir ledit duc a telx gaiges comme sera accordé entre
⟨   ⟩ parties. Et ou cas que ledit Thoumas voudroit faire voyage oultre mer ou
autres pelerinaiges, ou aler en Engleterre ⟨   ⟩ ou deux pour ses propres
afaires par temps de treves ou de paez, il porra avoir du duc son congé, lesqueu-
⟨   ⟩uz ledit Thoumas sera tenu de retorner a faire sondit service. Et ce tenir
et acomplir bien et loiaument o⟨   ⟩ctes parties en bonne foy l'un vers l'autre
sanz venir encontre. Donné et fait souz les seaux desdictes part⟨   ⟩geablement
le xiiijᵉ jour de may l'an de grace mil CCC soi⟨ ⟩ et troys.

> [*Parchment, sealed on two tongues, one seal gone. Arch. Dép. Loire-Atlantique,
> E 142, no. 4.*]

7. *Letters of Henry IV, king of England, 12 July 1401*

[*In left margin:*] Pur Gilibert Pelegrue, chivaler, de concordia per R. confirmata.

Le Roy a touz ceux qui cestes presentez letres verront, saluz. Come debat &
desacord fust par davant nous entre Gilibert autrement appellé Petit de Pelegrue,
chivalar, demandant, d'une part, e Guillem Amaniu de Madelhain, chivaler, sire de
Lesparra & de Rousan, d'autra part, sur ce que ledit Gilibert demandoit audit sire de
Lesparra que come Florimont jadiz sire de Lesparra, predecessor dedit Guillem
Amaniu sire de Lesparra, l'eust donné a terme de vie cent francs de rende chescun
an & boche en cort a soy & a troys varletz & fen & avena pour quatre chevaus,
moyan letre seellee de son. propre seel, lequiel don. en son. testament l'avoit con-
fermé; e ledit Guillem Amaniu sire de Lesparra qui en present est l'ayt contredit de
li paier ledit don., dont l'estoit dehu, a ce q'il disoit, le arreradgez pour le terme de
trois ans, lesquiels estimoyt a deux centz francs pour an, et sur ce nous suppliest
ledit Gilibert que li vousissoms fere compliment de justice. E ledit Guillem Amaniu
sire de Lesparra se deffendist que ne l'estoyt en non. tenuz de compleir sa domande
pour ascuns trespas que disoit que lidit Gilibert avoit comis vert li, pour lesquiels il
avoit pardu sa pension., & pour autres chouses q'il allegoit davant nous, dezquiels
chouses nous avoms ehy conysense. Nientmant nous, voulens nurrir pes & concorde
entre noz foialx liges & subgiz, pour especial entre ledit Guillem Amaniu sire de
Lesparra & ledit Gilibert, lesquiels nous tenoms & pansoms qu'ils soient loyals &
prodomes & vailans, si les avoms acordé pour voloir & assent de ambes dues les
parties pour la manier que s'ensuyt: c'est assavoir que ledit Guillem Amaniu sire de
Lesparra ait a paier audit Gilibert de Pelegrue pour tout que li puet demander a causa
de la annuauté surdite le somme de sinq centz francs diutz le terme de seinte Michel
qui vient en un an, e ledit Gilibert de Pelegrue, receu ledit paiemant, que ait a quipta
audit sire de Lesparra & a ses heirs tout quant que li porroit demander a cause des
chouses surdites, e que le soit tenu de rende la obligacion. & ententure qu'il a dudit
Florimont jadiz sire de Lesparra, & que d'assi en avant ils soyent bons amiz; lequel

nostre apuntament & acort ambedeux les parties si ont approé & loé & chescuin s'en est tenu pour contente, & promys chescun en droyt soy par davant nous de tenir ledit nostre [acort] & apuntament sens venir encountre. Si donoms en mandement a toutz noz officiers & ministres de nostre duché de Guyenne qui en present sont o par temps avenir seront, que en le cas que lesdites parties o aucune d'icelles fussent refusans o contradisans a tenir les chouses surdites, qu'ils les constreinhent a tenir pour les voies & remedies que de droit o de custume du paiis se darra fere. En tesmoignance de quelle chose a ycestes noz presentes letres nous avons fait mettre nostre graunt seal. Don. a Farnham le xij jour de juyllet l'an du grace mill. quatre centz primer & de nostre regne second.

Per litteram ipsius Regis de signeto.

[*Gascon Roll 2 Henry IV, P.R.O., C 61/108, m. 3.*]

9

'Mon Pais et ma Nation': Breton Identity in the Fourteenth Century

MICHAEL JONES

Contemporary writers provide evidence for the existence of a regional sentiment in the duchy of Brittany in the fourteenth century. Guillaume de Saint-André, secretary and biographer of Duke John IV, put into the mouth of his hero a patriotic speech at the point when the duke resolved firmly to defend his duchy against the king of France in 1379.[1] It is but one of a number of such expressions which indicate feeling for Brittany and an incipient nationalism. Saint-André argued that the duke was not the liege man of the king of France; Brittany and France were two separate entities and there was little respect amongst the Bretons for the French, an effeminate race of men with forked beards who

> Bien danczoint en salles jonchees,
> Et si chantoint comme serrenes,
> Les plus veulx ressambloint jeunes.[2]

Nor do the English fare much better despite acknowledgement of the assistance which they rendered to John IV in obtaining his duchy. The reader is exhorted to peruse Saint-André's book carefully and to draw from it the obvious lesson of history: the duke of Brittany, despite hardship and ill-fortune, has triumphed over his enemies, and by implication, established his rule.[3]

Another writer close to the duke and his court, who began the

---

1. In a work completed shortly after 1381, *Le Libvre de bon Jehan, duc de Bretaigne*, printed as an appendix to Jean Cuvelier, *Chronique de Bertrand de Guesclin*, ed. E. Charrière (2 vols., Paris, 1839), ii. 421–560. Cf. p. 521, lines 3025 ff.

> A eulx yrai-ge vrayement!
> Sanz plus tarder ne plus actendre
> G'iray a eulx pour les deffendre . . .
> Mon pais et ma nation

2. Ibid., p. 515, lines 2818 ff.   3. Ibid., pp. 459, 556, and *passim*.

Chronicon Briocense in 1394, shared these views.[4] In his final assessment of John IV he commented, 'suumque Ducatum Britannie et ejus libertates ac subditos contra quoscumque tuebatur et deffendebat atque in pace et tranquillitate servebat'.[5] Attempting to characterize the temperament of certain races, the author of the *Chronicon* described a world remote from his own era in which Greeks were vain, Romans prey to jealousy, Lombards greedy, Franks cruel and proud, Saxons treacherous, Bretons brave or foolhardy, Slavs drunkards, Saracens debauched, Jews oppressive, and Spaniards disorderly and abominable.[6] His dislike of contemporary Englishmen emerges every time he mentions the Saxons from whom they were descended.[7] Both the compiler of the *Chronicon* and Saint-André display an interest in Breton origins. Saint-André refers to the illustrious descent of his master from Brutus;[8] in the *Chronicon* emphasis is laid on the Breton language as the purest surviving form of ancient Trojan.[9] But these individual touches apart, the ideas, and the phraseology in which the authors expressed them, on the origins and identity of Brittany, the distinctiveness of its people, and the separateness of its institutions, follow a pattern common to many regions of western Europe. Professor Rubinstein, writing on Florence, comments generally that the beginnings of political thought are 'always closely related to the awakening of the interest in history, and in the early periods of society, interest in the past appears to be inseparable from the observation of existing conditions and from the expression of prevailing ideas'.[10] In a medieval Italian context the example of Rome provided the starting point for a historical investigation of urban state origins, identity, and development; in northern Europe origins were more often sought in the legends about Troy.[11] The differences between peoples inhabiting the various parts of Europe were crudely delineated; xenophobia predominated and, as in the Breton cases just cited, much description was as derivative as it was obligatory. The early parts of the

4. Partially edited in Morice, *Preuves*, i. 7–102. A new edition is in progress; *Chronicon Briocense: Chronique de Saint-Brieuc. Texte critique et traduction* (henceforward *Chronique de Saint-Brieuc*), ed. G. Le Duc and C. Sterckx, i (Paris, 1972). For possible authorship, see below, pp. 163–4.
5. Morice, *Preuves*, i. 78.   6. *Chronique de Saint-Brieuc*, i. 84.
7. Ibid. 50–54, 94, 118, and *passim*.
8. *Chronique de Bertrand de Guesclin*, ii. 447, lines 631 ff.
9. *Chronique de Saint-Brieuc*, i. 74 and 114.
10. N. Rubinstein, 'The Beginnings of Political Thought in Florence. A Study in Medieval Historiography', *Journal of the Warburg and Courtauld Institutes*, v (1942), 198.
11. B. Guenée, *L'Occident aux XIVe et XVe siècles. Les États* (Paris, 1971), pp. 124–30.

Chronicon Briocense, for example, depend heavily and not surprisingly on Geoffrey of Monmouth's *Historia Regum Britanniae*.

The search for a regional identity in the Middle Ages thus meets a number of obstacles; those which faced contemporaries when they wanted, for a wide variety of reasons, to describe or encourage regional differences; those which face historians of our own day trying to grasp the significance of abstract ideas to men of a remote period. Beginning from the documents, there is nothing exceptional in the way Breton chronicles, letters, legal and administrative documents make reference to 'le pais de Bretaigne' and 'la nation de Bretaigne'. The words *pais* and *nation* had evolved in French in a fairly direct manner from their classical counterparts, *patria* and *natio*. One's land of birth, *patria*, might be a region as large as a duchy or even a kingdom. It could also be a much smaller unit. These words were but two of the many medieval synonyms of 'province', a word later used to describe the various major geographical and administrative regions of France.[12] In Brittany men referred to the 'pais de Rays', to the 'pais de Dinannais', to the 'pais de Guérande' and so on.[13] From Isidore of Seville, who was himself summarizing classical usage, medieval man learnt that *natio* simply described a group of men having a common origin—*multitudo ab uno principio orta*[14]—like the students of the Breton nation at the University of Angers or the butchers of the Breton nation at Paris in the 1390s. Yet familiar phrases might take on new shades of meaning in the mouths of the duke and his advisers, as we shall see.

In the present century historians of all opinions have discussed at great length the characteristics of nationalism. It is not my intention to rehearse the many arguments; modern nationalism had medieval origins.[15] This essay attempts to discover how far the feelings of the

12. G. Dupont-Ferrier, 'Sur l'Emploi du mot "province", notamment dans le langage administratif de l'ancienne France', *Rev. Hist.* clx (1929), 241–67; Dupont-Ferrier, 'De quelques synonymes du terme "province"', ibid. clxi (1929), 278–303; Dupont-Ferrier, 'Le Sens des mots "patria" et "patrie" en France au Moyen Âge et jusqu'au début du XVIIe siècle', ibid. clxxxviii (1940), 89–104, citing Breton examples; B. Guenée, 'État et nation en France au Moyen Âge', ibid. ccxxxvii (1967), 17–30; and P. S. Lewis, *Later Medieval France. The Polity* (London, Toronto, and New York, 1968), pp. 1–4.

13. See Arch. Dép., Loire-Atlantique, E 147, no. 5, contemporary endorsement of a ducal *alliance*, 11 August 1379: 'Obligacion sur mons. Robin de Lanvalay et mons. Rogier de Beaufort et autres chevaliers et escuiers de Dinanaies pour servir le duc contre touz, etc.'

14. Guenée, 'État et nation en France', p. 19.

15. Gaines Post, *Studies in Medieval Legal Thought* (Princeton, New Jersey, 1964), pp. 434 ff.; Guenée, *L'Occident*, pp. 14–15 and 296–302.

Bretons were a spontaneous expression of a sense of regional identity, and how far they were the product of political and administrative activity on the part of the duke and his advisers, consciously encouraging such sentiments.[16] It will also investigate some of the forces that were operative to counteract the growth of regionalism; limitations of space prevent a full discussion of all the points raised, but it is hoped that this sketch will illustrate, from the case of Brittany, some of the characteristics of what Professor Galbraith aptly described as 'the primary groupings of the Middle Ages . . . the provincial or regional nationalities'.[17]

The great principalities of France, like the national state which eventually absorbed them, came into being and flourished only as a result of the constant attention of their rulers to the problem of creating loyalty to themselves and to the much more intangible concept of a regional state.[18] Evidence for this in Brittany can be found in the views elaborated by lawyers, representing the duke, and by writers at the ducal court, in the changing formulae and practices of the ducal chancery, in the visual symbolism of the coinage in daily use and the heraldic representation of ducal authority, in court ceremonial—all reminding ducal subjects of their common history, inheritance, and tradition.[19] The defence of a provincial society with its own privileges is neither novel nor limited to Brittany in fourteenth-century France. At the very moment when, according to Professor Guenée, in a broad sense a 'French' political community recognized that it formed an ethnic community,[20] the movement for provincial charters of liberties had just

16. I should like to thank John Le Patourel and Malcolm Vale for their help and criticism in the preparation of this essay.

17. V. H. Galbraith, 'Nationality and Language in Medieval England', *T.R.Hist.S.*, 4th ser. xxiii (1941), 114. He also remarks (p. 113), 'A nation may be defined as any group of people who believe they *are* one; and their nationalism as the state of mind which sustains this belief. Broadly speaking the sentiment of nationality is much the same in quality at all times and in all places. Its minimum content is love, or at least awareness, of one's country, and pride in its past achievements, real or fictitious; and it springs from attachment to the known and the familiar, stimulated by the perception of difference—difference of habits and customs, often too of speech from those of neighbouring peoples.'

18. See Lewis, *Later Medieval France*, pp. 59–77.

19. Some of these points are discussed below; others can only be mentioned briefly in passing, yet their importance is obvious, particularly where, as with chancery formulae and coinage, the pretensions of the dukes, their emulation of French royal practice and the infringement of royal sovereignty, can easily be discerned. For example, the adoption of the style 'par la grace de Dieu' around 1417, see *Lettres et mandements de Jean V, duc de Bretagne*, ed. R. Blanchard (5 vols., Nantes, 1889–95), i, p. xxxiv.

20. About 1318 (Guenée, 'État et nation en France', p. 21).

achieved expression.[21] The various 'nations' of France were to survive for another two centuries at least. Some historians have reacted too sharply against the tradition which sees French history purely in terms of the centralization of the country under an absolutist monarchy,[22] but there is still a danger that provincial feeling as an element in the history of France in the late Middle Ages can be under-rated, even though the techniques used by the provincial rulers owed much to royal example.

From the time when parts of the Armorican peninsula were settled by immigrants from southern Britain, Breton history followed a slightly different course from that of the rest of the kingdom of France. The failure of Charlemagne to incorporate fully the future area of the duchy into his empire and the dominance of the dukes of Normandy over the counts of Brittany in the eleventh and twelfth centuries reduced contact with the evolving French monarchy. The relationship of the duke, *sensu lato*, to the king of France was not regulated precisely until the homage agreements of the thirteenth century and the grant of peerage in 1297.[23] Although Philip III and Philip IV had begun to interfere in the affairs of the duchy, Brittany still stood somewhat apart from the kingdom at the beginning of the fourteenth century,[24] when certain sections of Breton society began to express views on the nature and status of the duchy. In 1314–15, for example, it is perhaps symbolic that such aspirations as there were in the duchy were channelled by the duke into obtaining the confirmation of legal privileges conceded by the Capetians in 1297, with additional restrictions on royal sergeants who had recently begun to operate on a more extensive scale in the duchy.[25] There was no general movement of the Breton nobility and, when such movements did occur in the fourteenth century, they favoured the strengthening of ducal power against any attempt by the king to exercise more direct rule in the duchy.[26] But Breton attempts to limit the extension of royal interference through its local representatives such as

21. A. Artonne, *Le Mouvement de 1314 et les chartes provinciales de 1315* (Paris, 1912), *passim*.
22. See Lewis, *Later Medieval France*, pp. 195–9.
23. J.-Fr. Lemarignier, *Recherches sur l'hommage en marche et les frontières féodales* (Lille, 1945), pp. 115 ff.; and P. Jeulin, 'L'Hommage de la Bretagne', *A. Bret.* xli (1934), 380–473.
24. H. Touchard, in *Histoire de la Bretagne*, ed. J. Delumeau (2nd ed., Toulouse, 1973), pp. 170–4.
25. Artonne, *Le Mouvement*, pp. 48–49.
26. In 1334, for example (R. Cazelles, *La Société politique et la crise de la royauté sous Philippe de Valois* (Paris, 1958), pp. 140–2), and in 1379 (see below, p. 163).

the *baillis* of the Cotentin, Touraine, and Poitou, through the appointment of royal clerks to important benefices, and through the acceptance
of appeals from the ducal courts in the *Parlement* of Paris, reflect a
general movement. This found supporters even in regions which had a
much more intimate and longer connection with the crown, as well as
amongst those who lived in the great fiefs on the periphery of the kingdom; Flanders, Burgundy, and Guyenne in particular.[27] With varying
degrees of emphasis, regional awareness based on a whole range of
ethnic, linguistic, cultural, artistic, political, and administrative traditions can be found in areas which lacked even the apparent unity of
the duchy of Brittany.

Recent works on the economy and social structure of the duchy have
tended, quite rightly, to insist on the huge range of geographical and
social diversities to be observed there.[28] Nevertheless in the fourteenth
century contemporaries did recognize the separateness of the duchy
behind well-defined frontiers. Sergeants in charge of those banished by
sentence of the ducal courts, for example, were ordered to take prisoners
'dehors le duche jusques a Pontorson, et aporter relation de [les] avoir
fait passer la riviere de Coaynon, comme il est de coustume'.[29] The exact
limits of the duchy were often known with extreme precision—in the
fifteenth century boundaries were even marked by posts bearing the
ducal arms.[30] Where the geographical bounds did not correspond to the
modern conception of a frontier, as in the marches separating the duchy
from Anjou and Poitou to the south of the Loire, the customs prevailing
in these areas were sufficiently defined for the inhabitants to know under
what law they lived, who their political master was, and for disputes to
be amicably settled between the duke of Brittany, and, say, the count of
Poitou.[31] When contemporaries referred to events 'in partibus Britannie' there was little ambiguity; they meant within the duchy of Brittany,

27. See R. Cazelles, 'Le Parti navarrais jusqu'à la mort d'Etienne Marcel', *Bulletin
philologique et historique (jusqu'à 1610) du comité des travaux historiques et scientifiques*
(1960), part ii. 845 ff.
28. H. Touchard, *Le Commerce maritime breton* (Paris, 1967), pp. 5–86; and J.
Meyer, *La Noblesse bretonne au XVIIIe siècle* (2 vols., Paris, 1966), i, pp. xii–xiii, and
passim.
29. Morice, *Preuves*, ii. 654.   30. Ibid. ii. 1660.
31. E. Chenon, 'Les Marches séparantes d'Anjou, Bretagne et Poitou', *Nouvelle
revue historique de droit français et étranger*, xvi (1891), 18–62 and 165–211; M. Jones,
Ducal Brittany 1364–1399 (Oxford, 1970), p. 124; in 1371 Mag. Jean Vitrier, king's
secretary and a native of Bouzillé (dép. Maine-et-Loire) described himself as 'in finibus
Andegavie et Britannie oriundus' (*Monuments du procès de canonisation du bienheureux
Charles de Blois, duc de Bretagne, 1320–64*, ed. F. Plaine (Saint-Brieuc, 1921), p. 174.)

whose inhabitants 'the gretteste rovers and the gretteste thevys'[32] had acquired a reputation for bravery and daring, qualities essential in their careers by land and sea, as royal mercenaries and in the *routier* companies, as sailors and pirates.[33]

In the context of fourteenth-century Brittany, it is possible to examine administrative developments under John IV (1364–99), in order to see how he was able to use the existing political situation to further claims to rule an independent duchy.[34] It has been traditional to view the civil war fought between the Montfortists and their English allies and the Penthièvre-Blois party, as the great turning point in the history of the duchy. In the first phase of the war the Montfortists established their claim to succeed; this was recognized by Charles V at the time of the first Treaty of Guérande (1365). A second phase, in which John IV's struggle with his one-time ally, Olivier, sire de Clisson, with other members of the Breton nobility and with his sovereign, was punctuated by the duke's exile (1373–9), the second Treaty of Guérande (1381) and a series of agreements which led to a more permanent peace with Clisson, and was finally concluded in 1395. As a result, warfare, though not continuous nor simultaneously affecting the whole of the duchy, was an important factor in maintaining disturbed conditions, creating tensions in Breton society, and providing John IV with the excuse, as well as the need, to develop a more extensive administrative machine. In these conditions increasing institutional maturity was encouraged by the quickening pace of political life, with more business for ducal courts, the *Parlement* and the beginnings of the *Etats*. Contrasting ducal administration before the civil war with that functioning afterwards, the government can be seen changing from a largely private, personal type, characteristic of feudal society in its prime, to an administration of a public nature with fixed institutions and personnel, small though numbers often were in central offices like the Chancery and *Chambre des Comptes*. As records accumulated, traditions developed and the expertise of ducal officers in using them to support ducal pretensions and authority increased. The civil war, the troubles of John IV's reign, and French distraction by the war with England, allowed the duke to

---

32. *The Libelle of Englyshe Polycye*, ed. G. Warner (Oxford, 1926), p. 9.
33. For Bretons in French royal armies see below, p. 162; as mercenaries see L. Mirot, 'Sylvestre Budes et les Bretons en Italie', *B.E.C.* lviii (1897), 579–614 and lix (1898), 262–303; and as sailors and pirates see Touchard, *Le Commerce, passim*.
34. See Jones, *Ducal Brittany*, for a more detailed account of these developments.

build up a *de facto* position of independence on which his fifteenth-century successors were to build. Pursuing policies at variance with the wishes of his sovereign, and even of his one-time guardian, the king of England, like his contemporaries, the cadet sons of John II of France and their cousins, John IV was concerned with power for his own ends. Yet it is inaccurate to suggest that it was only after the civil war that separatist feelings emerged in Brittany;[35] the war enabled the duke to cast off a number of restraints. His legislative competence, previously restricted by deference to seigneurial privilege and criticism, increased.[36] A more modern taxation system, taking into account seigneurial interests once again, was imposed with a fair degree of success after 1364, supplementing the financial monopolies and an expanded demesne available to dukes prior to the war.[37] Individual bishops, seigneurs, and towns might oppose ducal authority as they had done with impunity before 1341,[38] but by the reign of John IV, few were able to maintain their opposition for long, unless they were able to command the support of the king of France, like the citizens of Saint-Malo between 1387 and 1415.[39] The political balance within the duchy was tipping much more towards the duke and his officers in their attempts to limit privilege other than that granted and authorized by the duke. But it needs to be stressed that the ideological foundations of ducal action had not greatly changed as a result of the civil war; opportunities to make claims to independence a reality had simply improved.

Some evidence for this view can be gathered from the dukes' fulfilment of the obligations entered into when accepting the peerage in 1297. With reservations the dukes had generally served the king in the various capacities expected of them as peers in his court and army. Possessing the attributes of sovereignty, the king could hear appeals from the duchy, though only under two conditions (false judgement and denial of justice)—conditions, which were constantly being infringed, but which the king, especially in times of weakness, could only

35. A traditional view most recently reaffirmed in the otherwise excellent chapter by Touchard, in *Histoire de la Bretagne*, ed. Delumeau, pp. 187–8.

36. B-A. Pocquet du Haut-Jussé, 'La Genèse du législatif dans le duché de Bretagne', *Revue historique de droit français et étranger*, 4ᵉ sér. xl (1962), 351–72.

37. M. Jones, 'Les Finances de Jean IV, duc de Bretagne (1364–1399)', *Mémoires de la société d'histoire et d'archéologie de Bretagne*, lii (forthcoming).

38. B-A. Pocquet du Haut-Jussé, *Les Papes et les ducs de Bretagne* (2 vols., Paris, 1928), i. 234 ff. and 425.

39. Touchard, *Le Commerce*, pp. 83–85.

confirm.[40] He could also attempt to levy taxation in the duchy, publish royal *ordonnances* there, and interfere in the duke's issuing of coinage. Several of these matters were still claimed as royal prerogatives in the late fourteenth century, but by then John IV had been able to ensure that such claims had no practical importance.[41] Elements of ambiguity were introduced into the actual ceremony of liege homage. John IV and his advisers argued in 1366 that it was simple homage, a position they restated in 1381. This was repeated at future ceremonies until Louis XI, with a characteristically bold stroke (though unprofitable in the short-term) attempted to bring Francis II to heel by ignoring the form of words recently used in the ceremony, and insisting on the subject-status of the duke.[42]

In the case of homage the records used to back up ducal claims were not very convincing.[43] But there are other instances where the use of traditional arguments, enshrined in a series of legal briefs and other documents of an official or semi-official nature, shows how late-four-teenth-century claims for the powers of the duke and the status of his duchy depend substantially on a position adopted prior to the civil war. The *locus classicus* for such claims is in the dispute between John de Montfort and Charles de Blois for the succession to John III in 1341.[44] Many of the statements then made had already been adumbrated before the *Parlement* of Paris in 1336, in the case of John III *versus* Marie, countess of Saint-Pol, who was claiming a share in the succession to Duke John II (d. 1305).[45] Some of them are of interest for contemporary views of the character of French peerages in general. It was stated, for instance, that

les dictes parries et baronnies [de France] furent fondees premierement et entraduytes riches et puyssantes pour les noblesces et juridicions garder et pour la deffense des

40. Arch. Dép., Loire-Atlantique, E 110, no. 3, original letters of Philip IV, February 1297 (see Morice, *Preuves*, i. 1121), confirmed by Philip V in March 1317 and Charles IV in 1323 and 1324 (Arch. Dép., Loire-Atlantique, E 110, nos. 12, 13, and 15). Particularly notable are a series of letters from Philip VI, between 23 April and 16 June 1328, chiefly addressed to the *Parlement* of Paris to send back to Brittany any cases it had received contrary to customary form, and to respect ducal privileges, which were confirmed in accordance with letters of 1303, 1316, 1318, and 1319 (ibid., nos. 18–26).

41. Jones, *Ducal Brittany*, pp. 2–4 and 114 ff.; Morice, *Preuves*, ii. 629–33.

42. B-A. Pocquet du Haut-Jussé, 'Une Idée politique de Louis XI: la sujétion éclipse la vassalité', *Rev. Hist.* ccxxvi (1961), 383–98.

43. Jeulin, 'L'Hommage de la Bretagne', pp. 419–33.

44. 'Some Documents relating to the Disputed Succession to the Duchy of Brittany, 1341', ed. M. Jones, *Camden Miscellany*, xxiv (1972), 1, 15–70, and 75–76.

45. Ibid., pp. 4–5.

pays ou elles sont et especialment du Royaume, et que le Roy se en peust mieuz aydier, quant mectier en avient, quar de tant est il plus noble, plus fort et plus puyssant comme il a plus nobles et puyssanz subiez, les quielx ne seroyent puyssanz ne nobles si les dictes parries ou baronnies se partoyent, quar toute chose devisee est mains force de soy meymes que ne est une ensemble unie.[46]

Other points are similarly made about the weaknesses which follow from the division of great lordships among several heirs. The disadvantages affect not merely the lord, but ultimately 'le Roy et le Royaume' if the power of such lordships is diminished by division. The majority of the arguments used in 1336, however, with their claims resting on 'historical' foundations were intended to support the conclusion that 'le duc de Bretaigne ne la duche ne sont pas de autel condicion comme les autres pers et parries de France'.[47] As far as succession to the dukes was concerned, the proctors of John III argued that they stood above the customary laws of the duchy applicable in the case of noble successions. Even though they could find support for the indivisibility principle in the laws applied to other recent peerage successions, they pressed a much more dangerous line: 'Item, que ou temps passe la terre de Bretaigne fut Royaume . . . Item, que le Roy ou les Roys de Bretaigne pour le temps ne recognoissoyent nul soverain en terre. . . .'[48]

By 1341, then, royal lawyers were becoming familiar with some of the more extravagant Breton claims that the acceptance of the peerage by the duke in 1297 had not resulted in any diminution of his prerogatives as successor to former 'kings' of Brittany. The duchy was a jewel in the crown of France, a 'vroie escharboucle reluisant et erradiant en ilcelle',[49] but the duke's privileges, his 'regalities', were not to be shared with subject or far-off sovereign because Brittany possessed 'les droiz et nobleces de royaulme'.[50] Feelings might have been somewhat mollified by the critical qualification 'exceptee la soveraynete et le resort de son parlement que il volut que fust au Roy notresire'[51] for this was, of course, the key issue when new and ever more precise definitions of what constituted sovereignty threatened to undermine the ability of a duke to rule in his duchy, even if there were goodwill towards the

46. Arch. Nat., K 1152, no. 49, m. 1.   47. Ibid., m. 8.

48. Ibid., mm. 1 and 8; see Post, *Studies*, pp. 453 ff. For the use of similar arguments in fifteenth-century Burgundy, see J. Richard, ' "Enclaves" royales et limites des provinces. Les élections bourguignonnes', *A.B.* xx (1948), 107; and Y. Lacaze, 'Le Rôle des traditions dans la genèse d'un sentiment national au XVe siècle: La Bourgogne de Philippe le Bon', *B.E.C.* cxxix (1971), 303–85.

49. *Camden Miscellany*, xxiv (1972), 57.

50. Ibid., p. 23.   51. Ibid., p. 5, n. 19.

sovereign.[52] Yet if John III's lawyers thought in 1336 that their arguments about indivisibility and male succession might appeal to Philip VI,[53] in the light of royal succession problems since 1316, their boldness in pressing John's claims in these terms, in their definition of some of the particular characteristics of the duke's prerogatives,[54] must have put royal lawyers on their guard. Repetition of these claims in 1341 reveals a similar lack of sensitivity to royal views.[55] To a large extent, the issue of the Breton succession in 1341 was already predetermined by the close personal ties between Philip VI and his nephew, Charles de Blois, before the disputants reached court.[56] Royal advisers had a facility for producing arguments to buttress a decision politically favourable to the king on the question of important successions;[57] Breton claims to virtual independence espoused by Montfort cannot have helped his cause. They were, all the same, to be used with increasing frequency by his son and his successors. Repetition did not validate the authenticity of historical claims made on behalf of the dukes, but it did help to implant in the minds of their subjects an idea of those claims.[58]

Formal occasions for publicizing regional feelings were presented by meetings of the *Parlement*, and subsequently by meetings of the *Etats*, where the duke could consult thirty or more major nobles, the leading ecclesiastics, his legal officers, and representatives of the commons.[59] As a supplication to the king in 1384 stated:

Toutesfoiz quil en est doubte et que bon semble au prince, les prelaz, barons et commun doudit pais ou chose leur estre necessaire, tant de subsides que autres choses, au proulfit doudit pais le faire, len le fait, et pour laubsence de dun ne de dous

52. P. Chaplais, 'La Souveraineté du roi de France et le pouvoir législatif en Guyenne au début du XIVe siècle', *M.A.* lxix (1963), 449–69; J. Favier, 'Les Légistes et le gouvernement de Philippe le Bel', *Journal des Savants* (1969), pp. 92–108.

53. Arch. Nat., K 1152, no. 49, especially mm. 1, 2, 4, and 8.

54. Ibid., m. 8: 'Item, que de telles noblesces usa celi . . . duc qui ores est quar il a son parlement ou len appelle de ses senechalx et a la garde et les regalles des yglises quant elles vaquent et plusours autres noblesces *que ne ont pas les autres pers ou barons* (interlined) qui seront autres foyz decleries si mestier est . . .'; and *Camden Miscellany*, xxiv (1972), 5.

55. *Camden Miscellany*, xxiv (1972), 31, 34, 38, and 62–63.

56. On 17 April 1341, just a fortnight before the death of John III, Philip VI ordered a *vidimus* to be made of the terms of his confirmation of the marriage contract between Charles and Jeanne de Penthièvre, originally issued on 4 June 1337 (Arch. Nat., K 42, nos. 37, 37 *bis*, and 37 *ter*).

57. See *Camden Miscellany*, xxiv (1972), 4 and 9–10.

58. See below, pp. 163–4.

59. B-A. Pocquet de Haut-Jussé, 'Les Faux États de Bretagne de 1315 et les premiers états de Bretagne', *B.E.C.* lxxxvi (1925), 388–406.

ne tarde pas, puis la maire et plus saine partie se y abssant, et il est avise par le prince et son consaill ainssi le faire, *quia quod principi placuit legis habet vigorem.*[60]

But it was generally in the smaller ducal council that policy was formed and 'le conseil étant le reflet direct de la puissance ducale, sa competence est pratiquement illimitée'.[61] Its composition, at least for the late fourteenth century, is fairly well established. Even in the early years of John IV's reign, after the bitter struggles of the civil war and despite the presence in it of a few Englishmen, the council reflected a good cross-section of the duchy's nobility, the leading churchmen, and those with legal and administrative experience, often gained in the service of the late Charles de Blois.[62] In effect, the duke was not alone in being able to influence opinion about regional identity. His advisers, whether owing their position to social status or professional expertise, were also in a position to do so. It is interesting, therefore, to examine their opportunities for education in order to assess what kind of formative experiences and intellectual traditions they brought to their work as ducal councillors. In particular, a number of recent studies have emphasized the position of lawyers in the creation and maintenance of many specific characteristics of later medieval administrations, and it might be expected that the same would be true for Brittany.[63]

French historians have long assumed that education at a primary level was readily available in the later Middle Ages. Simeon Luce wrote, 'on ne peut guère douter que pendant les années même les plus agitées du quatorzième siècle la plupart des villages n'aient eu des maîtres enseignant aux enfants la lecture, l'écriture et un peu de calcul'. A. Dupuy, writing about fifteenth-century Brittany agreed.[64] Recent historians, more cautious than their forbears and anxious to document such wide claims, have been able to show that even if schools were not to be found in every parish, they were numerous enough in some areas.[65] From chance references in Breton sources, it can certainly be established that besides schools in the leading towns of the duchy, there were many, run

60. Morice, *Preuves*, ii. 457–8.

61. B-A. Pocquet du Haut-Jussé, 'Le Conseil du duc en Bretagne d'après ses procès-verbaux', *B.E.C.* cxvi (1958), 140.

62. Jones, *Ducal Brittany*, pp. 38–40 and 55–57.

63. Bibliography in Guenée, *L'Occident*, pp. 51–53.

64. S. Luce, *Histoire de Bertrand du Guesclin* (Paris, 1876), pp. 15–16; A Dupuy, *Histoire de la réunion de la Bretagne à la France* (2 vols., Paris, 1880), ii. 377–81.

65. For example, B. Guenée, *Tribunaux et gens de justice dans le bailliage de Senlis à la fin du Moyen Âge vers 1380–vers 1550* (Paris, 1963), pp. 186–8.

by parish priests or by professional schoolmasters, which flourished, at least briefly, in the countryside. Saint-Yves Helori learnt grammar just after the mid thirteenth century from the parish priest of Pleubian, who later accompanied his star pupil to the University of Orléans.[66] Schools existed at Machecoul and Bourgneuf in the *pays de Rays* in the mid fourteenth century.[67] At an inquiry held at Vannes in 1402, Jean Loppin, advocate in the court of the bishop's official, testified that he had gone to school at Landaul where Geoffroy Nesindre, master of sciences, grammar, and logic, was his mentor. Loppin had himself taught grammar at Muzillac around the year 1366 and had then directed a grammar school at Vannes.[68] This evidence is significant since the diocese of Vannes, one of the poorest in the duchy, appears to be the one which sent fewest students on to the universities.[69] That the lack of formal higher education was not in itself an impediment to lucrative and important office is shown from the case of Loppin himself or that of Rolland Poencé. Loppin had been befriended at Vannes by Mag. Jean le Thiec and Mag. Pierre de Cancouet, respectively official of the bishop and collector of apostolic dues. So well had he deputized for Cancouet during his absences from the diocese that he succeeded him as receiver for the chapter of Vannes, and began to take on commissions from neighbouring parishes which enabled him to practise as an advocate.[70] Poencé, a married clerk and native of the parish of Goudelin in the diocese of Tréguier, aged about fifty-three when he deposed at the inquiry at Angers in 1371 into Blois's sanctity, had chosen a secular career. As a clerk and notary he had served fifteen years 'in curia senescallorum' before becoming *alloué* and lieutenant to the seneschal of Guingamp. At about the same time he was appointed secretary to Blois and held this position for fifteen years until Charles's death, and for the last four years he had also been seneschal of Cornouaille.[71] But among the secretaries of Charles de Blois there were men with university degrees, the duke

66. *Monuments originaux de l'histoire de St-Yves*, ed. A. de la Borderie *et al.* (Saint-Brieuc, 1887), pp. 8, 15, 36–37, and 41.
67. 'Cartulaire des sires de Rays', ed. R. Blanchard, *Archives historiques de Poitou,* xxviii (1898), xviii; Arch. Nat., 1 AP 606, fo. 75, accounts rendered to Alienor de Thouars, 10 June 1360: 'Mise de vin: Item, 1 pipe au mestre de l'escole (de Bourgneuf).'
68. Arch. Dép. Morbihan, 58 G 1, fos. 83–85 ᵛ; see *Inventaire sommaire, Morbihan, série G*, ed. J. de la Martinière, G. Duhem and P. Thomas-Lacroix (Vannes, 1940), ii. 165. Other witnesses, too, made reference to their schooling.
69. Pocquet, *Les Papes*, i. 226, and below, pp. 158–9.
70. See above, n. 68.
71. *Monuments*, ed. Plaine, pp. 135 ff.

had himself received a clerk's education and he liked to dine with learned men.[72]

A factor which may have militated against the growth of a specifically Breton intellectual outlook or tradition in the fourteenth century was the lack of a *studium generale*.[73] Bretons seeking higher education had to leave the duchy. The influence of the schools of the Loire valley, and of Paris, where four colleges were established by the early fourteenth century for Breton students, may be suspected where it is at first difficult to demonstrate.[74] There are hints of the influence of this academic training on the circle of ducal advisers, amongst whom must be numbered in the reign of John III the compilers of *La très ancienne coûtume*, with its borrowings from Roman law and the customary law of Anjou and Touraine.[75] At an earlier date, Saint-Yves had gone on to Orléans University after Paris, whence he returned to Brittany to practise as an official in the ecclesiastical courts of the archdeacon of Rennes and the bishop of Tréguier. Yet contact with wider cultural horizons in cosmopolitan universities did not automatically obliterate provincial attitudes. In the case of Saint-Yves, on his return to the duchy, not only did he display his newly acquired knowledge of the law and an increasing asceticism (marked by the use of his copy of the *Decretals* as a pillow), but also the appropriate Breton stance in opposition to royal attempts to levy taxation in the duchy.[76] Many Bretons were to follow his example in obtaining an education outside the duchy; by the later fourteenth century, an increasing proportion of those who returned can be found in the service of a duke, who was pledged to the defence of a regional political identity.

There does, however, appear to have been an interesting change with regard to the popularity of particular universities, if the evidence of the rolls for benefices, submitted to the pope, can be relied upon for tracing the careers of Bretons in the absence of matriculation records.[77] Paris

72. For example, ibid., pp. 44–46, 56–60, and 84–89, for secretaries; 11–16 and 54 for duke's education; 30 and 56 for dining habits.

73. Documents concerning the abortive attempts by John V to found a university at Nantes in 1414, and its subsequent establishment in 1460, can be found in *Les Statuts et privilèges des universités françaises depuis leur fondation jusqu'en 1789*, ed. M. Fournier (3 vols., Paris, 1890–2), iii, nos. 1588–95.

74. *Histoire de la Bretagne*, ed. Delumeau, p. 165.

75. *La Très Ancienne Coûtume de Bretagne*, ed. M. Planiol (Rennes, 1896), pp. 7–11; cf. J.-Ph. Levy, 'La Pénétration du droit savant dans les coûtumes angevins et bretons au Moyen Âge', *Tijdschrift voor Rechtsgeschiedenis*, xxv (1957), 1–53.

76. *Monuments Originaux*, ed. de la Borderie *et al.*, pp. 28 and 46.

77. The rolls present disadvantages for statistical analysis; there is no means of

maintained its importance for those who wished to enter the higher faculties of theology, canon law, and medicine, and cases can be cited of Breton graduates of Orléans and Angers transferring to Paris to continue their studies and to teach.[78] Paris was also the university most favoured by Bretons from the dioceses of Quimper, Saint-Brieuc, Saint-Pol-de-Léon, and Tréguier. Saint-Malo produced a number of graduates but the other four Breton dioceses sent only a handful each of students to Paris.[79] Yet the number of Paris graduates entering directly into the ducal administration was small, and by the 1370s, Orléans had lost ground to Angers. There the Breton element, more numerous even than at Paris, although only comprising one of the six nations, appears to have dominated the university.[80] The majority of Bretons came from the dioceses of Rennes, Saint-Malo, Nantes, and Quimper. In the case of the first three, the proximity of Angers, its emphasis on law and the recent strong patronage of Louis, duke of Anjou, son-in-law of the late Charles de Blois, may have attracted them. As for the diocese of Quimper, its over-all educational record deserves more attention than it can receive here, since it provided the highest number of Breton students at Paris and Orléans,[81] and comes second in the list for Breton students at the three universities under discussion. There was a long tradition of learning at Quimper but it is also indicative of contemporary concern with educational matters which appears to be more evident there than in any other Breton chapter in the late fourteenth century.[82]

---

telling what proportion of university members are included, or even, on occasion, whether the man for whom a benefice was being sought was resident.

78. Statements about Paris University are based on *Chartularium Universitatis Parisiensis*, ed. H. Denifle and E. Châtelain (4 vols., Paris, 1889–97), ii (1286–1350) and iii (1350–94).

79. Calculations based on ibid. ii, nos. 1164–5; and iii, nos. 1263, 1265, 1304, 1307–8, 1426, 1429, 1431–7, 1496, 1539, 1541, and 1563, show that Breton dioceses were represented by the following totals of teachers and students for the period 1349–88: Quimper, 71 names; Saint-Brieuc, 52; Léon, 49; Tréguier, 36; Saint-Malo, 16; Nantes and Vannes, 5 each; Rennes and Dol, 4 each. These figures cannot be used as absolute numbers; some names are repeated in different rolls (see also above, p. 157, n. 77).

80. Statistics for Angers are calculated from *Les Statuts*, ed. Fournier, iii, nos. 1894–8. For the period 1362–93, 382 Breton names appear on the rolls as opposed to 242 at Paris from 1349–88. Totals, by diocese, as for Paris, are: Rennes, 113 names; Saint-Malo, 74; Nantes, 65; Quimper, 35; Vannes, 25; Dol, 21; Tréguier, 20; Saint-Brieuc, 16; Léon, 13. See A. Coville, *La Vie intellectuelle dans les domaines d'Anjou—Provence de 1380 à 1435* (Paris, 1941), pp. 506 ff. for the history of the University of Angers.

81. *Les Statuts*, ed. Fournier, iii, nos. 1888–91, give the following figures for Orléans for the period 1378–94; Quimper, 11 names; Rennes and Tréguier, 9 each; Léon, 7; Saint-Malo, 6; Nantes, 3; Dol and Saint-Brieuc, 2 each; Vannes, 0.

82. For Geoffroy le Marhec, bishop of Quimper (1357–83), see *Chartularium*, ed. Denifle and Châtelain, ii. 1164 and note; for the chapter library and its use, see *Cartulaire*

Angers was dominated by legal studies, and out of 286 bachelors in the Faculty of Law for whom benefices were sought in 1378, 117 were definitely of Breton origin; in 1393 the figures were 49 Bretons out of 96. In 1378 at least 84 out of 188 scholars were Bretons; in 1393, 44 out of 95.[83] Among the bachelors and scholars were a future chancellor of the duchy, bishops, abbots, ducal secretaries (including Guillaume de Saint-André), and notaries.[84] Among those with higher degrees, 22 out of 73 licentiates in law in 1378 at Angers were Bretons, while the corresponding number in 1393 was 12 out of 22.[85] Guy de Cleder, described in 1363 as 'legum doctoris ordinarie in eodem studio regentis et qui jam per septem annos vel circa rexit',[86] was a councillor of Charles de Blois and his wife, whom he represented at Guérande in 1365, and also of John IV. He was still trying to accumulate more benefices as a professor at Angers in 1393.[87] Hugues de Keroulay, a doctor of both laws, professor at Angers in 1378, was later in John IV's council and became bishop of Tréguier, following a standard career pattern.[88] There were two Raouls de Caradeuc from the diocese of Quimper. One was doctor of both laws as early as 1371 and may still have been teaching as late as 1418; it is more likely, however, that the survivor then was the second Raoul, described as a bachelor in decretals in 1378.[89] One of them, at least, undertook diplomatic missions for John IV and sat on his council,[90] many members of which in the 1380s and 1390s had been

---

de l'Église de Quimper, ed. Abbé Peyron (Quimper, 1909), nos. 334–5, 385, 401, and 429 In 1349 there is mention of Guillaume, son of 'magistri Guidomari rectoris quondam scolarum gramaticalium de Kemper Corentino et Margareta filia Francisci Pergamenarii eius uxor' (ibid., no. 300).

83. *Les Statuts*, ed. Fournier, iii, nos. 1896–8.

84. For Robert Brochereul, chancellor 1396–9, ibid., no. 1897; for bishops, see below, p. 160; for Jean le Bart, future abbot of Saint-Melaine, and for Saint-André, see ibid.; for Jean Hilari and Geoffroy Coglais, ducal secretaries in the 1380s, see ibid., no. 1898; for Guillaume Chauvin, priest, and later a notary, see ibid. Breton notaries as a group deserve further study; twelve are named in the 1371 *procès* alone (*Monuments*, ed. Plaine, *passim*).

85. *Les Statuts*, ed. Fournier, loc. cit.

86. Ibid., no. 1895. In 1369 he received a dispensation for non-residence (Pocquet, *Les Papes*, i. 380, n. 4).

87. Jones, *Ducal Brittany*, pp. 39, 58, and 85; *Les Statuts*, ed. Fournier, iii, no. 1898.

88. Ibid., no. 1897. As archdeacon of Désert he witnessed a ducal protestation on 28 October 1380 (Morice, *Preuves*, ii. 296). For lists of Breton bishops, see *Series Episcoporum*, ed. P. B. Gams (2nd ed., Leipzig, 1931).

89. *Les Statuts*, ed. Fournier, iii, nos. 1896–7; *Monuments*, ed. Plaine, p. 414; M. Fournier, *Histoire de la science du droit en France*, iii (Paris, 1892), 199.

90. See Nantes, Bibliothèque Municipale, MS. 1703, no. 3[ii], 17 February 1382, Mr. Raoul de Caradeuc and Mr. Guy de Cleder in the ducal council; Arch. Dép., Loire-Atlantique, E 92, no. 20, 27 October 1382, appointment of these two and Nicolas du

contemporaries at Angers in the 1370s. This pattern persisted into John V's reign.[91]

It has recently been demonstrated that friendships made at the university amongst future members of the *Parlement* of Paris survived into later life.[92] But how far Breton councillors shared more than a similar academic training with each other, and how far their master shared anything more than political confidences with them, remain intriguing mysteries. The most distinguished Breton bishops, like Geoffroy le Marhec, bishop of Quimper (1357–83),[93] and Everart de Trémaugon, bishop of Dol (1382–6),[94] were not very close to the duke, and other Breton bishops who became cardinals in this period were drawn away from the duchy to Avignon and Rome. Those who remained, like Keroulay, Bonabé de Rochefort, bishop of Nantes (1392–8),[95] and Gacien de Monceaux, bishop of Quimper (1408–16)[96] had been trained in law, and like Henry and Guy le Barbu, Richard de Lesmenez, and Guillaume le Briz, received their bishoprics largely as a reward for administrative services to the duke.[97] There is some evidence that members of noble families, from the most important to the lesser gentry, were likewise fitting themselves for ducal service by attending the University of Angers.[98]

The cultural interests of the nobility as a whole for this period still remain uninvestigated. It would appear, however, that they did not take any specifically Breton form.[99] Their main concern was with the build-

---

Perche, to deliver 12,500 francs to Charles VI; and ibid., H 352, no. 1, 13 December 1382, ducal order to the seneschal of Nantes, on complaint of the prioress of Bourg des Moustiers, witnessed by Cleder and Caradeuc, drawn up by Saint-André as ducal secretary.

91. See Coville, *La Vie intellectuelle*, p. 512.

92. F. Autrand, 'Les Librairies des gens du Parlement au temps de Charles VI', *Annales E.S.C.* xxviii (1973), 1241.

93. See above, p. 158, n. 82.

94. See A. Coville, *Everart de Trémaugon et le Songe du Vergier* (Paris, 1933).

95. Listed amongst the *nobiles* at Angers in 1378 as a clerk of Nantes diocese and scholar in laws (*Les Statuts*, ed. Fournier, iii, no. 1897).

96. Amongst the second year scholars in 1378 (ibid.), ducal secretary and councillor from the 1380s. For some of the terms of his will, see *Cartulaire*, ed. Peyron, no. 494.

97. See Pocquet, *Les Papes*, i, *s.n.*

98. *Les Statuts*, ed. Fournier, iii, no. 1897. A key example is Robert Brochereul, sire de la Sicaudais, a minor seigneury in the *pays de Rays*, who rose to be chancellor of the duchy (see above, p. 159, n. 84) and who married his daughters into the prestigious families of Montfort and Montauban (a scion of whom was a contemporary at Angers, *Les Statuts*, ed. Fournier, iii, no. 1897). See Jones, *Ducal Brittany*, pp. 59 and 99; and A. Du Paz, *Histoire généalogique de plusieurs maisons illustres de Bretagne* (Paris, 1619), pp. 550–3.

99. It would be interesting to know who owned the early fifteenth-century copy of

ing and decoration of their castles and manors rather than with academic matters.[100] Some ducal servants did dabble with subjects of a conventional kind. Guillaume de Saint-André, besides his historical work and the daily chores of his secretarial duties, was the author of a laboured paraphrase of an earlier *Jeu des échecs moralisés*. This lacks intellectual sparkle, although there are one or two pleasing observations.[101] It reveals, as do surviving lists of books owned by clerics and notaries,[102] the essentially conservative character of Breton cultural life at a point when more stimulating and astringent works were already causing excitement in literary circles in Paris,[103] and when a more learned and artistic tradition flourished at the court of Charles V and his brothers.

The lack of originality and general poverty of Breton court life is reflected in the duchy at large by the failure of most testators to make provision for educational foundations, and by the absence from most wills of manuscripts, apart from devotional manuals.[104] Most interest was directed towards aspects of religious devotion,[105] though there was some awareness amongst non-clerical elements of the population of the importance of learning. Numerous Breton witnesses at the inquiry in 1371 claimed to be *illiteratus* in the exact medieval meaning of that word.[106] However, many knights and esquires, whose calling did not in the first instance require them to be able to write, could by the late

---

Le Songe du Vieil Pèlerin, sheets of which were later used to wrap documents in the *Chambre des Comptes* at Nantes (Arch. Dép., Loire-Atlantique, Parchemins, non classés, liasses 5 and 15). I hope to examine this aspect of the nobility elsewhere; my remarks stem from an examination of the few surviving fourteenth-century accounts.

100. H. Waquet, *Art Breton* (Paris, 1960), pp. 65–72.

101. F. Lecoy, 'Guillaume de St-André et son "Jeu des échecs moralisés"', *Romania*, lxvii (1942–3), 491–503.

102. See *Mélanges historiques bretons* (Société des Bibliophiles Bretons, Nantes, 1883), pp. 192–6, for the sale of certain books once belonging to Mag. Guillaume Hequenoille, chanter of Rennes cathedral, 1338–71. They included a *Code*, a *Digest*, a *Decretum* together with a commentary on it, a *Sext*, a psalter, and a *Golden Legend* (which was also the favourite reading of Charles de Blois, see *Monuments*, ed. Plaine, p. 30). Mag. Pierre Dorenge, an important notary living at Nantes, frequently employed by the duke, left at his death in 1395 only four books which he thought fit to mention in his will: a breviary, a bible, a *Golden Legend*, and an '*Ystorias scolasticas*' (Arch. Dép., Loire-Atlantique, H 483).

103. Autrand, 'Les Librairies', pp. 1220 and 1237–41.

104. A convenient list of some surviving wills can be found in A. Perraud, *Étude sur le testament d'après la coûtume de Bretagne* (Rennes, 1921), pp. 251–61.

105. For example, see Morice, *Preuves*, ii. 658–60 and 716–21, for the wills of Jean, vicomte de Rohan (1395), and his wife (1401).

106. *Monuments*, ed. Plaine, pp. 131, 156, 176, and 179. Among those who claimed to be literate was Michel Barbelot, ducal barber, who had been a servant of the Carthusians of Paris (ibid., p. 162).

fourteenth century at least sign their names.[107] This indicates some acquaintance with the rudiments of learning. But, it must be emphasized, this was not distinctively Breton. Like the duke and his court, the *noblesse* and clergy followed French traditions, even when, like Mathieu Bovis (an otherwise unknown clerk of the diocese of Léon, who finished copying a manuscript of the sayings of St. Augustine in 1358), their feelings towards the French lacked charity.[108]

The attitudes of the Breton *noblesse* towards France were bound to be ambivalent. There was always primitive patriotism and loyalty to one's homeland. *Pugna pro patria* was a well-known adage.[109] Those ignorant of it could exemplify its spirit as did Yvo d'Alnet, a Breton esquire, held prisoner at Poitiers around All Saints' Day, 1370.[110] Provoked beyond endurance by the reproaches of a Gascon man-at-arms who claimed that Gascons were better fighters and more loyal than Bretons, Yvo sought leave before the court of the seneschal of Poitou to wage battle for the honour of his countrymen, despite the superior size of his opponent, the Bourc de Caumont, who had already accounted for three men in such duels. Having admittedly taken the precaution of vowing himself to the saintly Charles de Blois, whose name (*in gallice*) he had had embroidered on his sleeve as a token, he nevertheless considered it miraculous that he had defeated and killed the Bourc.

Yet France offered tempting prospects to the Breton *noblesse*, many of whom had followed Bertrand du Guesclin into the royal armies.[111] The royal administration absorbed the talents of a number of Bretons: Paris University provided an outlet for those of the most highly trained Bretons.[112] Guillaume de Saint-André describes du Guesclin's dilemma in 1379:

> Glequin qui Connestable estoit,
> Trop grand dueil en son cueur avoit,
> De la guerre et dissention,

---

107. See Arch. Dép., Loire-Atlantique, E 137–48, *passim*, for a series of letters of fealty, obligations, *alliances*, etc., bearing signatures of the *noblesse* for the late fourteenth century.

108. L. Delisle, *Le Cabinet des Manuscrits de la Bibliothèque Nationale* (4 vols., Paris, 1868–81), i. 492.

109. Post, *Studies*, p. 436.   110. *Monuments*, ed. Plaine, pp. 247–9.

111. P. Contamine, *Guerre, état et société à la fin du Moyen Âge. Études sur les armées des rois de France, 1337–1494* (Paris and The Hague, 1972), pp. 155–7 and 162–3.

112. M. Fournier, *La Faculté de Décret de l'Université de Paris au XVe siècle* (Paris, 1895), pp. 127 ff.

> Estant entre sa nation,
> Et les Francois que il amoit.[113]

When the duke was at loggerheads with France, Breton pensioners of the king found that their lands and all the other ties of family alliance, the tangible and intangible links, which bound a man to his native soil, were bound to suffer. In the years 1379–81 they decided that the price to be paid for the restoration of peaceful conditions should not be the sacrifice of the virtual autonomy achieved by successive dukes.[114]

It was the task of the duke and his councillors to build on this shaky foundation of political loyalty. They turned increasingly to various aids which would help them to foster natural feelings of loyalty. Propaganda for their point of view took legal and literary, visual and symbolic form, as they sought to create a ducal mystique which reflected, in a shadowy form, that which surrounded the king of France.[115] With regard to the duke's legal claims, not only did he make representations at Paris, based on the claims current in the days of John III, but there is some evidence to show the deliberate popularization of these views of the duchy's history and status. At an inquiry into ducal prerogatives carried out in 1392, as at a similar inquiry in 1455, a wide range of witnesses testified to the verity of the pseudo-legal and historical justifications of ducal pretensions which stemmed directly from arguments advanced before the civil war.[116] It would seem that witnesses may have been carefully chosen beforehand and primed on the answers required; some certainly replied in terms suspiciously close to the wording of earlier council statements on ducal rights.[117] An exercise like the 1392 inquiry also helped to condition Bretons and encouraged expression of their regional identity. A similar purpose may have been behind the literary work of Saint-André and the writer of the *Chronicon Briocense*. The use by the latter of original documents *in extenso* and the imaginative fabrication of spurious documents to authenticate actions of earlier rulers of the duchy which surviving historical evidence failed to corroborate, betrays a man closely in touch with ducal ideas at this

---

113. *Chronique de Bertrand de Guesclin*, ii. 536, lines 3526–30. Cf. B.-A. Pocquet du Haut-Jussé, 'La Dernière Phase de la vie de Du Guesclin; l'affaire de Bretagne', *B.E.C.* cxxv (1967), 142–89.

114. Morice, *Preuves*, ii. 214–18 and 273–80. I hope to study Breton pensioners of France elsewhere.

115. See Lewis, *Later Medieval France*, pp. 81–84.

116. Morice, *Preuves*, ii. 595–7 and 1651–68, and see, for instance, *Camden Miscellany*, xxiv (1972), 23.

117. See Morice, *Preuves*, ii. 457–8.

stage.[118] The *Chronicon* was shaped to contemporary needs; it built on existing popular traditions and encouraged loyalty to the fledgling state.[119]

Since the kings of France, supremely blessed by God, who had endowed them miraculously with gifts like the coronation oil, the sacred *oriflamme*, and the ability to touch for the king's evil, used such methods to build up their power,[120] it is not remarkable that the dukes of Brittany, who had their kings and saints of old, should imitate them. John IV was naturally at pains to stamp out the cult of his defeated rival, Charles de Blois, but payments by him in 1393 'pour enchasser partie des reliques de Saint Salomon et de Saint Grallon jadis roys de Bretaigne predecesseurs de monseigneur . . .'[121] were a small investment for the potential otherworldly assistance these long-deceased monarchs might provide. Nor was this the first time in the fourteenth century that chieftains of the late Roman or Carolingian periods were recalled. John's father ransacked all sources for evidence to support his claims to succeed John III in 1341. His lawyers alleged that 'croniques et escript-tures' showed conclusively 'quil ot plusours rois en Bretaigne ou temps passe et le premier fut Salemons qui ot guerre contre Charlles le Grant, le Roy Cohel et le Roy Chouable et le Roy Arbams et plusours autres qui sont nommez aes ystoires de Bretaigne . . .'[122] and some of the implications drawn from these views have already been mentioned. But Charles de Blois, for all his Valois connections, came to value these Breton traditions sufficiently to have himself portrayed in a window at one of his favourite convents in the company of his saintly predecessors, Salomon and the other 'kings' of Brittany, whose cult he encouraged.[123] Other visual symbolism included the use of ducal armorial bearings displayed on buildings, especially on property taken into the ducal

118. The most likely author so far suggested is Mag. Hervé le Grant. In addition to arguments advanced by M. Pocquet du Haut-Jussé ('La Dernière Phase', p. 145), it can be noted that Hervé was probably responsible for a copy of the thirteenth-century *Livre des Osts*, which included the revised Breton version of the homage owed to France, current from 1366 (Arch. Dép., Loire-Atlantique, E 132, fos. 18–19ᵛ), and also a copy (ibid., fo. 2) of the forged charter mentioning the nine baronies of the duchy, which is also found in the *Chronicon Briocense* (Morice, *Preuves*, ii. p. xxv; A. de la Borderie, *Étude historique sur les neuf barons de Bretagne* (Rennes, 1895), p. ii).

119. For a fine fabrication, see the pseudo-charter of 689 issued by 'Alanus Dei Gratia Letauiorum seu Armoricanorum Britonum Rex' (*Chronique de Saint-Brieuc*, i. 216–24).

120. Lewis, *Later Medieval France*, pp. 65 ff.

121. Arch. Dép., Ille-et-Vilaine, I F 1111 (3 September 1393).

122. *Camden Miscellany*, xxiv (1972), 23.

123. *Monuments*, ed. Plaine, pp. 53, 67, and 137.

safeguard.[124] The right to the arms of the duchy was a subject of controversy in 1341 and in later diplomatic negotiations.[125] Their impact on the imagination was often all too vivid. Witnesses at Angers in 1371 deposed that they recognized Blois in visions by the arms of Brittany which he bore.[126] The *Chronicon Briocense* recounted, with more than its usual disregard for historical niceties, a story about King Arthur adopting ermines in place of three gold crowns on an azure field.[127] The ducal coronation service, and other occasions for ceremonial display, like the chapters of the Order of the Ermine, founded in about 1381, would likewise have accustomed Bretons to seeing symbolic and heraldic representation of ducal authority.[128]

But there were limitations to the extent of this persuasion and when lawyers could argue that 'le pais de Bretaigne est un pais distinct et separe dautres'[129] such limitations should be noted. In particular, it may indeed appear strange that ducal propagandists did not exploit, in the defence of a regional identity, the Celtic element, which, like Low Dutch in Flanders, Tout thought 'made for the regional unity of those regions under their duke or count'.[130] Even though many of the supporters of John de Montfort had come from the principal Breton-speaking regions, the only evidence of appeal to the Breton language as a rallying point for the disaffected lies in indirect remarks in the *Chronicon Briocense*.[131] The sum total of written Breton surviving for the whole of

124. For example, *Cartulaire de l'abbaye de St-Sulpice-la-Forêt*, ed. Dom Anger (Rennes, 1911), pp. 318–20 (18 June 1392); 'Item, pour taille et faire bannieres dermines a mectre sur les porrtes du chastel et de la ville de Doul et sur la grant tour, et pappier armaye darmes a mectre es barriers, portes, maisons et moulin, pour taele pappier et sallaire des paintres . . . xv s.', accounts of Jean le Fauchoms, receiver of the *régale* of Dol, 1391–2 (Arch. Dép., Loire-Atlantique, E 63, no. I, m. 3); see F. L. Cheyette, 'The Royal Safeguard in Medieval France', *Studia Gratiana*, xv (1972), 645–6.

125. *Camden Miscellany*, xxiv (1972), 49 and 52–53; Morice, *Preuves*, i. 1590 and ii. 582.

126. *Monuments*, ed. Plaine, p. 395.

127. *Chronique de Saint-Brieuc*, i. 198; see, also, G. Brault, 'The Use of Plain Arms in Arthurian Legend and the Origin of the Arms of Brittany', *Bulletin bibliographique de la société internationale arthurienne* (1966), pp. 117–23.

128. *Camden Miscellany*, xxiv (1972), 60 and n. 101, for coronation. The early history of the Order of the Ermine is obscure, but see Jones, *Ducal Brittany*, p. 140. The deference of Charles V to Breton sensibilities is seen in his allowing coinage circulating in the duchy during the duke's exile to bear the legend *Moneta Britannie*, and ermine spots (ibid., p. 56, n. 1 for references).

129. Morice, *Preuves*, ii. 457.

130. T. F. Tout, *France and England, their Relations in the Middle Ages and Now* (Manchester, 1922), p. 16.

131. Jones, *Ducal Brittany*, p. 11; *Chronique de Saint-Brieuc*, i. 74.

the fourteenth century, apart from the occasional names of places,
people, and particular Celtic customs, amounts to six short lines of
indifferent verse from a clerk of sensual and scatalogical tendencies
(who was more at home in Latin than in Breton) and a couple of
phrases noted down after a riot at Vannes in 1398.[132] It is well attested
that Breton was spoken widely, and not just by the peasantry, west of a
line running approximately from Saint-Brieuc to the *pays de Guérande*.
Four interpreters were required to assist in the taking of evidence into
the sanctity of Saint-Yves;[133] at Angers in 1371, Alain Tardif, *lector* at
the Franciscan convent of Angers, and Even de Haya, esquire, 'Brit-
tones Brittonizantes' acted in the same capacity.[134] On that occasion,
too, Erard de Léon, aged fifty-five, knight, sire de Fremèreville, in the
diocese of Amiens, but a cadet of the Léon family of Finistère, deposed
that he had known a Breton-speaking servant of Count Guy de
Penthièvre, whose sight had been restored through the intercession of
Guy's son-in-law, Charles de Blois 'et hoc scit quia Britonnicum
Brictonizans bene et congrue loquebatur; et hoc scit iste quia dictum
ydioma Brictonicum bene novit', even though he had been absent 'a
patria Brittanie' for thirteen years.[135] Parish priests in the four dioceses
of *Bretagne-bretonnante* must have been able to speak the vernacular in
order to hear confessions,[136] though it is doubtful whether all their
diocesans could have easily emulated them.[137]

As for the dukes, Charles de Blois, despite preference for his estates
in the Trégorrois, his above-average ability for study and his didactic
manner, never learnt to speak Breton,[138] and there is no conclusive
evidence that the other fourteenth-century dukes, who favoured living
in the Vannetais, were any more successful. It can be argued, of course,
that this state of affairs is only natural since the dukes came of families of
French descent and were, if only with moderate enthusiasm, imbued

132. J. Loth, 'Le Plus Ancien Texte suivi en Breton', *Revue Celtique*, xxxiv (1913),
241–8; E. Ernault, 'Encore du Breton d'Ivonet Omnes', ibid., pp. 249–52; Arch. Dép.,
Morbihan, 58 G 1, fo. 53 ᵛ: 'et quando idem magister Yvo exivit portam Sancti Paterni
omnes tam viri quam mulieres de burgo Sancti Paterni ceperunt clamare quod eciam
Sancti Paterni clauderentur, dicendo britanice, "Ferwet, ferwet, ferwet, donet avant",
quod est dicere, "Claudite, claudite, claudite, ipsi, ipsi, venerunt . . ." '.
133. K. H. Jackson, *A Historical Phonology of Breton* (Dublin, 1967), pp. 35–36;
Monuments originaux, ed. de la Borderie *et al.*, pp. 122–3.
134. *Monuments*, ed. Plaine, p. 318.
135. Ibid., pp. 393–5.
136. Ibid., pp. 398–400, for an example.
137. See Pocquet, *Les Papes*, i. 201–3 and 226 ff.
138. *Monuments*, ed. Plaine, p. 48.

with the traditions of French chivalric culture.[139] But in England where the same is largely true of both Edward I and Edward III, these kings appealed to their subjects for the defence of the English language when threatened by France.[140] In Wales, Owen Glyn Dŵr followed suit, in measures to preserve Welsh identity through its distinctive speech, at the time of his revolt against the English.[141] Flanders, like Brittany, was divided linguistically; Louis de Mâle, cousin to John IV of Brittany, one of his closest friends and whose political ambitions were very comparable, flattered his Flemish-speaking subjects by corresponding with them in their native tongue.[142] Only in modern times has the conjunction of the vernacular and nationality in Brittany self-consciously imitated the pattern set by French, Italian, and English in the later Middle Ages.

The growth of regional identity in Brittany at this time was slow and uncertain. Basic elements of unity were provided by geography, by a shared administrative and political experience, and by emotional loyalty to the duchy and a Breton people. But there were weaknesses in the ducal position. The attraction of service in the royal army and administration for the politically dominant *noblesse* of the duchy was a major factor in undermining the ducal position in 1372, as it was to be in the later fifteenth century.[143] The continuing attraction of the French court, and the ideals for which the monarchy stood, robbed the movement for Breton autonomy of some of the psychological appeal which might have been nurtured by the development of a cultural life entirely separate from that of royal France. Furthermore until 1460, it was necessary for Bretons who wished to obtain higher education, to travel outside the duchy, especially to universities in the kingdom or established in a rival ducal principality. Yet within the ducal court, which was to be overhauled and modernized by the guardian of John V, Philip,

139. See Sarah V. Spilsbury, 'On the Date and Authorship of *Artus de Bretaigne*', *Romania*, xciv (1973), 505–22, for possible interest at the ducal court in Arthurian romances at the beginning of the fourteenth century.

140. Tout, *France and England*, pp. 94 and 140 ff.

141. J. E. Lloyd, *Owen Glendower* (Oxford, 1931), p. 120; and see pp. 46–47 for an appeal to the king of Scotland, to the Irish and Welsh supporters, based on their common ancestry from Brutus, and the Saxon oppression of his nation.

142. C. A. J. Armstrong, 'The Language Question in the Low Countries: The Use of French and Dutch by the Dukes of Burgundy and their Administration', *Europe in the Late Middle Ages*, ed. J. R. Hale, J. R. L. Highfield, and B. Smalley (London, 1965), p. 392.

143. Jones, *Ducal Brittany*, pp. 72–76; Arch. Nat., KK 79, for payments by Charles VIII to Bretons, 1485–91.

duke of Burgundy, in the years following the death of John IV, the aspirations are apparent and they were not novel. Some of the methods used to project an image of the duchy, based on a widely held view of its history, backed up by propagandist activities, show the real importance attached to the establishment of a Breton identity. From 1364, at least, it was deliberate ducal policy to shape the natural and spontaneous expressions of sentiment in 'nostre nacion de Bretaigne'.[144]

144. B.N., MS. lat. 9093, fo. 11, notarial instrument, 10 December 1364, of ducal pardon to the bishop and citizens of Quimper for supporting Blois, 17 November 1364.

Ecclesiastical Reform and the Politics of the Hundred Years War during the Pontificate of Urban V (1362–70)

J. J. N. PALMER and A. P. WELLS

In the latter half of 1364 Pope Urban V was called upon to make a critical political decision. In the face of strong competition from France, Edward III had secured for his son Edmund the hand of Margaret of Burgundy, 'the richest heiress in Christendom'. The terms of the alliance had been settled, the date of the marriage fixed. All that was required to make Edmund of Langley the prospective ruler of a vast Flemish 'empire'—which would eventually comprise Calais, the duchies of Brabant and Limburg, and the nine counties of Flanders, Burgundy, Artois, Rethel, Nevers, Mark, Guînes, Ponthieu, and (possibly) Hainault—was a papal dispensation from consanguinity. Such dispensations were normally granted as a matter of course; but, prompted by Charles V of France, Urban refused Edward's application.

All this is well enough known.[1] What has not been recognized, however, is the consequences of Urban's refusal. For Edward III did not accept this decision as final; and in an attempt to force the pope to change his mind, launched a sustained and increasingly bitter attack upon him.[2] Both England and the papacy were seriously affected by the ensuing conflict. For if Edward had to concede the loss of a Flemish 'empire' for his son, Urban V witnessed the destruction of the programme of ecclesiastical reform with which he had inaugurated his

---

1. F. Quicke, *Les Pays-Bas à la veille de la période bourguignonne, 1356–1384* (Brussels, 1947), pp. 75–85.

2. J. J. N. Palmer, 'England, France, the Papacy and the Flemish Succession, 1361–1369', *The Hundred Years War: Bristol Colloquium Papers*, ed. J. Sherborne (forthcoming).

pontificate. This programme was first thrust to one side, then attacked by Edward III in pursuit of his political ends, and finally destroyed by the pope himself in his unavailing efforts to counter the aggression of the English king. One of the most serious reforming measures of the later medieval papacy thus fell victim to the dynastic imperatives of the Hundred Years War.

In order to appreciate the impact of the political conflict provoked by Urban's refusal of a dispensation, we must first examine his programme of reform and the difficulties which it had initially encountered.

The main purpose of this programme was to improve the calibre of the clergy, and in particular of the higher clergy. To this end Urban set himself from the beginning of his pontificate to increase the educational opportunities available to clerks. He founded *studia* and colleges, encouraged the foundation of new universities, revised the statutes of existing institutions, and supported some 400 students at his own cost. But Urban was enough of a realist to appreciate that these measures could produce no lasting results unless he simultaneously improved the prospects of graduates. Any such improvement had, of course, to be at the expense of the unlettered clerk, and above all at the expense of the unlettered pluralist. Hence the central feature of Urban's programme was an attack upon pluralism: pluralism in any form. This point is crucial. The object of all previous legislation on this subject had been to limit the number of benefices with cure of souls that could be held by a clerk, whereas the object of Urban's legislation was to limit the number of sinecures that could be held by a clerk. Earlier legislation had been designed to keep the pastoral benefices of the church out of the clutches of excessively greedy pluralists, in order to promote the spiritual welfare of parishioners; Urban's legislation was designed to prevent the concentration of the fat prebends of the church in the hands of a few favoured clerks, in order to distribute the wealth of the church more widely among the lettered clergy. Urban's legislation on pluralism thus diverged sharply from that of all his predecessors.[3] It was a radical programme of ecclesiastical reform, a programme that went a long

---

3. This has not been appreciated. Only A. H. Thompson, in his excellent sketch of the history of legislation against pluralism ('Pluralism in the Medieval Church', *A.A.S.R.P.* xxx (1915), 35–73), took the measure of Urban's reforms; but even he failed to gauge their true significance, owing to his belief that John XXII's bull *Execrabilis* anticipated Urban's legislation against the holding of sinecures in plurality. This is erroneous; see A. Deeley, 'Papal Provision and Royal Rights of Patronage in the Early Fourteenth Century', *E.H.R.* xliii (1928), 503–4.

way to meet the rapidly growing criticism of corruption within the church.[4]

All these features are clearly apparent in the first of Urban's reforming measures, *Horribilis et detestabilis*,[5] issued in February 1363.[6] In the preamble Urban thundered:

Oh how horrible and detestable is the cupidity—condemned by God and men alike —which perverts the souls of those reprobate clerks, quite incapable of study themselves, who nevertheless hold an excess of benefices, while innumerable prudent, wise, and learned men, studying in the schools and elsewhere, have no benefice at all!

The prescriptions which followed aimed to reverse this lamentable state of affairs. For the future, academic qualifications were to determine ecclesiastical preferment. Hence, clerks with no academic qualification were to be limited to a single benefice, while doctors of theology and of canon and civil law could hold as many as four benefices up to a total value of £300 per annum.[7] Between these extremes, a bachelor (*intitulans*) could hold two benefices, provided that their annual value did not exceed £120; and a master (*titulans*) could have three benefices, worth up to £200.[8] Anyone holding more than was permitted was to resign the excess within two months; and those who failed to do so would *ipso facto* incur excommunication and deprivation of all their benefices, these being reserved to the pope.

Despite this threat of excommunication and deprivation, *Horribilis et detestabilis* was almost completely ineffective. Petrarch, it is true,

4. The 'insatiable ambition' of clerks in their 'unbridled pursuit of benefices' (see below, p. 171 n. 9) was taken by reformers to be the fundamental evil of the late medieval church; see for instance, E. Delaruelle, E. R. Labande, and P. Ourliac, 'L'Église au temps du Grand Schisme et de la crise conciliaire, 1378–1449', *Histoire de l'Église*, ed. J. B. Duroselle and É. Jarry, xiv (Paris, 1964), pp. 295 ff. and 885 ff.

5. *Annales Monastici*, ed. H. R. Luard (5 vols., R.S., 1864–9), iii. 413–14.

6. The text in the Annals of Dunstable (ibid.) is dated only 1 February, without year. The annalist says that the bull was sent into England *anno gratiae* 1363 which could, of course, mean 1363 or 1364 new style. John of Reading and Thomas Walsingham give 1363 (*Chronica Johannis de Reading et Anonymi Cantuariensis, 1346–1367*, ed. J. Tait (Manchester, 1914), p. 156; *Historia Anglicana*, ed. H. T. Riley (2 vols., R.S., 1863–4), i. 298), and their testimony is to be preferred to that of the continuators of Higden's and Murimuth's chronicles who give 1364 (see *Polychronicon Ranulphi Higden*, ed. J. R. Lumby (9 vols., R.S., 1865–86), viii. 413 and 436; and A. Murimuth, *Chronica sui temporis*, ed. T. Hog (English Historical Society, 1846), p. 197).

7. According to the valuation of the tenth or, failing such valuation, 'according to the true common estimation'.

8. *Titulans* and *intitulans* lend themselves to a number of interpretations; but the context of the constitution, taken in conjunction with the description of its terms in the *Scalachronica* of Sir Thomas Gray (ed. and trans. H. Maxwell (Glasgow, 1907), p. 171), suggests the interpretation adopted in the text.

believed otherwise and congratulated Urban on having 'curbed the unbridled pursuit of benefices and [having] compelled those of insatiable
ambition to make do with a single living. Well done! For is it not
shameful to see some overladen with revenues, while others—better
than they—live in need?' This judgement was echoed, although in more
restrained language, by Urban's contemporary biographer.[9] But against
this testimony there can be set an overwhelming mass of documentary
evidence.[10] For England there is no mention of *Horribilis et detestabilis*
in the *Calendar of Papal Letters* or the *Calendar of Papal Petitions*, while
the accounts of the papal collector in England show that in the two
years following its publication there were only four cases in which an
English clerk was deprived for plurality, and that in every case the
deprivation failed to take effect. Continental sources reveal a similar
pattern. The published *Lettres communes* of Urban V, which concern
the whole of Europe, show that in the nine months following the publication of *Horribilis et detestabilis*, Urban failed to deprive a single
pluralist. For France, Sweden, Bohemia, Denmark, Poland, the Netherlands, and the diocese of Constance, the published papal letters and sup-
plications contain no reference or allusion to *Horribilis et detestabilis* or
to its execution; and for the dioceses of Cambrai, Tournai, Thérouanne,
and Liège, for which all relevant papal letters have been published, there
were less than a dozen cases of deprivation in the whole of Urban's

---

9. F. Petrarch, *Epistolae seniles*, l. vii, ep. i; S. Baluze, *Vitae paparum avenionensium*,
ed. G. Mollat (4 vols., Paris, 1914–27), i. 378.

10. *Accounts rendered by the Papal Collectors in England, 1317–1378* (henceforward
Accounts), ed. W. E. Lunt and E. B. Graves (Philadelphia, 1968), pp. 252, 253, 255, 306,
381, and 382; *Lettres communes d'Urbain V*, ed. M. H. Laurent and M. Hayez (*B.E.F.A.R.*,
3r° sér., v bis, 1954–67, in progress); *Lettres secrètes et curiales d'Urbain V se rapportant à
la France*, ed. P. Lecacheux and G. Mollat (*B.E.F.A.R.*, 3° sér., v, 1902–55); *Acta pontificum Svecica* (= *Diplomatarium Svecarum Appendix*), I: *Acta cameralia*, i (1348–70), ed.
L. M. Bååth (Stockholm, 1936); *Monumenta vaticana res gestas Bohémicas illustrantia*, ed.
F. Jeńsovský, iii (Prague, 1944); *Acta Pontificum Danica: Pavelige aktstykker vedrørende
Danmark*, i, ed. L. Moltesen (Copenhagen, 1904), 236–312; vii, ed. A. Krarup (Copen-
hagen, 1943), 105–46; *Diplomatarium Danicum*, 3rd ser. vii (1364–6), ed. C. A.
Christensen and H. Nielsen (Copenhagen, 1972); *Monumenta Poloniae Vaticana*, II:
Acta camerae apostolicae, ii, ed. J. Ptaśnik (Cracow, 1913); III: *Analecta Vaticana*, ed. J.
Ptaśnik (Cracow, 1914); *Supplieken gericht aan de pausen Clemens VI, Innocentius VI en
Urbanus V, 1342–66*, ed. R. R. Post (The Hague, 1937); *Römische Quellen zur Konstanzer
Bistumsgeschichte zur Zeit der Päpste in Avignon, 1305–1378*, ed. R. Rieder (Innsbruck,
1908); *Lettres d'Urbain V*, ed. A. Fierens and C. Tihon (Analecta Vaticano-Belgica, ix,
xv, 1928–32); *Suppliques d'Urbain V*, ed. A. Fierens (Analecta Vaticano-Belgica, vii,
1914); *Die päpstlichen Kollektorien in Deutschland während des XIV Jahrhunderts*, ed. J.
P. Kirsch (Paderborn, 1894); *Les Collectories pontificales dans les anciens diocèses de Cambrai, Thérouanne et Tournai au XIV° siècle*, ed. U. Berlière (Analecta Vaticano-Belgica,
x, 1929).

pontificate. Finally, the accounts of the papal collectors in Germany, Hungary, and the province of Rheims mention only four cases of deprivation for plurality of sinecures, and two of these were ineffective. *Horribilis et detestabilis* was evidently a resounding failure.

In order to appreciate the significance of Urban's later measures, it is essential to grasp the reasons for this failure. The English chronicler who blamed the selfish opposition of those with vested interests to protect[11] was no doubt fundamentally correct. But there is a more immediate explanation: *Horribilis et detestabilis* was drafted with such ineptitude that patrons and pluralists were never seriously threatened.[12] Its most glaring deficiency in this respect was its failure to define 'benefice'. In the context of previous legislation against pluralism, 'benefice' had acquired a semi-technical meaning, i.e. a living with cure of souls, and it was therefore essential to spell out in plain language that *Horribilis et detestabilis* applied to sinecures. Failure to do so opened the door to evasion on a large scale. Those clerks who held sinecures in plurality—the majority—could blithely pretend that the constitution did not apply to them and simply ignore it. They could do so with impunity because the Curia held no record of benefice holders, and had to depend upon the pluralists themselves to volunteer information about their sinecures. It is difficult to believe that many would have jeopardized their livings when they could persuade themselves that the constitution applied only to benefices with cure. Even those who were foolish enough to do so could still defeat the purpose of the constitution by engaging in litigation; for those responsible for the drafting of *Horribilis et detestabilis* inexplicably omitted the standard prohibition of appeals against its stipulations.

These flaws must soon have become apparent to the Curia, for little over a year later Urban issued a mandate which was specifically designed to make good the deficiencies of his original legislation. This mandate, dated 25 April 1364, ordered all secular and religious clerks then in residence at Avignon, together with those who customarily resided there, who held more than a single benefice, to deliver within

11. *Polychronicon Ranulphi Higden*, viii. 413 and 436.
12. This might suggest that the text in the Annals of Dunstable is an inept précis, rather than an accurate copy, of the original. Certainly, it is uncharacteristically succinct. Apart from this, however, it bears the hallmarks of a chancery product. Both its *arenga* and its abbreviated *Nulli ergo* clause are typical of chancery practice, and the intervening text shows no trace of the joins which a précis might be expected to leave. But the most convincing proof that these inadequacies of drafting were in the original, is the care subsequently taken to eliminate precisely these weaknesses (see below).

one month to the papal chamberlain a list of the 'names of their priories, dignities, parsonages, administrations, offices, churches, canonries, prebends, annuities, and benefices, together with their value and their assessment for the tenth . . . as well as any expectations or chaplaincies, or any perpetual offices attached to their benefices'. Anyone failing to make a return was *ipso facto* deprived of all his benefices, which were reserved to the pope; and no appeals against the stipulations of the mandate were to be admitted.[13]

This mandate had been carefully considered and was meticulously drafted. It stopped all the loopholes in *Horribilis et detestabilis*. In the first place, it defined 'benefice' with strict precision; secondly, it prohibited appeals; and finally, it provided the Curia with the information which would enable it to check that any future legislation was observed.

The trial run at Avignon evidently revealed no flaws in this administrative process. The returns were made as stipulated;[14] and by the autumn, Urban was sufficiently confident to extend its application to the whole of Christendom. On 24 September 1364 the mandate was reissued, now addressed to all archbishops and their suffragans. They were required to summon diocesan synods at which they were to order all those who held more than a single benefice of any description—with or without cure—to make within a month a return of all such benefices to the ordinary of the diocese in which they resided. Within a month of receiving these returns, the diocesan was required to deliver them to his archbishop, who was to forward them to the Curia within a stipulated period. All those who failed to make their return within the given period were to be *ipso facto* deprived of all their benefices. Once again, appeals were prohibited.[15]

Thus, by the autumn of 1364, Urban had laid secure foundations for the successful implementation of his reform programme. The deficiencies of his initial legislation had been made good; and a sound administrative process had been devised, tested, and set in motion. But before this process could yield results, the political conflict with England, which was eventually to destroy the whole programme, intervened.

13. Reg. Vat. 246, fos. 172ᵛ–4; inaccurately calendared in *Lettres secrètes d'Urbain V*, i, no. 923; and in *Lettres d'Urbain V*, ed. Fierens and Tihon, i, no. 1115.
14. This appears from the English returns of 1366: *Registrum Simonis de Langham* (henceforward *Reg. Langham*), ed. H. C. Wood (C. & Y.S., 1956), pp. 81–82 and 85–86; *Registrum Simonis de Sudbiria* (henceforward *Reg. Sudbiria*), ed. R. C. Fowler (2 vols., C. & Y.S., 1927–38), ii. 170.
15. *Lettres d'Urbain V*, ed. Fierens and Tihon, i, no. 1261.

Although tension between Edward III and Urban V did not reach crisis proportions until Urban's formal refusal to grant a dispensation for the Flemish marriage in December 1364, there had twice, before this date, been hints of the crisis to come. And on both these occasions Edward had linked his negotiations for a dispensation with Urban's ecclesiastical reform: *quid pro quo*.

The first episode occurred in September 1363 when Sir Nicholas Loraine was sent to Avignon to pursue negotiations for the dispensation[16] and simultaneously to protest against infringements of Edward's 'regale'.[17] The nature of these infringements was made clear by the parliament which met in the following month to debate the 'attacks made upon the franchises of Holy Church'.[18] The outcome of this debate was a strongly worded protest to Urban from king, nobles, and commons against the number of reservations issuing from the Curia which, they alleged, were more numerous than ever before. Edward taxed the pope with devising new and yet more onerous reservations than any practised by his predecessors; went on to catalogue the evils to which this practice gave rise; and concluded with the warning that if the pope did not allow patrons to enjoy the legitimate exercise of their patronage, not only would there be no one left in England willing to endow a church, but existing patrons would even try to disendow the churches founded by their ancestors.[19]

This protest was not without foundation, for Urban's reservations had been on a scale which had eclipsed those of even his most predatory predecessors. On 5 January 1363 he annulled all expectations granted by Innocent VI; on 10 June he reserved to himself all benefices previously collated to by Innocent, even where his collation had been ineffective, and also all benefices reserved by Innocent and vacant at the time of his death; on 30 June he reserved all benefices of papal collectors and

---

16. Palmer, 'England, France, the Papacy and the Flemish Succession'.

17. L. Mirot and E. Déprez, *Les Ambassades anglaises pendant la Guerre de Cent Ans, 1327–1450* (Paris, 1900; reprinted from *B.E.C.* lix–lxi, 1898–1900), nos. 227–8.

18. *Rot. Parl.* ii. 275.

19. B.L., Add. MS. 24062, fo. 163, undated; but the references to the summons of the bishops of Coventry and Lichfield and of Lincoln, the abbots of St. Alban's and Chester, and the archdeacon of Lincoln to the Curia, indicate the year 1363, and this is supported by the reference to the extent of the pope's reservations (see p. 176 and n. 20 below), and by the failure to mention the summons of the earl of Arundel (who was summoned in 1364). Finally, the letter mentions the support of the lords and commons for the king's protest, which must be a reference to the Parliament of October 1363, which we know met to debate attacks upon 'the franchises of Holy Church' (see *Rot. Parl.* ii. 275).

sub-collectors; on 4 August all patriarchates, archbishoprics, bishoprics, and all monasteries of all orders; and on 1 September all benefices of cardinals and papal officials.[20] Finally, of course, *Horribilis et detestabilis* itself had reserved to the pope the benefices of all those who failed to observe its stipulations.

In view of all this, it is important to emphasize that Edward's reaction was surprisingly mild, and revealed no fundamental hostility to Urban's reforms. He made no attempt to interfere with *Horribilis et detestabilis*, and the many references to it in English chronicles show that it was widely published.[21] If it produced little result, it failed on its own demerits. At this stage, therefore, Edward's aim was simply to exploit Urban's desire for reform in order to secure the dispensation he so urgently required.

This aim is even more clearly apparent in the second episode which occurred in the summer of 1364 on the eve of the publication of Urban's new administrative measures.

In the last week of July 1364, Sir Nicholas Loraine returned to Avignon to conclude his earlier negotiations, while his companion, Sir Nicholas Tamworth, was sent to the French court to enlist the co-operation of Charles V against impending papal legislation against pluralists.[22] The correspondence provoked by Tamworth's embassy has fortunately survived and illuminates in some detail the pressure exerted by Edward III at Avignon in the autumn of 1364.[23] He complained that,

the said pope (so we are informed) intends to issue, or has already issued, an ordinance proclaiming that no clerk may hold more than one or two benefices of a certain annual value. Those who hold more are to be deprived of the surplus, even though some of them have held these benefices in the time of the pope's predecessors, as gifts from popes, princes, prelates, and other patrons, their friends, in return for their service, their status, or from some other consideration. In the past, these clerks have maintained great estate, and have cared for their parents, their friends, and others; but now they will be such poor and miserable beggars that they will be quite incapable of managing their benefices, let alone of serving their prince or any other

20. C. Lux, *Constitutionum apostolicarum de generali beneficiorum reservatione ab anno 1265 usque ad anno 1378 emissarum* (Breslau, 1904), pp. 42–44; J. R. L. Highfield, 'Relations between the Church and the English Crown (1349–1378)' (unpublished Oxford D. Phil. thesis, 1952), pp. 45–50.

21. See above, p. 171, nn. 5–6 and 8.

22. Mirot and Déprez, *Ambassades*, nos. 238–9.

23. B.L., Add. MS. 24062, fos. 187ᵛ and 151ᵛ; É. Perroy, 'Charles V et le traité de Brétigny', *Le Moyen Âge*, xxxviii (1928), 262. The letter published by Perroy is dated 18 August (1364), and those in Add. MS. can confidently be dated July 1364 (fo. 187ᵛ) and *c.* September 1364 (fo. 151ᵛ) by reference to it.

honourable person. This is harsh, even sinful, and it could do great harm to our kingdoms. For the pope will receive the first fruits of all benefices voided by his ordinance—a very considerable sum indeed—thus despoiling our realms of their wealth; and when he has waxed rich on the goods of *our* subjects, then he will subjugate princes and kingdoms to his will.

In his reply Charles V undertook to send the abbot of Cluny to Avignon to discuss with the pope 'the ordinance which he desires, and intends, to issue against the clergy of *your* kingdom, depriving them of their benefices'.

Finally, in September, the abbot of Cluny reported to Edward that he had petitioned the pope:

on behalf of yourself and of my lord, the king of France, that if he issued an ordinance against pluralists, he should show consideration to those clerks who are regularly employed on your business and on that of the king of France. I gave good reason why he should do this—as I have written at some length to my lord of Arundel and to your knight, Sir N[icholas] T[amworth]—but he was nevertheless extremely angry with me, and said that he was astonished that I, who knew the Canon Law better than any layman, should make such a request. In the end, however, he agreed that, when he issued the ordinance, he would show greater consideration to those clerks than to others, leaving them benefices appropriate to their status.

The message of all this was clear enough. Urban's projected reforms would demand of England very considerable sacrifices, and would bring corresponding advantages to the papacy: both would have to be paid for. And Urban would have had to have been very obtuse indeed not to have appreciated the price. His options were still open. Edward had so far taken no action against his reforms and Urban himself had yet to refuse the dispensation. But he chose to do so, and on 18 December 1364 formally published his decision.[24]

Urban's decision raised the conflict to a new level. The mild political blackmail of the earlier encounters now gave way to aggressive political action.

Edward's first move—in December 1364 or earlier[25]—was to undermine the administrative foundation of Urban's reform programme by preventing the publication of his September mandate ordering a return of benefices to the Curia. Although the act of prohibition has not survived, there can be no doubt that it was issued. For the mandate was certainly never published in England; and after an interval of eighteen

24. *Foedera* (original edn., 20 vols., 1704–32), vi. 457.
25. Edward evidently had prior warning of the pope's decision, for on 18 December he asked the count of Flanders to agree to a postponement of the marriage (ibid.).

months, Urban found it necessary to reissue the substance of the mandate with the addition of a number of clauses designed to minimize the possibility of further interference from the crown.

Having thus sabotaged the machinery of papal reform, Edward immediately attacked the reforms themselves. This was the main business placed before the parliament summoned in December 1364, which 'approved, accepted, and confirmed' the statutes of Provisors (1351) and Praemunire (1353).[26] The purpose of this re-enactment has puzzled historians since it appears to have added nothing of consequence to the original acts of 1351 and 1353. The only addition of any apparent importance was the insertion of a clause extending the competence of the statute of Provisors to cover appropriated benefices and those in royal and lay collation; but since these benefices were never seriously threatened by papal provision, this addition at least was gratuitous. However, the re-enactment was not superfluous. It has only appeared to be so because its significant additions lay in two clauses whose obscurity has hitherto concealed their purpose. Both these clauses were aimed directly at Urban's reforms. The first stipulated that all those who had sought, or should in future seek, papal provision to benefices, 'at present occupied by any person of the kingdom by reasonable title', would be liable to the penalties of the statutes of 1351 and 1353. In other words, no benefices rendered vacant by papal legislation against pluralists could be filled by papal provisors. This clause was both retro- and prospective, and would apply equally to clerks seeking provision to benefices rendered vacant by *Horribilis et detestabilis*, or by any future legislation. At a stroke, this threatened to destroy Urban's whole programme. In order to redistribute richer benefices amongst the better-educated clergy, he had to increase his own share in appointment to those benefices. The statute of 1365 would have reduced his share. It would have deprived him of the right to appoint to benefices rendered vacant by his legislation, even those benefices previously subject to papal provision. Hence, the main beneficiary of Urban's reforming legislation would be Edward III, the foremost patron of precisely that type of ecclesiastic whom the pope was trying to deprive.

The second important addition in the act of 1365 was a clause designed to make it effective. Whereas the implementation of the statute of Praemunire of 1353 had depended on the initiative and activity of the

26. *Rot. Parl.* ii. 284–5.

crown, that of 1365 gave to private individuals the right to institute proceedings against papal provisors, and stipulated that such provisors were not to be pardoned by the king without the express consent of the aggrieved party, and then only after the plaintiff had been satisfied. Anyone deprived of their benefice by papal legislation would therefore have a right of action in the royal court against the provisor who succeeded him. The papal provisor was thereby placed at the mercy of the English pluralist, and the fate of Urban's reforms in the hands of those who had a vested interest in their failure.

This legal and political broadside was accompanied by a general attack on papal provisors. Edward's first step—taken, once again, in December 1364—was to strengthen his defences. On 12 December he notified all sheriffs and the mayors and bailiffs of forty-eight towns that henceforth no one was to leave England without royal licence; that only recognized merchants were to be permitted to export money and bills of exchange; and that:

search shall be made in all ports within the king's power on either side of the sea that no person of whatsoever condition coming from the court of Rome to England or elsewhere beyond the sea bring letter patent, bull, instrument, process or aught else which may be to the prejudice of the king or any of his subjects, and none passing out of the realm to the court of Rome or elsewhere over sea carry letter patent, instrument, process or aught else which may turn to the like prejudice; and in case any shall pass out by the king's licence, he shall take oath and give security before the king in chancery not to make, sue nor procure any suit or impeachment of matters which may turn to the prejudice of the king, the laws, or of his subjects, on pain of being out of the king's protection and of forfeiture of life and goods, according to the statute made in the 27th year of the reign . . .[27]

On 26 December two or more searchers (*scrutatores*) were appointed in every major port to ensure that this last provision was fulfilled. Reissued at regular intervals, these measures were to remain in force until the end of the decade, by which time the *scrutatores* had become permanent officials accounting regularly at the Exchequer.[28]

With his defences in order, Edward launched his attack against provisors. His first thrust was delivered against aliens. On 15 December—a mere three days after closing the ports—Edward, complaining that the majority of fat prebends were 'now . . . held by strangers and aliens of foreign parts, *called provisors*, more truly robbers and destroyers',

27. *C.C.R.*, *1364-8*, pp. 90–91.
28. *C.P.R.*, *1364-7*, pp. 76–78, 139–40, 142, 279, 361–2, and 449; *C.C.R.*, *1364-8* pp. 135–8 and 141; P.R.O., E.101/396/2, m. 35; E.364/3, m. A.

ordered 'with the assent of the magnates and others, learned, of our council . . . that the temporalities of deaneries etc. of the foundation of our progenitors held by such aliens now void and as they fall void shall be taken into our hands. . . .'[29]

Although neither this measure against alien provisors, nor the re-enacted statutes of Provisors and Praemunire, were enforced to the letter, there was a very marked increase in activity against all provisors. From January 1365 down to the end of Urban's pontificate they were harassed at every turn: orders to arrest, imprison, fine, outlaw, or deprive them abound on the Close and Patent Rolls.[30] The unfortunate papal provisor bore the brunt of Edward's displeasure with the pope.

The last of Edward's major measures against Urban was to cut off his income from England. This too occurred in December 1364. An un-dated passage in the report of the papal collector, covering the years 1364–6, refers to 'an arrest placed on the monies of the Camera', and there can be no doubt that this 'arrest' dates from 26 December, when the *scrutatores* were empowered to confiscate all money and bills of exchange leaving the kingdom for other than legitimate commercial purposes. This ordinance was endorsed by Parliament in January 1365 and was reissued at intervals throughout the decade. The *scrutatores* were still accounting for receipts from this source as late as September 1369;[31] and the accounts of the papal collectors in England show that not a florin was remitted to Avignon between the beginning of 1365 and the summer of 1366. Finally, the same accounts reveal that the 'arrest' on papal moneys threw the routine of collection into considerable con-fusion. Arrears of Peter's Pence reached unprecedented heights in the mid 1360s, and the situation did not return to normal until 1370.[32]

In addition to prohibiting the outflow of normal papal revenue, Edward applied financial pressure in a number of other ways. The first Parliament to meet after the outbreak of the crisis, that of January 1365, debated a proposal for the total abolition of Peter's Pence; and in the

29. *C.P.R.*, *1364–7*, pp. 61–62.

30. Ibid., pp. 73, 78–79, 145, 201–2, 204–5, 207, 208, 217, 245–6, 277–8, 280, 283, 310, 336, 366, 369, 420, 433, and 447; *C.C.R.*, *1364–8*, pp. 106–7, 125–6, 227–8, 241, 277, 348, and 490; *C.P.R.*, *1367–70*, pp. 45, 49–50, 52–59, 60–67, 70–75, 109, 126–34, 143, 169, and 190.

31. *Accounts*, p. 226; Reading, *Chronica*, p. 163; *C.P.R.*, *1364–7*, pp. 76–78; and references above on p. 179, n. 28.

32. *Accounts*, pp. 225–6; W. E. Lunt, *Financial Relations of the Papacy with Eng-land*, *1327–1534*, Studies in Anglo-Papal Relations during the Middle Ages II (Cam-bridge, Mass., 1962), 9–11.

very next assembly, of May 1366, the lords and commons not only joined with the king in rejecting the pope's demand for the arrears of tribute, but also pledged themselves in advance to support the king if the pope should proceed against him 'par proces ou en autre manere de fait'.[33] Finally the unfortunate papal collector, John de Cabrespino, was harassed at every turn. He was denied the customary procurations, and his normal perquisites of office were withheld. Indeed life was made so uncomfortable for him that he spent the greater part of his five-year term of office at the Curia.[34]

Thus, in the few weeks which followed his refusal of a dispensation for the Flemish marriage, Urban was subjected to every possible ecclesiastical pressure. His legislation was attacked, his income depleted, and his patronage curtailed. This pressure was to be maintained until the end of the decade.

All this left Urban with little choice: he could either capitulate and grant the dispensation, or resign himself to a prolonged struggle. He chose the latter course; and on 30 October 1365, in a letter to the archbishop of Canterbury, he confirmed his refusal of a dispensation, repeated an earlier nullification (11 December 1364) of all general dispensations granted by his predecessors, and threatened Edward himself, his family, and his ministers with excommunication, and all English territories with interdict, if they proceeded with the marriage.[35]

Having fired this salvo, Urban had all but exhausted his armoury; his remaining weapons were mainly of small calibre, and apt to recoil upon their user. In reply to Edward's financial measures, for example, all that Urban could do was to demand the arrears of the tribute (unpaid since 1333) and the intercalary fruits of the see of Canterbury following Archbishop Islip's death in 1366.[36] Neither demand produced a penny, and both served to consolidate opinion behind the king. Again, in the face of Edward's attack on provisors, Urban's only practical resort was to make more extensive use of his right to provide to bishoprics, indulging in multiple translations in 1366 and 1368, and impeding for almost a year the appointment of William of Wickham to the see of Winchester (1366–7). While these provisions may have served to em-emphasize papal prerogatives—they were probably designed to do just

33. Reading, *Chronica*, p. 163; *Rot. Parl.* ii. 290.
34. Lunt, *Financial Relations*, ii. 661–2; *Accounts*, pp. xxxvi–xxxvii, xxxix.
35. *Lettres d'Urbain V*, ed. Fierens and Tihon, i, no. 1624.
36. Ibid., no. 1505; *Accounts*, p. 1.

that—it was the king's ministers, and hence the king himself, who enjoyed the practical benefits. Finally, when Urban attempted to use an English bishop as an instrument against the king, the unfortunate prelate, William Lynn of Chichester, was driven into exile at the Curia (at Urban's expense), while his confiscated temporalities went to swell the royal coffers.[37] Like his other measures, this too was counter-productive.

In devising means to combat Edward's pressure therefore, Urban found himself in a dilemma, a dilemma which was particularly acute where his reforms were concerned. For to counter Edward's attack on this front might jeopardize the reforms themselves. This probably accounts for his procrastination. Edward had prevented the publication of the September mandate at the end of 1364, and had directly attacked the reforms themselves in the Parliament of January 1365; but it was not until May 1366—sixteen months later—that the pope retaliated, with the bull *Consueta* (3 May 1366).[38]

The terms of this bull were draconic. All clerks possessing more than a single benefice or expectation—'benefice' being broadly defined to cover every type of ecclesiastical preferment—had to make returns to their ordinaries within six months; and in making this return, they were to 'elect' their two favoured compatible benefices. Within a further month, these returns were to be dispatched to the metropolitan, who was then to forward them to the pope within the following four months. To ensure that *Consueta* did not suffer the fate of the previous mandate, the responsibility for making his return was placed squarely on the shoulders of the individual clerk, who was ordered to make it by 'this edict of public monition', which 'edict' was to have as much force 'as if the individual had been personally informed of its content'. If he failed to comply within the stipulated six months, the clerk was *ipso facto* deprived of all but his two favoured benefices, the remainder being reserved to the pope; and if he procrastinated for more than one more month, he was *ipso facto* deprived of his elected benefices, these too being reserved.

Two features of this bull demand special attention. First of all, its severity. Every clerk, of any description, had to elect two compatible benefices. No exceptions were allowed; and since Urban did not ask for information about the qualifications (academic or otherwise) of the clergy, the clear implication of this measure was that all clerks were to be

37. Highfield, 'Church and Crown', pp. 138–40.
38. *Reg. Langham*, pp. 1–5.

restricted to one or two benefices: exactly as Edward himself had anticipated in his correspondence with Charles V in the summer of 1364. Secondly, *Consueta* was directed only against the English clergy. The mistaken belief that it was a constitution of general application is due to a misreading of its preamble. Urban himself stated quite clearly that it applied 'to the clerks of the kingdom of England' alone.[39] Taken together, these two features indicate that by the mid 1360s Urban's programme of reform had degenerated into a political attack on the English civil service. *Consueta* was the product, not of Urban's desire for reform, but rather of the politics of the Hundred Years War.

By using his legislation for political purposes, Urban irretrievably ruined his reform programme without obtaining any corresponding political advantage. Indeed, *Consueta* did him nothing but harm; for both the severity of its prescriptions and their manifest unfairness turned the body of the English clergy against the pope. This is very apparent in their returns to *Consueta*, submitted to the Curia in January 1367; for in making these returns, the clergy employed every conceivable device to thwart the pope.

In this they were aided by a single but fatal flaw in the drafting of *Consueta*. The flaw occurs in the crucial passage prescribing the 'election' of two compatible benefices. It reads,

otherwise all and singular—notwithstanding any appeal which they or others may lodge before us or their ordinaries within the aforesaid term—who do not effectively comply with our aforementioned mandate and reasonable warning are, after the lapse of the said six months, forever deprived of all their priorates, dignities, parsonages, administrations, churches, canonries, prebends, benefices, offices, and expectative graces which they shall have presumed to retain in excess of two benefices (which must be compatible) which they, within the said [sixth] month, shall have elected to be retained before their ordinary, their priorates, dignities, parsonages, administrations, churches, canonries, prebends, benefices, and offices being reserved to our disposition. And if they presume to retain these said priorates, dignities, parsonages, administrations, churches, canonries, prebends, benefices and offices, of which (as stated) they shall have been deprived, for one month beyond the said term, then let it be known that they are then *ipso facto* deprived of the other two compatible benefices which we (as stated) have permitted to be retained, these similarly being reserved to our collation and disposition . . .

There are three possible interpretations of this clause: (*a*) that all pluralists should elect two compatible benefices, resigning all others;

39. Reg. Vat. 256, fo. 58ᵛ.

(*b*) that all pluralists should simply elect two compatible benefices but take no further action; (*c*) that only those who failed to make their return should elect two compatible benefices. Serious objections can be made to any one of these interpretations, for all lead to absurdities. Hence, it was open to the individual clerk to choose whichever he preferred (or whichever he happened to grasp).

The majority of pluralists naturally opted for the interpretation which best suited their interests and assumed that the act of making a return absolved them from the need of selecting two benefices.[40] Not a single clerk in the dioceses of Canterbury, Lincoln, Worcester, Salisbury, Winchester, or Chichester made an 'election', their example being followed by the majority in other dioceses. A number of those who took this course went one step further and protested vigorously against the threat to their sinecures. William of Wickham, the richest pluralist in England, provides an excellent example. Wickham held eleven benefices, one with cure and ten without cure. In listing each of these ten sinecures he reiterated insistently, 'non curatum et compassibile cum curato beneficio', thereby implicitly questioning Urban's right to deprive him of his sinecures. His lead was followed by nine important pluralists in the diocese of London and by others elsewhere.

Even those who felt obliged by their understanding of the critical clause of *Consueta* to elect two benefices did so under protest. Gilbert de Thornton of Llandaff, for example, concluded his return with the statement that if he was constrained by 'any papal constitution, mandate or precept' to elect two compatible benefices, then he did so under protest, and always saving his right to all his other benefices. Similar protests were made by clerks in the dioceses of St. David's, Exeter, London, Ely, Coventry and Lichfield, Bath and Wells, and Rochester; but none was more eloquent than that of one Mag. Roger de Otery, whose form of protest was adopted by every clerk in the diocese of Hereford:

40. The London returns are printed in *Reg. Sudbiria*, and those for the remainder of the Canterbury province in *Reg. Langham*; there are no extant returns for the York province, nor for Bangor and St. Asaph. Other copies of the diocesan returns are preserved in some episcopal registers: for example, *The Register of John de Grandisson, Bishop of Exeter, 1327–1369*, ed. F. C. Hingeston-Randolph (3 vols., Exeter, 1894–9), iii. 1248–62; *Registers or Act Books of the Bishops of Coventry and Lichfield: 1st and 2nd Registers of Robert de Stretton, 1358–85; an abstract*, ed. R. A. Wilson, William Salt Archaeological Soc., new ser., vols. viii and ix, 1905–7, pt. ii. 216–23; Lincolnshire Archives Office, Episcopal Register xii: Buckingham's Register of Memoranda, fos. 43–47; Kent Archives Office, DRC/R4: Register of Thomas Trillek, fos. 342 ᵛ–5; but these copies reveal no substantial difference from those in *Reg. Langham*.

And let it be observed that, according to the sacred canons, a good and industrious and lettered person could and would know how to govern two or ten churches better than another sort of person is understood to govern one and serve its altar, whether resident or non-resident, provided that he live well and spend well what he receives therefrom. And I say also that of the custom of the church of England it has been and is wonted, accustomed and approved from a time whereto the memory of man runneth not contrary, and has been suffered by the church of Rome, that the bishops and other patrons of the said realm of England might make provision to well-deserving clerks of benefices, especially without cure, in any number whatever, without any sort of contradiction or offence to the apostolic see.[41]

Like Wickham, but more explicitly, Otery was reminding the pope that 'well-deserving clerks' could hold benefices without cure 'in any number whatever, without any sort of contradiction or offence to the apostolic see'; and, like Wickham, Otery was implicitly questioning Urban's right to alter this 'custom of the church of England'.

In addition to exploiting the ambiguities of *Consueta*, the English clergy resorted to other expedients designed to thwart the pope. Perhaps the most favoured of these expedients was the frequent reference to the fact that particular benefices were in royal or lay patronage, or in lay fee. One-fifth of the pluralist clerks in the diocese of Coventry and Lichfield drew attention to this fact, as did others in London, Exeter, Lincoln, Hereford, and Salisbury. The purpose of these comments was nowhere made explicit, and it is not entirely clear. It is possible that these pluralists were simply reminding the pope that to deprive them of such benefices would not profit him, since the lay patrons would certainly collate if the benefices were voided. Or perhaps they intended to draw his attention to the political dangers of depriving the protégés of lay patrons. Perhaps they had both objects in mind; but in any case it seems clear, from the frequency with which this formula was employed, that pluralists considered it a form of defence.

Passive resistance took two further forms. Some pluralists falsified their returns, others failed to make them. Amongst the latter, the case of John Wycliffe is notorious. But Wycliffe was by no means the most prominent defaulter. Humphrey de Charlton, brother of the bishop of Hereford, made no return, nor did the famous astronomer, Simon de Bredon, or Nicholas de Hethe, or Roger de Chesterfield, prominent royal clerks. The list could be considerably extended: for example, Alan de Sherington, William Dalton, William Denby, and Richard de

41. *Reg. Langham*, pp. 44–45; trans. A. H. Thompson, 'Pluralism', *A.A.S.R.P.* XXXV (1919–20), 227–9.

Radford were all known pluralists.[42] Falsification of returns is more difficult to detect; but one can point to the case of John de Welbourne,[43] and also to the highly suspicious number of clerks who claimed to hold two compatible benefices—the permitted maximum: in the diocese of Norwich, for example, eighteen of the twenty pluralists stated that they held only two compatible benefices; and in the diocese of Chichester, only four of the sixteen admitted to having more. In the light of these facts, the suggestion that 'the returns were made with a promptness and exactitude which is in itself a testimony to the deference and respect with which the English clergy regarded the Holy See',[44] can scarcely be maintained. Rather they serve to illustrate the hostility provoked by Urban's legislation and the determination of the English clergy to evade its consequences.

The opposition of the English clergy provided Edward with an opportunity which he was quick to exploit. In the spring of 1367, when the returns of the English clergy would have reached Avignon, the 'Flemish question' had reached a new and critical phase. Since the publication of Urban's threat of excommunication in October 1365, Edward had concentrated on building a system of anti-papal alliances in Provence and North Italy.[45] But Urban had not been cowed; and in March 1367 retaliated by issuing the dispensation which was to enable Philip of Burgundy, brother of Charles V, to marry Margaret of Flanders.[46] To counter this, Sir John Cobham was sent to the Curia in the early summer of 1367 armed with threats of intensified political and ecclesiastical pressure if concessions over the Flemish marriage were not forthcoming.

The aggressive tone of this embassy was set by the first major item of Cobham's credence.[47] Edward had been negotiating a marriage alliance

42. A. B. Emden, *A Biographical Register of the University of Oxford to A.D. 1500* (3 vols., Oxford, 1957–9), i. 257–8, 390–1, 408–9, 538–9 and 568; iii. 1541–2; Emden, *A Biographical Register of the University of Cambridge to 1500* (Cambridge, 1963), p. 302; *Accounts*, pp. 252, 289, 294, 295, 296, 341, 345–7, 381, 386, and 388; *Cal. Papal Registers: Petitions to the Pope, 1342–1419* (London, 1896: repr. 1971), i. 514, 526, and 536–7.

43. C. J. Godfrey, 'Pluralists in the Province of Canterbury in 1366', *Journal of Ecclesiastical History*, xi (1960), 27, n. 1.

44. Ibid., p. 24.

45. Palmer, 'England, France, the Papacy and the Flemish Succession'.

46. J. J. Vernier, 'Philippe le Hardi, duc de Bourgogne. Son mariage avec Marguerite de Flandres en 1369', *Bulletin de la commission historique du département du Nord*, xxii (1900), 101.

47. J. R. L. Highfield, 'The Promotion of William of Wickham to the See of Winchester', *Journal of Ecclesiastical History*, iv (1953), 51–53.

with the Visconti—the pope's principal enemies in Italy—and Urban had asked him to desist. The king replied:

that he had many sons to marry who were advanced in years, and that it would be dangerous to let time pass; and that the only other brides as attractive and as wealthy . . . were denied to his sons by lack of a dispensation, the which—together with many other advantages—was denied to the king by the pope. Therefore, it seemed to the king and the said lords of his great council that it would be harmful to the king to forgo the said marriage—unless sufficient profit and advantage were offered to him and his said son elsewhere, equal to that offered by Milan. And so far no such offer had been made.

Having threatened the pope with an Anglo-Milanese alliance if the Flemish dispensation was not forthcoming, Cobham turned to the 'other advantages . . . denied to the king by the pope'. These all related to Urban's attack on English pluralists. At the outset, Cobham protested most strongly against the demands made on behalf of the pope by his recent envoy, Mag. Alexander Neville: demands which were so outrageous that the king could only imagine that they had been maliciously concocted by Neville himself 'in order to move the king against the church, which God forbid'. Unfortunately, the precise nature of these demands was not stated; but it is clear from their context that they concerned Urban's recent legislation, and it is equally clear that they had indeed 'moved the king against the church'.

Having protested against *Horribilis et detestabilis* and *Consueta* in principle, Cobham then dealt with particular cases of deprivation. Once again, Neville was cast as the villain and castigated for 'moving the pope against the king and certain of his subjects', so that he, the pope, had deprived many worthy clerks of their benefices, granting them to insufficient and unworthy men. Had the pope been truly informed of the merits of those he had deprived, he would (Edward felt sure) rather have increased the number of their benefices (!). Anticipating this, the king had not allowed the deprivations to take effect; but he nevertheless required Urban to annul the measures he had taken, to confirm the royal clerks in their benefices, and to desist in future from depriving the royal clerks 'of the benefices to which they had good title and possession': in other words, to abandon his reforms.

In return for this, the king promised that 'in order to nourish true love between the church and his kingdom, which he greatly desired', he would treat papal provisors with the same consideration which the pope showed to royal nominees. In short, if the pope would moderate his extreme demands, his provisions would meet with greater success; but this, in its turn, depended upon a favourable response to the political concessions demanded in the first part of Cobham's credence. This was the classical tactic of English diplomacy in its dealings with the Curia: to seek political concessions by applying pressure to papal provisions. It was a tactic which Edward could now employ with greater assurance than ever before owing to the support which Urban's legislation had ensured he would receive from the English clergy.

On the political level, Cobham's embassy was a complete failure. At the beginning of November 1367, Urban annulled all vows made by Edmund of Langley and Margaret of Flanders, thus freeing Margaret to contract marriage with Philip of Burgundy, whose dispensation was now renewed.[48] Edward retaliated by arresting Urban's envoy, Alexander Neville; by concluding the marriage alliance with the Visconti; by sending his son, Lionel, to aid Bernarbò Visconti; by ordering the English companies in Italy to support the Visconti against the pope;[49] and by continuing to harass papal provisors in England.

But although the political struggle continued unabated, the ecclesiastical duel was virtually at an end. The pressure of the king, coupled with the united opposition of the English clergy, had convinced the pope that both his genuine efforts at reform and his political abuse of those measures were equally doomed to failure. By the summer of 1367, this had become unmistakably clear. Between September 1366 and August 1367, for example, Urban had deprived eleven pluralists of a total of thirteen benefices; but in every case, both deprivation and subsequent provision were ineffective as the collector's accounts reiterate with monotonous regularity: 'non habuit effectum dicta amotio', 'non habuit effectum ista privatio . . . quia non fuit executa', 'dicta privatio/ provisio nunquam habuit effectum', 'dicta privatio non habuit effectum, nec provisio', etc.[50] Indeed such was the fear inspired by the second statute of Provisors and by Edward's harsh treatment of those who had the temerity to accept provisions to benefices from which his clerks had been ousted, that papal provisors now hastened to resign the graces which they had so injudiciously accepted: 'renuntiavit gratie ex causa rationabili', 'non est gratiam prosecutus ex causa certa et rationabili',

---

48. *Documents pour servir à l'histoire des relations entre l'Angleterre et la Flandre. Le Cotton MS. Galba B 1*, ed. E. Scott and L. Gilliodts van Severen (Brussels, 1896), p. 516.

49. Palmer, 'England, France, the Papacy and the Flemish Succession'.

50. *Accounts*, pp. 252, 253, 255, 289, 291, 294, 295–8, 306, 341, 342, 345–51, 381, 382, 385–90, 392, and 393.

etc.[51] When the pope could not induce clerks to accept provision to such benefices, it was clearly futile to continue the struggle. Having failed to deprive a single pluralist of a single English benefice after four years of persistent effort, Urban accepted defeat. There were no more deprivations after Cobham's embassy.

The net result of the struggle was unfortunate for both England and the papacy. Only Charles V could show a profit: he secured the Flemish marriage. Edward's major ambition had been frustrated; but even he could count some gains: the solid support of the English clergy, the diminishing number of papal provisions, and an increase in his royal patronage. For Urban, however, the effects were all bad: the destruction of his cherished reform, loss of revenue, decrease in patronage, and a legacy of bad-feeling between England and the papacy which was to contribute in no small measure to the consolidation of the Schism. All this stemmed from Urban's refusal to grant a dispensation. By thus allowing himself to become involved in the politics of the Hundred Years War, Urban had been inexorably led to subordinate the ecclesiastical interests of the church to the political interests of France.

51. Ibid., pp. 295, 298, 306, 346, and 349.

INDEX